THE NEW WORLD
OF AMERICAN VERSE

The current landscape of American poetry embraces every region of the country. Since World War II, small presses and literary magazines have sprung up across the nation. Now, A GEOGRAPHY OF POETS uncovers the grass roots direction of current poetry that includes native Americans, issue-oriented poets writing about black life, gay consciousness, and ecology, and numerous other schools united by their locales and ethnic viewpoints. From this swelling chorus of poets arises a new geography of American verse that at last recognizes the stunning variety of its voices.

A
Geography
of Poets

AN ANTHOLOGY OF
THE NEW POETRY

Edited by Edward Field

A GEOGRAPHY OF POETS:
AN ANTHOLOGY OF THE NEW POETRY
A Bantam Book
Bantam edition / January 1979

COPYRIGHTS AND ACKNOWLEDGMENTS

The copyright notices listed below
and on pages 543-552 constitute an
extension of this copyright page.

AI: All poems from Cruelty; *copyright © 1970, 1973 by Ai. By permission of Houghton Mifflin Company.*
ALTA: "Never Saw a Man in a Negligee," from No Visible Means of Support, *and "I Don't Have No Bunny Tail on My Behind," from* Poems and Prose. *Other poems from* I Am Not a Practicing Angel; *copyright © 1970 by Alta. By permission of the author.*
AMMONS, A. R.: All poems from Diversifications; *copyright © 1975 by A. R. Ammons. By permission of W. W. Norton & Company, Inc.*
ANDERSON, JACK: "Going to Norway," from City Joys, *published by Release Press; copyright © 1975 by Jack Anderson. By permission of the author.*
ASHBERY, JOHN: "Mixed Feelings," from Self Portrait in a Convex Mirror; *copyright © 1972, 1973, 1974, 1975 by John Ashbery. By permission of the Viking Press. "Farm Implements . . . ," from* The Double Dream of Spring; *copyright © 1966, 1967, 1968, 1969, 1970 by John Ashbery. By permission of the author.*
AUBERT, ALVIN: All poems from Feeling Through; *copyright © 1975 by Alvin Aubert. By permission of the author.*

ISBN 0-553-12441-2

Published simultaneously in the United States and Canada

Bantam Books are published by Bantam Books, Inc. Its trademark, consisting of the words "Bantam Books" and the portrayal of a bantam, is Registered in U.S. Patent and Trademark Office and in other countries. Marca Registrada. Bantam Books, Inc., 666 Fifth Avenue, New York, New York 10019.

PRINTED IN THE UNITED STATES OF AMERICA

Contents

Introduction

Introduction

Today there are about 2500 poets listed in the *Directory of American Poets*—and that includes only the widely-published ones—but back in World War II when I began writing not only was there no directory but American poetry was a small, exclusive cult, an unnoticeable underground in a few cities and universities.

I first became aware of the world of poets through meeting a poet in my bomber group when I was stationed at an airbase in England. He used to go on London weekends to the Gargoyle Club to which many literary people belonged, and he would bring back stories of the English and American poets he met there—Stephen Spender, Dunstan Thompson, Harry Smith, George Barker, and others. The Americans were mostly on the London staffs of the army publications, *Yank Magazine* and *Stars and Stripes*. I heard of the doings of these fabulous people and longed for my friend to invite me to go with him, but he never did, for I had just started to write and did not merit being included in that elegant company.

In fact, I had just discovered that there was such a thing as *modern* poetry—poetry actually written by *living* poets —the ones I'd studied in school were all dead. On my own passes into London, between bombing missions, I bought books by the poets I was hearing about now for the first time: T. S. Eliot's *The Wasteland*, Dylan Thomas' early works ("This wine I drink was once the grape/ This bread I break was once the oat . . ."), Edith Sitwell ("Jane, Jane,/ tall as a crane . . ."). With only an ordinary American high school education behind me I knew less than nothing about poetry and read these books by "the moderns" with excitement but with comprehension. Secretly I preferred Rupert Brooke with his soft romanticism of another era:

> Breathless, we flung us on a windy hill,
> Laughed in the sun and kissed the lovely grass . . .
>
> ("The Hill" by Rupert Brooke)

But I'd gotten my first glimpse of what seemed to be a glittering world that was the antithesis of what passed the stifling small town I came from.

Back home from the war, I determined to make myself over into a brilliant, witty intellectual like those poets I admired from afar. I studied at New York University and attended with the devotion of a religious convert the poetry readings at the YMHA Poetry Center—at that time the only place such things went on. (It was not until a few years later that Dylan Thomas was brought over by the Poetry Center and the era of poetry readings around the country began.) Instead of going to classes I hung out with the literary/bohemian set in the college cafeteria where we felt superior to the masses of students around us.

I gradually became familiar with the masters of modern poetry, each with a distinctive style of his or her own. All seemed more or less obscure but I pretended to understand what they were doing and imitated them. Reading e. e. cummings I threw out capitals and punctuation, but then I read T. S. Eliot and tried to be austere. I read the formidable magazines—*Poetry* (Chicago), *Partisan Review*, *Kenyon Review*—where to have your work accepted meant that you were part of an incredibly exclusive society. That was what I aimed for.

I never thought for a minute about how I would earn a living—of course, I was going to school on what was to me the luxury of the G.I. Bill. For my friends and me, becoming an artist involved a vague fantasy of enlisting in a crusade for truth and somehow saving mankind. Furthermore, we had the idea that it would "solve our lives." Unlike the bourgeois ruts we were expected to follow, it was a revolutionary path that gave one room to develop, that allowed all the kinky corners of one's nature to be expressed. You didn't have to conform. It seemed to us possible through art to get over our problems, become a realized being—a saint, a hero, a giant, somebody you wanted to be.

I dropped out of school and went to Paris and sat in Left Bank existentialist cafés and, with a cup of coffee (the price of sitting there) growing cold, working on my poems. When my money ran out I came home and tried to continue living like an old artist. But in those gray years of the early fifties—the Cold War, the Korean War, McCarthyism and blacklisting, the Rosenbergs' execution —when the literary community seemed to shrink into a little neurotic group at the San Remo bar in the Village, there was nothing to do but go into therapy, having found that art did not change the frustration, guilt, and anxiety I was crippled by. Clearly art was not enough.

There was a movement back to religion with T. S. Eliot and W. H. Auden leading the way, but despite them, it sounded to me like you had to give up your mind. And politics, even if we all gave lip service to being radical, was suffering from exhaustion after the war and the recent disillusionment of most of the intellectual community with Marxism.

My shaken belief that poetry would rescue me was now bolstered by the new hope that psychoanalysis would put me back together again. But there was a conflict between the two, because my psychiatrist really wanted me to be practical about my life and get a job (not that you can't be practical and a poet, but I didn't see that then). I did work from time to time (jobs in factories and warehouses that satisfied my romantic self-image). Nevertheless I went on writing and even began publishing my poems in the highbrow magazines I so believed in.

Poetry was then dominated by a board of higher beings called the New Critics—people like John Crowe Ransom at Kenyon College and Yvor Winters at Stanford University —whose ideas I barely understood. What the New Criticism meant to me was that a poem had to be revised again and again and the more revisions you made, the closer to a masterpiece it would be. Poets used to brag about how many revisions they made, even into the hundreds. I saw the goal of all this work more as "correcting" myself than the poem, revising what I was: those authorities did not accept poets like me who had the misfortune to be clumsy and stupid, ashamed of themselves, from humble, immigrant parents, and obviously Jewish. All traces of this had to be deleted from the poem until it became a beautiful object with elegant diction and syntax, with meanings that would only emerge from close analysis. (Even if I reject all that today, it was good training, and now that it is no longer dogma it's useful for poetry workshops.)

The poets I liked, I often liked for the wrong reasons—
W. H. Auden, for example, whose little tender moments
and campy jokes I loved but whom I found otherwise
impenetrable:

> Come to our well-run desert
> Where anguish arrives by cable
> And the deadly sins
> May be bought in tins
> With instructions on the label.
> ("For the Time Being")

and Hart Crane, whose romantic, self-destructive life made
me a passionate *devoté*, even though his complex images
often had little meaning for me. If none of the poets said
anything directly about my life, I accepted that because I
knew that modern poetry was supposed to be obscure. That
was one of the words on its banner with which it had
charged into battle against Victorianism and sentimental
Edwardianism and the yahoo culture of American pro-
vincialism. Obscurity gave you class, meant you were deep.
Until I was obscure I knew I never would be really ac-
ceptable (the occasional poem I had published did not
convince me otherwise), and how I'd get to be obscure
I had no idea.

My bible in the late forties and early fifties was the
Oscar Williams' *Treasury of Modern Verse* which set the
canon for modern poetry of that time. In it were the titans,
today all dead. My image of them was compounded of
gossip and fantasy: T. S. Eliot, indisputable king of poetry,
an American who ruled from his editorial offices at Faber
& Faber, London's most prestigious publisher; W. H. Auden,
English but living in America, the most serious contender
for the crown; William Butler Yeats, who had had the
monkey gland operation for virility and subsequently wrote
his greatest poems; Wallace Stevens, who incomprehensibly
worked as an insurance executive and William Carlos
Williams, a pediatrician (one wondered in both cases
how this could be compatible with being a poet); the
spinsterish Marianne Moore who lived in a historic Brook-
lyn far from the slum Brooklyn of poor immigrants I knew
about, and insisted that what she wrote was "ordered
prose"; Hart Crane who had leaped off a boat in the
Caribbean into shark-infested waters; e. e. cummings

with his typographical peculiarities who moved from early political satire to fey whimsy; Robert Frost, somewhat suspect for his folksy tone and regular verse; even the virulent anti-semite, Ezra Pound, doing time in a mental institution for having broadcast propaganda for the Fascists during the war, though visited by a constant stream of admirers among the non-political young.

I puzzled with friends over the fascinating difficulties of the poems, digging out meanings, searching for clues, putting hints together—this was called "close textual analysis." These poems were sacred and if I couldn't understand them I assumed the fault was mine. Understandable or not, it was obvious that they were magnificently wrought.

The great revolution in the teens and twenties that these poets created lost poetry whatever popular audience it had ever had. Except for Frost, the poets preferred it that way. The emphasis on symbols and images rather than on linear meaning and pleasing rhythms and rhymes removed poetry from any possibility of being a popular art.

It is true that in the thirties a radical wave of poets tried to bring poetry back to "the people," incorporating the social concerns of the Depression into their poetry, but this ended with World War II and it was not until the mid-fifties that this impulse emerged in a different form.

At that time we were all startled by the news of the "Howl" trial in San Francisco. A movement of public poetry readings had begun out there with great popular success, but when Allen Ginsberg read his poem "Howl," he was prosecuted for obscenity. The ensuing publicity along with the furor over Jack Kerouac's novel *On the Road* was the beginning of what came to be called the Beat Generation. Just when American poetry, in the hands of the disciples of Eliot, Pound, Stevens et. al, had become even more refined, self-conscious, and academic, along came the Beats who brought into question all the rules of the poetry establishment. They substituted a new principle: write directly about your own experience, write it down as it comes and don't change a word. They not only rejected the cult of impersonality but also its practice of revision after revision that had been a sacred tenet for so long and driven so many poets crazy. In response to their new attitudes, terms like 'bard' and 'wordslinger' came into fashion.

With their unconventional behavior the Beats made a

very colorful show as they took to the road, giving group readings around the country. The media loved them. Poetry readings in cafés, often accompanied by jazz, spread all over. Poetry became easy to write, and long chanting poems based on Walt Whitman's biblical line came into fashion:

> I saw the best minds of my generation destroyed by
>   madness, starving, hysterical naked,
> dragging themselves through the negro streets at
>   dawn looking for an angry fix . . .
>   ("Howl" by Allen Ginsberg)

The theory behind this was William Carlos Williams' idea that the line should follow the breath and not be based on any arbitrary foot like the iambic of traditional English metrics. You placed your trust in inspiration (inner breath). Also you trusted your experience and no longer hid your background, sex life, and the other aspects of your being who you were.

The leaders of this movement—Ginsberg, Ferlinghetti, Corso, and Kerouac—all came from New York, and it was strange to me at first that they had chosen San Francisco as their literary home rather than Paris, as my friends and I had. But I saw that theirs was the more realistic choice—in San Francisco you could work, go on welfare, or get unemployment insurance to finance your poetry career, and you could hitchhike out there and back.

At the same time the Beats were catching on, and loosening up poetry, even affecting someone as much in the modern tradition as Robert Lowell. There was another less flamboyant movement in New York City, later to be called the New York School made up of poets involved in the emerging abstract expressionist art scene. These poets, Frank O'Hara, John Ashbery, Kenneth Koch and others, were mostly Harvard graduates. They saw New York as the newly-emerged cultural capital of the world just as Paris had been a generation earlier. They adopted its surrealism and tried to create in New York the kind of lively atmosphere—with plays, art openings, and other events—that was associated with the surrealist-dada period in Paris of the twenties. If the San Francisco movement was populist, the New York poets were aristocrats, but just as American. They moved easily between the city and the summer colony in the Hamptons at the far end of Long Island. Their activities were above all inextricably involved with the art world—galleries, museums, and magazines, as well as the painters' bars and studios.

Their poetry seemed tossed off; it had a carelessly elegant style:

> It is 12:20 in New York a Friday
> three days after Bastille Day, yes
> it is 1959 and I go get a shoeshine
> because I will get off the 4:19 in Easthampton
> at 7:15 and then go straight to dinner
> and I don't know the people who will feed me . . .
> ("The Day Lady Died," by Frank O'Hara)

They made the city their playground and if they suffered, it did not show in their poetry. I was always amazed at how much at home they seemed to be in a city where I felt at that time so cut off from everyone.

There was another group of poets in the fifties all connected in some way with the super-innovative, short-lived Black Mountain College in North Carolina. The Black Mountain poets were characterized by an intense if narrow intellectuality. Their leader was Charles Olson with his "composition by field" and "projective verse" theories, which attempted to rescue poetry from the printed page where it had been embalmed, and reawaken appreciation of the breath and the syllable and the echoes of ancient languages in the words.* His poems had a kind of Homeric

*For his own explanation of his theories see Olson's *Selected Writings*, edited by Robert Creeley (New Directions, 1966).

voice, sounding like jazzy translations of classical odes:

> The lordly and isolate Satyrs—look at them come in
> on the left side of the beach
> like a motorcycle club! And the handsomest of them,
> the one who has a woman, driving that snazzy
> convertible
>   Wow, did you ever see even in a museum
> such a collection of boddisatvahs, . . .
> ("The Lordly and Isolate Satyrs")

Others in this group were Denise Levertov, who had come from England a short time before; Robert Creeley, known for the "skinny poem," meaning it looks long and thin on the page; Robert Duncan, with the voice and intensity of a medieval mystic.

These movements plus a lot of other avant-garde poets (the ones around the Bay Area were called the San Francisco Renaissance) were collected by Donald Allen in the Grove Press anthology *The New American Poetry, 1945-1960*, establishing the fact that something revolutionary was taking place, challenging the tight academic formalism of the New Criticism. But if these groupings had some validity everybody in them sounded different. Meanwhile, there were still many poets who belonged to none of them. Poets like May Swenson, Louise Bogan, and Theodore Roethke went on writing their own way no matter what anyone else was doing.

Still, poetry was widely affected by the radical changes that began in the mid-fifties with the Beats and became nationwide in the protest movements and rebellions of the sixties. It was a romantic period with its civil rights and anti-Vietnam activism, communes, mysticism, drugs, sexual freedom, an alternative culture that developed its own arts and crafts as well as politics. Among the young it became hip to write poetry. I myself let my hair grow longer, took up wearing beads and Indian shirts, bought a VW bus with a bed in the back.

There was also a rise in ethnic consciousness. The struggle for Black civil rights and the revolutionary movement that arose from it gave birth to a new generation of Black poets. Leroi Jones, well known as a Beat, changed his name to Amiri Baraka and joined the battle for Black power, working in the Newark community. He and Gwendolyn Brooks have influenced many younger Black poets, some of whom like Don L. Lee and Sonia Sanchez were published by Broadside Press in Detroit, or like Carolyn Rodgers and Nikki Giovanni, by major publishing houses.

Numbers of Chicano and native American poets began to emerge, speaking not only of their heritage but of the struggle to survive in the white man's world. Some Hispanic poets, working out their bilingual predicament, produced work that freely mixed English and Spanish. Other poets of various ethnic backgrounds (Jewish, Armenian, Chinese, Polish, etc.) were also exploring and expressing their particular identity in their work. Back in the forties, aside from a few Black poets like Langston Hughes and Owen

Dodson, and the Jewish poet Charles Reznikoff, there were few evidences of such ethnic awareness in poetry.

The Kennedy administration was sophisticated enough to give government recognition to the arts, leading in 1965 to the establishment of the National Endowment for the Arts which financed literary magazines and small-press publication of books, sent poets to teach in the schools, and later gave grants to individual poets.

This upsurge of public interest in creativity also affected academic life. More and more poets were being hired by universities to teach, and graduate programs were set up leading to advanced degrees in creative writing. These have been turning out competent poets every year, many of whom go off to teach all over the country, running poetry workshops themselves, and often convincing school administrations to grant budgets for poetry readings. Not all young poets follow this course—there are many alternatives to the academic life—but it has meant that some can make a comfortable career of poetry.

I did it in a non-academic way. I worked at a variety of jobs to support myself, sometimes even writing my poems on office typewriters when the boss wasn't looking. It was only at the age of thirty-eight, after receiving twenty-two rejections by publishers, that I won the Lamont Award in 1963 and my first collection was finally published, and, to my surprise, widely praised. Since that time I've been able to make a living largely by going on poetry-reading tours.

In doing so, I began to discover a lot of good poets everywhere I had never heard of before. In New York we were always aware that there were some poets out there in the hinterlands. New England aside (that was next door), there was Theodore Roethke in the Northwest, famous not only as a poet but as a teacher; the legendary figure of Robinson Jeffers building a stone house with his twin sons in Big Sur; Kenneth Rexroth who would later play father to the Beat movement and the San Francisco Renaissance; John Crowe Ransom teaching the principles of the New Criticism at Kenyon College. But it was to New York that most young poets had always come, fleeing the provinces where life for a poet was an ordeal. (He might go back when he was famous but it was usually to the safety of a university.)

It was strange to discover that most of the young poets

I met on my tours did not feel that they had to come to New York to "make it," and seemed perfectly at home out there where they lived. Nor could they be thought of as "regional" in the old sense, completely identified with the folklore and traditions of their immediate area. I found they were in touch not only with English and American poetry but with Latin American and Asian poetry, as well as the oral literatures of native Americans and Africans.

Though some were born in the areas they still live in—like Wendell Berry in Kentucky, Kathleen Norris in South Dakota, Ted Kooser in Nebraska, James Welch in Montana, Robert Bly in Minnesota—most have moved there in the last twenty-five years—Richard Shelton (born in Idaho) in the Southwest desert, Ron Koertge (born in Illinois) in Southern California, Greg Kuzma (born in New York) in Nebraska.

In one generation, really overnight, the populace that had always been hostile to the eccentric and alien has gotten used to the unconventional behavior of the long-haired young. Writing poetry is not considered just for sissies anymore. When I began writing, the poetry world looked toward England, the image of poet being the English gentleman or the New England spinster. Today's image (post-Beat, post-hippie) is more cowboy/hobo or slut/yenta.

Wherever I go now I come across an indigenous poetry scene with its own small presses, magazines, and poetry readings. The complaint I hear from poets everywhere is that New York publishers, editors and critics refuse to recognize what is happening.

I discovered that there was enormous hostility to New York on various grounds, not only that the commercial publishers are here and effectively control the literary market place, but also that any city is evil and the country is good. New York as the financial capital is especially evil, standing for Capitalism and Imperialism, as well as European influences which to the populist mind has always meant class structure and decadence. To this view is added the belief that New York and all cities are an ecological menace.

Out of this opposition to the Northeast and its literary establishment has grown up a nationwide counterculture mentality, polarized on the West Coast, that rejects European ancestry as well as our debt to Europe, adopting our Indians as spiritual forebears as well as teachers who know how to live on the land without wrecking it. It looks westward across the Pacific for religious instruction, mixing frontier anarchism with Buddhism, and has the usual bohemian commitment to health foods, drugs, and sexual freedom—to "naturalness."

> How rare to be born a human being!
> Wash him off with cedar-bark and milk weed
>   send the damned doctors home.
> Baby, baby, noble baby
> Noble-hearted baby
>
> One hand up, one hand down
> "I alone am the honored one"
> Birth of the Buddha.
>   ("Hunting" by Gary Snyder)

Traveling as I do for a living, I myself started to develop a more national view, and what was happening in the Southwest say, or the Midwest, began to seem just as exciting and important as poetry in the Northeast where, it is true, there is a particularly dense concentration of poets.

Today, for example, there is a lively poetry scene around Long Beach, California, with its own magazines and small presses. Against the clean background of blue sky, a sea with tropical islands that are camouflaged oil derricks, beautiful, bland people—the American Dream—poets like Charles Stetler, Ron Koertge, and Gerald Locklin are writing poems that are direct, funny, and often filthy.

On Saturday night the pimply young men go up to the record
    stores
and look through the albums.

They are waiting for a beautiful girl without morals
or panties to pick them up in the Soul Section,
but no one ever does.

                ("The Archetype" by Ron Koertge)

Their vernacular style, sassy and jaded, is at the opposite pole from the issue-oriented, righteous poetry of the Bay Area to the north.

Poets, come out of your closets,
Open your windows, open your doors,
You have been holed up too long
in your closed worlds.

* * *

Poetry isn't a secret society,
It isn't a temple either.
Secret words & chants won't do any longer.
The hour of *om*ing is over,
the time for keening come,
time for keening & rejoicing
over the coming end
of industrial civilization
which is bad for earth & Man.
("Populist Manifesto" by Lawrence Ferlinghetti)

Around Minneapolis and St. Paul a poetry center has developed not only around the Minnesota Poets Cooperative Press but also around the once-blacklisted radicals, Thomas McGrath and Meridel LeSueur. In the Pacific Northwest, the legacy of Theodore Roethke remains alive, setting particularly high standards for the young. In North Carolina alone there are the Southern Poetry Review, Red Clay Reader, Jargon Press, and Unicorn Press, among others.

Statistically it's phenomenal. Besides the 2500 poets in the Directory of American Poets, there are over 250 writing programs in colleges (leaving out poetry workshops in other schools), 3000 little magazines and small presses that publish poetry—and they are scattered all over.

While a number of anthologies present a good historical view of modern poetry, none reflects this new situation adequately—they start off with the big names about whom there is no question, but when it comes to present writers, they dwindle away uncertainly.

Excellence of course is the only criterion, but a current anthology should show how things are developing, make a point. In America today with poetry springing up everywhere and with such a variety of approaches, no one has been able to find a coherent pattern in it.

The last one that succeeded in doing this was Donald Allen's anthology at the start of the sixties, but even his categories—Beat, New York School, Black Mountain, San Francisco Renaissance, which might be said to have given birth to fuzzy labels such as Post-Beat, New York School/

Second Generation, and in reaction to them, Classical Revival or New Formalism—have really fallen apart under the impact of the variety of poetry being written today.

For the first time there are no recognized standards or any nationally powerful critics whose judgment is respected. (One of the few exceptions is Richard Howard with his landmark book of essays on forty-four contemporary American poets, *Alone With America*.) There's nothing that can be called a mainstream movement in our poetry—or an avant garde.

One night in Portland, Oregon, while I discussed the question of New York vs. The Rest of the Country with a group of young poets who had come to my reading there, it was suggested that an anthology giving each area of the country "equal time" would be the best way to make sense out of the new cultural decentralization. The young poets insisted it couldn't be organized in any other way if you were going to show how things were developing.

That was how the idea began. I decided to put together an anthology giving the same space to west of the Mississippi as to east of the Mississippi, dividing it all up into geographical sections—Southwest Desert, Great Plains, the South, Midwest cities, etc. By presenting the poets of each area I might reveal a whole world of poetry still undiscovered or ignored by the New York publishers. In the past, poetry was judged to be significant only when published by them (the two exceptions being Allen Ginsberg and Charles Bukowski whose reputations were established without ever publishing a book with a large house). But why should a publisher's decision, based as it is on economic questions, have anything to do with judging poetry? Today much of the best poetry is appearing in little-known small magazines and presses. I wanted to show how solidly this work could stand in the context of the established poets. And since I wanted a picture of the current scene and not a historical view, I would only include living poets, limiting them to work published in the last ten years (ultimately, I had to make a few exceptions to this).

One of my main objectives was to show where the poets are, but often they don't stay put. Many are floaters, going from job to job. Diane Wakoski, though teaching at the University of Michigan one term a year, is travelling the rest of the time. W. S. Merwin lives everywhere. Ralph Pomeroy migrates to a new city every few years—San Francisco, London, Halifax, Brussels, and currently New York.

The poems have been taken from the enormous small-press publishing scene as well as from the big publishers, and from the little magazines. I wrote poets for their latest work in manuscript, asked which of their poems they would recommend (though I didn't take their advice very often), and read and read and read. I even moved for several months to San Francisco to be sure I was being fair to the Western point of view—it is true that from there the great roster of poets in the East looks much less impressive, though they are published by the large houses far more often than the Western poets.

And, finally, how did I chose the poems? How do you tell a good poem from a bad one? There are no simple rules to go by, whether it is in free or formal verse. Some people look for an elaborate verbal surface, concrete images, a dense concentration of words, or "intensity." Others prefer a conversational style, dynamic chanting, or improvisational changes of voice based on jazz riffs. And still others respond to formal verse patterns and rhyme. There is no way to sum up briefly the elements that go into a poem that give it authenticity, or make a checklist to judge it by. I will refer the interested reader to the best handbook I know on the subject, *Western Wind* by John Frederick Nims (Random House, 1974).

But it might be useful to point out some changes poetry is going through in its work of exploring language and feeling: one healthy change in the last twenty-five years is that poetry is no longer divided into "light" and "serious." It was considered daring of Oscar Williams in his postwar anthology to put a section of light verse even at the end of the volume. Any humorous effects at that time put poetry into this category, though there were poets, of course, considered "lesser," like Ogden Nash, who specialized in it. If it was fun it couldn't be real poetry. Today this division has almost ceased to exist. Humor is a major element in many poets' bag of tricks, though it is still not widely understood that the shock in a poem that leads to laughter is as important as the shock that leads to tears and can be equally serious.

Periodically in the history of poetry the spoken language

takes over again from the formal. Today, poets are using more and more of their vernacular language with its street vocabulary and folk-syntax, and popular subject matter, as in John Ashbery's charming combination of the formal sestina with the characters of the Popeye cartoon:

> . . . It was domestic thunder,
> The color of spinach. Popeye chuckled and scratched
> His balls: it sure was pleasant to spend a day in the country.
> > ("Farm Implements and Rutabagas in a Landscape"
> > by John Ashbery)

A wider range of American voices is now heard in our poetry along with this use of the daily language, especially ethnic voices so long taboo:

> > Do you know my
> > Slap-a-hand, lend-a-hand main man?
>
> > Dirt-deep podner
> > Quick-reeling, nigger-feeling friend, then?
> > > ("Main Man Blues" by Eugene B. Redmond)

or:

> > > gramma thinks about her grandchildren
> > > they're losing the ways
> > > don't know how to talk indian . . .
> > > > ("the way & the way things are" by nila northSun)

In choosing the poems I tried to show the enormous variety of poetry today from the vernacular to the formal, though it ultimately came down to What I Like. I particularly looked for poems that say things that are not usually said in polite company, not just the use of dirty words or words that are otherwise offensive, but things coming out of your privateness—after all, poems are written in private when nobody is around to listen in on your secret dreams, your original thoughts that you're convinced the world would not understand or accept or might ridicule you for. I like poetry that tells me about the poet's life, the problems he's struggling with:

> > > You are not wanted
> > > I said to the older body
> > > Who was listening near the cupboards.
> > > > ("Periphery" by Ruth Stone)

that speaks from one's heart and is not ashamed to express the poet's ideals and yearnings for transcendence:

> When it is finally ours, this freedom, this liberty, this beautiful
> and terrible thing, needful to man as air,
> usable as earth; when it belongs at last to all . . .
> ("Frederick Douglass" by Robert Hayden)

poetry that's witty and full of jokes:

> Sisters,
> The Blue Nun has eloped with one
> of the Christian Brothers. They are living
> in a B&B Motel just out of
> Sacramento.
> ("With a Bottle of Blue Nun to All My Friends"
> by Madeline DeFrees)

poetry with ideas about life:

> You get to Gilead, let me know. That balm,
> supposed to be so good for human hurts
> —all wounds, holes, hollows, hungriness—
> you tell me if it's there, and how it works.
> ("Go Ahead; Goodbye; Good Luck; And Watch Out"
> by William Bronk)

poetry that is mysterious. I like to try to figure it out. One purpose of complications is to force you to pay close attention:

> It was round, orb being most nearly perfect,
> And warm perhaps, though hardly of any color,
> Smelling of spring, faintly, of hyacinth.
> It was not fruit, though on those trees first planted
> Eastward, of life and knowledge, it may have grown.
> ("The Gift" by Ann Stanford)

It used to be said that political poetry was just propaganda. And that poetry that deals with issues will be meaningless tomorrow when the issues are dead. I'm not sure I believe any longer that poetry can make anything happen in the world, but I'm not against poets trying, even if that limits the poem's life span:

Kissinger has made it, yall. He's the secretary
of state, U.S.A. The anglo-snakes have called him
mooing to their side, his bag-time with rocky helped
a lot. . . .
("Horatio Alger Uses Scag" by Amiri Baraka)

I've included poetry that is written loosely, almost like
prose:

daily courage doesn't count
we dont get diplomas for it.
i worked hard for 5 years with one man,
then had 3 years graduate training with another.
("Untitled" by Alta)

or tight, like riddles:

The full cloves
Of your buttocks, the convex
Curve of your belly, the curved
Cleft of your sex—

Out of this corn
That's planted in strong thighs
The slender stem and radiant
Flower rise.
("A Shallot" by Richard Wilbur)

These are some aspects of the poetry I've collected here.
But what I ultimately look for is a kind of magic. Poetry
really is magic as every child and adolescent instinctively
knows. These lines have been my touchstone:

Brightness falls from the air,
Queens have died, young and fair,
Dust hath closèd Helen's eye.
I am sick, I must die.
Lord, have mercy on us!
("In Time of Pestilence"
by Thomas Nashe, 1567-1601)

* * *

New Yorkers are convinced that everything good in
America eventually surfaces here and is recognized. But
this, if true, is certainly nothing to be smug about. Rather,
it is a responsibility not only to be open to new ideas from
all over but to let the rest of the country teach us. In

xlv

poetry at least this does not seem to have been true lately—the new wave of poetry has taken us by surprise. While no great figures have emerged yet, this discovery of America by its poets, and America taking its poets in, may be the most extraordinary phenomenon since the revolutionary changes poetry went through in the early part of the century.

The poets I have collected will typically go on moving around in the future from one region to another—that's the nature of modern life—and this configuration is necessarily tentative. We can only be grateful that the variety and mixture of influences have produced so impressive a body of poetry coming from every section of the country. And to celebrate this, I made this anthology. It is dedicated to the whole country, a New Yorker's attempt to pay a debt of recognition.

San Francisco/New York City, 1978

The
Northwest

HENRY CARLILE

Grandmother

No one remembered when she first discovered God.
Her conversion was sudden as a slammed door.
Outside, my grandfather beat the doorjamb with his fist,
But she, God-furious, would not relent.
Shut up like an oyster on a speck of dirt
She praised God in her bedclothes,
Read the Bible like a French novel,
And dreamed each night of Christ the Saviour,
The lightning bolt of revelation forking at her
From the black cloud of her Bible,
And the godhead stirring inside her like a sick sea.

Overnight her skirts grew longer and her temper shorter,
The black buttons on her boots crept higher and higher
On legs that had never seen the light.
Whenever she rode the cable car downtown
She pulled her bonnet tight around her ears
To let no evil word hiss through,
Her eyes magnified by scripture,
Split by the seeing lens and reading lens
Which could never look together,
Beholders of two worlds: one black and one white,
Negative, censored, and unprintable,
A damned world bleached of color.

Stern as an iron stove
She drove her children off to church,
Beat their bottoms with a willow
To make them kneel like thirteen sinful sheep,
Recalcitrant, flagellant, bleating at the altar,
Pinched upright in their pews,
Reciting alphabets of sin while the preacher,
A red-faced Russian with a beard as black as God,
Gospeled from the pulpit

3

And the congregation flapped their tongues,
Prophesying improbable forgiveness.

But nothing ever was:
The family scattered out like rabbits
From the sawed-off shotgun of the true faith
While Grandmother rocked in the cradle of belief,
Reading and praying, reading and praying,
Copying scriptures on tiny scraps of paper
That peeped like mice or children
From every nook and cranny of the old house:
From cookie jars and table drawers and kitchen
    cupboards—
Even from the Bible itself, marsupial with misconceptions,
Threatening every minute to explode,
Until one day her heart did,
And we hunkered in the shadow of her death,
A bad-luck come-to-nothing family
Wrong since genesis.

The Grief of Our Genitals

i

They droop like sad fuchsias from our bodies,
they stir blindly about like earthworms exposed to light,
they belong to us and yet we cannot own them,
we are attached like Siamese twins, one of whom is
    addicted,
we must share their insatiable appetites, their cravings,
and have no voice in the matter
but be as a master ruled by his dog.

ii

Dogs! How simple it is with them.
None of this complication:
Dogs do not need king-sized beds
lonely as deserted playfields.
Anywhere will do: lawn, sidewalk,
cemetery.
        They make love on our graves
and do not know how restlessly we sleep
with our arms full of dust
and lost opportunities.

4

In the tropic of Cancer,
through jungles of viney pubescence,
the soldiers are marching, are marching,
each with his tiny carapace like a shield
and fierce as a Hun living off the country.
We are invaded!
At midnight no remedy for this but strong spirits
and in the cure the flaming penance.

Dodo

Years they mistook me for you
chanting your name in the streets
pointing grubby fingers
Today in the natural history museum
I saw why
Dodo, you look the way I feel
with your sad absent-minded eyes
and your beak like a stone-age axe
Even your feathers—
Dingy and fuzzy
What woman would want them for a hat?

With a name like *Didus ineptus*
where could you go
wings too small to fly with
and feet so large and slow?
You were not very palatable
Men slaughtered you for sport
Hogs ate the one egg you laid each year
Sometimes I think I know how it feels
to be scattered over the world
a foot in the British Museum
a head in Copenhagen
to be a lesson after the fact
an entity in name only
and that taken in vain

MADELINE DE FREES

Letter to an Absent Son

It's right to call you son. That cursing alcoholic
is the god I married early before I really knew him:
spiked to his crossbeam bed, I've lasted thirty years.
Nails are my habit now. Without them I'm afraid.

At night I spider up the wall to hide in crevices
deeper than guilt. His hot breath smokes me out.
I fall and fall into the arms I bargained for
sifting them cool as rain. A flower touch could tame me.
Bring me down that giant beam to lie submissive
in his fumbling clutch. One touch. Bad weather
moves indoors: a cyclone takes me.

How shall I find a shelter in the clouds, driven by
gods, gold breaking out of them everywhere?
Nothing is what it pretends. It gathers to a loss
of leaves and graves. Winter in the breath.
Your father looked like you, his dying proportioned
oddly to my breast. I boxed him in my plain pine
arms and let him take his ease just for a minute.

With a Bottle of Blue Nun to All My Friends

1

Sisters,
The Blue Nun has eloped with one
of the Christian Brothers. They are living
in a B&B Motel just out of
Sacramento.

2

The Blue Nun works the late shift
in Denver. Her pierced ears
drip rubies
like the Sixth Wound.

This is to inform you
that the Blue Nun
will become Mayor of Missoula
in the new dispensation.
At fifty-eight she threw her starched coif
into the ring and was off to a late win
over Stetson and deerstalker,
Homburg and humbug,
Church and State.

When you receive this you will know
that the Blue Nun
has blacked out
in a sleazy dive
outside San Francisco.
They remember her in Harlem.
She still carried her needle case
according to the ancient custom.

5

You may have noticed
how the walls lean towards the river
where a veil of fog hides a sky diver's
pale descent. The parachute
surrounds her like a wimple.
That's what happens when Blue Nuns
bail out.
It's that simple.

The Odd Woman

At parties I want to get even,
my pocket calculator rounds everything off,
taught to remember. I'm not so good
at numbers, feel awkward
as an upper plate without a partner.
Matched pairs float from the drawing board
into the drawing room, ears touched
with the right scent,
teeth and mouth perfect.

The cougar jaw yawns on the sofa back,
his molars an art-object.
The old and strange collect around me.
Names I refuse pitched at my head
like haloes. This one is a dead-ringer.
It rings dead. I pat the head of the beagle
nosing in my crotch and try to appear
grateful. A witch
would mount the nearest broom

and leave by the chimney. At ten I plot
my exit: gradual shift to the left,
a lunge toward the bourbon. The expert hunters
are gutting a deer
for the guest of honor. Soft eyes
accuse my headlights. I mention early
morning rituals. A colleague
offers to show me the door I've watched
for the last hour.

We come to my coat laid out
in the master bedroom, warm hands curled
in the pocket. I know
how a woman who leaves her purse behind
wants to be seduced. I hang mine
from the shoulder I cry on.
Say goodnight to the Burmese buddha,
hunters in the snow,
and leave for the long river drive to town.

VI GALE

After Illness

Mother's home early, out of bed,
already squeezing the forbidden coffeepot.
She crosses the kitchen critically noting
what's been done in her absence.

Copper and kettles don't hold her long.
She snaps on the white plastic radio
to a Scandinavian hour strictly
from garlanded maypoles and midsummer revels.

"Listen," she says, stomping her foot,
(helpless in rage and affection
plus total exhaustion, we cringe for her stitches)

"thirty Rättvik fiddlers in skinpants!"

Hurting

A whole week. Barely.
My feet take me around
but I forget why.
Mouth's been to the dentist.
Hands don't read my head.
Ears ring the telephone.
Moon's knocked to one side
and I choke in fluids.

Eventually, they tell me,
the yelling quiets down
inside, but it takes
a while. It takes a while.

TESS GALLAGHER

Keeping You Alive

My mother, a great believer in presences,
has mended you four times
with bedside appearances. Recognition,
a congenial cave, takes everyone in
the same. We are told your mouth,

grown fat around some inward sound,
has buried our names.

A nurse disarms us
of our flowers. Your son
shakes you, he shakes
the tablets down. But you come up, old valentine,
red and choking for breath.
I too am here, who straddled your knees
for songs and charged you
a nickel to come to dinner.

Now you have neither songs
nor knees, and will not eat your dinner,
I am the one who buries the spoons
with your slippers, who sings
and sings in the deepening well
of your sleep.

The Ballad of Ballymote

We stopped at her hut
on the road to Ballymote
but she did not look up
and her head was on her knee.

What is it, we asked.
As from the dreams
of the dead her voice came up.

My father, they shot him
as he looked up from his plate
and again as he stood and again
as he fell against the stove
and like a thrush his breath
bruised the room
and was gone.

A traveler would have asked directions
but saw she would not lift her face.
What is it, he asked.

My husband sits all day in a pub
and all night and I may as well
be a widow for the way he beats me
to prove he's alive.

What is it, asked the traveler's wife,
just come up to look.

My son's lost both eyes in a fight
to keep himself a man
and there he sits behind the door
where there is no door
and he sees by the stumps
of his hands.

And have you no daughters for comfort?

Two there are an gone to nuns
and a third to the North
with a fisherman.

What are you cooking?

Cabbage and bones, said she. Cabbage
and bones.

To You on the Broken Iceberg

I'm speaking from the half
at the horizon; that's me waving
as though this were only vacation, the Titanic
of our hopes ploughing on
without us, passengers intact. They
haven't missed us
yet. Adrift near the dance floor, our cabin
still pretends we're inside, its "Do Not
Disturb" a partner to everyone.

So now we're both Captains: my salute
to yours. These slick clouds make us
stand for ourselves, the matching ships
we always yearned for. Yes, that's you
waving back as though this were only
happening and me yelling: "Snoweyes,
I'd know you anywhere." Look, I'm still

in my wedding clothes after all
these centuries, the live sieve of my skin,
run through with ice. Spilled hands
on the hard water, my part
was never so calm. Waves close over
and over a sky we took for land.

11

Welcome this sun or not
it's the same: even this melting
lifts the sleepless ship toward grass.

JOHN HAINES

The Legend of Paper Plates

They trace their ancestry
back to the forest.
There all the family stood,
proud, bushy and strong.

Until hard times,
when from fire and drought
the patriarchs crashed.

The land was taken for taxes,
the young people cut down
and sold to the mills.

Their manhood and womanhood
was crushed, bleached
with bitter acids,
their fibres dispersed
as sawdust
among ten million offspring.

You see them at any picnic,
at ballgames, at home,
and at state occasions.

They are thin and pliable,
porous and identical.
They are made to be thrown away.

The Child in the Rug

Better a bug in the dust underfoot
than a human child without a voice.

So when visitors came to her room
she rolled herself in a rug,
lay on the floor and listened.

Fear of the closeness of strangers,
of a word driven deep in her dumbness,
sent her to grieve in a tunnel,

and to think she was all right there,
that she needed no more than this:
to listen to others
through a wall of string,

safe with her moths and pins,
threads of the flowerprints
coming loose from her sky of wool.

The Cauliflower

I wanted to be a cauliflower,
all brain and ears,
thinking on the origin of gardens
and the divinity of him
who carefully binds my leaves.

With my blind roots touched
by the songs of the worms,
and my rough throat throbbing
with strange, vegetable sounds,
perhaps I'd feel the parting stroke
of a butterfly's wing . . .

Not like my cousins, the cabbages,
whose heads, tightly folded,
see and hear nothing of this world,
dreaming only on the yellow
and green magnificence
that is hardening within them.

The Goshawk

I will not walk on that road again,
it is like a story one hesitates to begin.

You find yourself alone,
the fur close about your face, your feet
soft and quiet in the frost.

Then, with a cold, rushing sound,
there's a shadow like the death-angel
with buffeting wings,
his talons gripping your shoulder,
the bright beak tearing and sinking . . .

Then, you are falling, swept
into the deepening red sack of a voice:

"Little rabbit, you are bleeding again;
with his old fire-born passion
the Goshawk feeds on your timid heart."

The Color

It was simply a dark,
laboring mass.
Now and then it gave off
some half-stifled
animal noises.

A group of idle people
were watching.
Curious, they drew close,
and someone prodded
the mass with a stick.

Because it was hungry,
it reached out a brown,
tentative finger.
A mouth,
suddenly appearing
in its sweating flesh,
opened and closed.

The people were frightened,
a woman screamed.

They all drew back
into themselves,
and immediately
began building walls.

14

Spilled Milk

When I see milk spilled on the table,
another glass overturned,
I think of all the cows who labor in vain.

So many tons of forage spent,
so many udders filling and emptying,
forest after forest
stripped for paper cartons,
the wax from millions of candles melting . . .

A broad sheet of milk spills across
the tables of the world,
and this child stands
with a sopping sponge in his hand,
saying he never meant to do it.

KENNETH O. HANSON

First of All

First of all it is necessary
to find yourself a country
—which is not easy.
It takes much looking
after which you must be lucky.
There must be rocks and water
and a sky that is willing
to take itself for granted
without being overbearing.
There should be fresh fish
in the harbor, fresh bread
in the local stores.
The people should know
how to suffer without
being unhappy, and how to be happy
without feeling guilty. The men
should be named Dimitrios

Costa, John or Evangelos
and all the women should be
named Elena or Anthoúla.
The newspapers should always
lie, which gives you something
to think about. There should be
great gods in the background
and on all the mountain tops.
There should be lesser gods
in the fields, and nymphs
about all the cool fountains.
The past should be always
somewhere in the distance,
not taken too seriously
but there always giving perspective.
The present should consist of the seven
days of the week forever.
The music should be broken-hearted
without being self-indulgent.
It should be difficult to sing.
Even the birds in the trees should
work for a dangerous living.
When it rains there should be
no doubt about it. The people
should be hard to govern
and not know how to queue up.
They should come from the villages
and go out to sea, and go back
to the villages. There should be
no word in their language
for self-pity. They should be
farmers and sailors, with only
a few poets. The olive trees
and the orange trees and the cypress
will change your life, the rocks
and the lies and the gods
and the strict music. If you go there
you should be prepared to leave
at a moment's notice, knowing
after all you have been somewhere.

Bouzouki

Listening to rock 'n roll
on the American Armed
Forces radio station in Athens
Evangelos says Americans
are crazy and changes the station
to bouzouki where the voice
of Kazantzides makes its way
despairing through a world
of broken promises, anonymous
letters and the basic Greek emotions.
This is the music to break
plates to. It simply leaves
no stone unturned.
Every day a new landscape
and the heart, peeled like an onion.

GWEN HEAD

Slug

How can he dare to cross me,
this oozing footless tube,
lifting his alert pronged head
in the cuckold's gesture?

Long ago his nation
cast off the security of shells
and now go proudly naked
relying for safety
on the *realpolitik*
of sheer slug numbers.

Clearly he glories
in each nuance of slug calligraphy,
those sly paths of silver
that chronicle the progress
of appetite, and answer
the urgent appeals of the rain.

Perhaps he incarnates
the slug king of legend
who lay for seven days and seven nights
besotted in a saucer of beer
but did not drown

and who, by this test,
won his dappled queen
and with her dangled upside down
on a glittering rope
of commingled slime
convulsed and tranquil
as a hypnotist's pendulum.

Then together they passed
through the exorcist's circles
of slug bait unharmed
and will feast forever
on trilliums and tulips

if I choose to stay my foot.

I don't, but stand a moment musing,
their sticky deaths the mucilage
holding me earthbound
by all that is at once
most vulnerable
most destructive.

Stinging Nettle

Its disguise resides in the commonplace.
The ancient shabby needle of the fields
plies its trade among blackberries, under dock,
or apes the sprawling pungency of mint.
Stalks upright, leaves opposite, toothed, of an attenuated
heart shape, its flowers loll in pendulous racemes
so little showy they seem an irritant,
like lint or a fallen eyelash.
Dioica, incomplete, of one sex only,
they inhabit, like Godwin and Wollstonecraft, two houses
to express the furious rectitude of their separateness.

You know the rest. Under the microscope
the leaves and stems bristle

with narrow metallic volcanoes.
Brushed, they erupt in poison, invisible, adamant
as unrequited love;
                                but should you, in rage
and pain, crush the offending
branch, the blood of the nettle will surely heal you,
just as, scalded, the spiteful shoots
turn tame and nourishing.
                                Further, the caterpillar
of the ravishing Admiral Skipper
feeds only on stinging nettle; and perhaps the butterflies
too are immune, and return
each summer in frivolous flight like loveletters
among the stern catkins.

One final warning. The plant is perennial.
Its roots multiply deep, in hiding.
Its pain, like that of childbirth, is strangely effaceable.
Forgetful, you too may grasp it time and again
in an open field, among flowers.

JIM HEYNEN

Tourist Guide: How You Can Tell for Sure
When You're in South Dakota

You drive down MAIN STREET
of the first town you come to.

There's a traffic light.
Always. Prestige.

When it sees you coming
it turns red.

You stop and you're exposed,
and you know it.

A thin cowboy's rabid dog
eyes you from the pool hall.

Then a thick old man
thumps down from the curb.

He's in front of your car
when the light turns green.

Something slow meets your eye.
An eye meets your eye.

You smile.
It doesn't.

You try to drive away.
The whole world stalls.

ROBERT HUFF

The Ventriloquist

(In Memory of J. P.)

Four years ago, dear old ventriloquist,
Your outcast voice, as pickled as von Zell's,
Buzzed chandelier, bounced off the hamster cage,
Balked, cracked, and broke out cackling
From your frozen daiquiri
To charm my daughter toward your dentures propped
Across the room (*The posh part of the skull!*).
An eerie death piece on the radio.

Before it died your throat had such control
That my ears now can't tell who's listening.
Today, they say, this foxglove in the park
Tells me your father couldn't understand
Why marriage was for you against the law.
One orange poppy, overweight, intones:
I drank to get myself away from me.
A model sailboat whispers: *Cutty Sark* . . .
Hart Crane and I loved crew cuts, liked to park,
Liked green, long, sun, deep, seals, beds, loved the dark.

20

Comes then from a motel in Florida—
Via this bobbing lily or the gills
Of some deep-feeder, sheepshead, carp
Your last cast as the final unclear sound
Your body must have tried to make your voice
Become its echo, emptying the tub
Of all but what remains. Found you that way,
Still buoyant, said the clerk; your belly
Full of blood, the doctor said, internal
Hemorrhage; no teeth in your head.
They too submerged beside an empty bed.

Dear lonely creature, kind ventriloquist,
You had a trick of playing with your mouth
Right to the end—I hear it in this park,
Tuning me in before you flew down South,
Speak through the blighted chestnut: *Was a lark.*

The Smoker

Sitting down near him in the shade,
I watch him strike a match on his white cane.
He burns his finger but displays no pain.
This smiling blind man with a hearing aid

Smokes by the hour. Now he's blowing rings.
He measures in the smoke and takes more care
To shape his mouth for pumping circled air.
He fathers hundreds of round hoverings.

I offer: It's too warm; it ought to rain.
His only comment is a smiling cough.
Maybe he's got his hearing aid turned off
To keep such interference from his brain,

Or can't hear through the haze, or won't let sound
Disturb his gentle passion. Who can tell
What he envisions with his sense of smell
Heaving my presence at him by the pound?

I never blame him when he comes in dreams
A slow smile smoking, circled to the thighs,
And screws both of his thumbs into my eyes
And will not stop to listen to my screams.

RICHARD HUGO

What Thou Lovest Well,
Remains American

You remember the name was Jensen. She seemed old
always alone inside, face pasted gray to the window,
and mail never came. Two blocks down, the Grubskis
went insane. George played rotten trombone
Easter when they flew the flag. Wild roses
remind you the roads were gravel and vacant lots
the rule. Poverty was real, wallet and spirit,
and each day slow as church. You remember threadbare
church groups on the corner, howling their faith
at stars, and the violent Holy Rollers
renting that barn for their annual violent sing
and the barn burned down when you came back from war.
Knowing the people you knew then are dead,
you try to believe these roads paved are improved,
the neighbors, moved in while you were away,
    good-looking,
their dogs well fed. You still have need
to remember lots empty and fern.
Lawns well trimmed remind you of the train
your wife took one day forever, some far empty town,
the odd name you never recall. The time: 6:23.
The day: October 9. The year remains a blur.
You blame this neighborhood for your failure.
In some vague way, the Grubskis degraded you
beyond repair. And you know you must play again
and again Mrs. Jensen pale at her window, must hear
the foul music over the good slide of traffic.
You loved them well and they remain, still with nothing
to do, no money and no will. Loved them, and the gray
that was their disease you carry for extra food
in case you're stranded in some odd empty town
and need hungry lovers for friends, and need feel
you are welcome in the secret club they have formed.

Invasion North

They looked soft floating down. White puffs that glowed
in sunlight like dandelion seed. And they landed
softly in the snow, discarded the billowing white silk,
formed squadrons based on types of weapon
and started marching at us, one drum rolling,
armor gleaming on their breasts. We tried to joke
inside the igloo fortress but we timed
the punchlines badly. Finally, the captain said
we'd better load. They were two miles off and closing.

They closed fast. The drum roared loud as cannon.
God, they were big. White uniforms and makeup.
Our mascot polar bear broke his titanium chain
and ran. The last order I remember from the captain
was retreat. I remember being alone. The wind against
my face. The walrus. Flashes on the horizon.
I knew without seeing it our fortress was destroyed.
And I knew somehow the enemy soldiers, those women
in military nylon had beaten us. I cried.

Of the entire garrison, I am the only survivor.
Lord, it's cold, wandering this ice alone. My radio
still works. The conquering women have offered me
the captain's skeleton, have promised amnesty
if I come in. They broadcast every day at noon
and again at nine on clear nights. They must think
I'm a fool. I've developed a terrible arsenal
in case I'm taken and I've stockpiled berries,
roots and dry meat, enough to last fifty years.

Landscapes

If I painted, I'd paint landscapes. In museums
I stop often at van Ruysdael, and the wind he painted
high in European oaks gives license to my style.
I move the barn two feet. I curve the hill down
more dramatic. I put a woman on the hill against
the light, calling me to dinner. The wind I paint
is low and runs the grass down dancing to the sea.

In no time I have aged the barn stark gray.
Obviously, my cows hate no one. My wife

23

across the field stays carved out solid on the sky.
My tossed kiss stings her through the waves of heat
plowed dirt gives off in August. My tossed worm
drifts beneath the cutbank where I know trout wait.
As long as wind is pouring, my paint keeps farming green.

When wind stops, men come smiling with the mortgage.
They send me the eviction notice, postage due.
My cows are thin and failing. My deaf wife snarls
and claws the chair. The creek turns putrid.
I said fifty years moss on the roof is lovely.
It rots the roof. Oaks ache but cannot stir.
I call van Ruysdael from my knees on the museum floor.

In uniforms like yours you'll never understand.
Why these questions? The bank was wrong. The farm
is really mine. Even now along these pale green halls
I hear van Ruysdael's wind. Please know I rearranged
     things
only slightly, barn and hill. This is real: the home
that warps in August and the man inside who sold it
long ago, forgot he made the deal and will not move.

Places and Ways to Live

Note the stump, a peach tree. We had to cut it down.
It banged the window every wind. Our garden
swayed with corn each summer. Our crops were legend
and our kindness. Whatever stranger came, we said,
"Come in." We ran excited. "Someone's come to see us."
By night we were exhausted. The dark came early
in that home, came early for the last time soon.

Some nights in motels, I wake bewildered by the room.
Then I remember where I am. I turn the light on
and the girl's still there, smiling from the calendar
whatever the year. When I'm traveling, I'm hurt.
I tune in certain radio stations by heart,
the ones that play old tunes like nothing worthwhile's
happened since that funeral in 1949.

When I'm in the house I've bought, I don't dwell on
the loss of trees, don't cry when neighbors move away
or dogs get killed by cars. I'm old enough to know
a small girl's tears are fated to return, years from now

24

in some Berlin hotel, though I seem to sit unfeeling
at the window watching it all like a patron.
I'm taking it in, deep where I hope it will bloom.

That is the crude self I've come to. The man who says
suffer, stay poor and I can create. Believe me, friends,
I offer you your homes and wish you well in them.
May kisses rain. May you find warm arms each morning.
May your favorite tree be blooming in December.
And may you never be dispossessed, forced to wander
a world the color of salt with no young music in it.

LAWSON FUSAO INADA

Making Miso

> *For Noboru Muramoto, author of* Healing Ourselves

Muramoto knew all this as a child.
But then he had the old country
around and behind him,
the people being whole and natural.

We try hard in Henry's rented kitchen,
huge as California
Jews and Japs
looming to his quick direction.

Muramoto moves, as they say,
"without question."

But we do it, or try,
and yet still have to ask
why
"March is such goood time
for making miso."

A sack of koji, a sack of soy,
hands
full of sea salt from Mexico.

Even the beans are Wisconsin,
leaping into the teeth of pigs.

These are the big
ingredients,
plus some decent water,

a touch of time some Sunday,
dipping your reach
deep to your being in the cask.

Sit back. Relax.
What you do for the next
nine months is your business.

Then you see summer coming,
what valley heat does to yeast . . .

This is the wisdom of the East:

Miles was surely conceived
on your mother's birthday,
your anniversary, when some
instructions
released you into Camp.

Toti greeted into a tadpole
on precisely the night
Lester Young's folks were making
love and great music
to a full winter moon
in Woodville, Mississippi.

Making miso is easy.
The simplest task.
All you have to do
is do it, with your full being,
and know how to love, and eat, and laugh.

DAVID KHERDIAN

For My Father: Two Poems

1

Our trivial fights over spading
the vegetable patch, painting the
garden fence ochre instead of blue,
and my resistance to Armenian food

in preference for everything American,
seemed, in my struggle for identity,
to be the literal issue.

Why have I waited until your death
to know the earth you were turning
was Armenia, the color of the fence
your homage to Adana, and your other
complaints over my own complaints
were addressed to your homesickness
brought on by my English.

2

My father always carried a different
look and smell into the house when he
returned from the coffee houses in Racine.
Playing in the streets we would stop,
walk quietly by, and peer in thru the
cracked doors at the hunched backgammon
players, their Turkish cups at their elbows.

Years later, reading the solemn and bittersweet
stories of our Armenian writer in California,
who visited as a paperboy coffee houses in
Fresno, I came to understand that in these
cafes were contained the suffering and
shattered hopes of my orphaned people.

SANDRA MC PHERSON

His Body

He doesn't like it, of course—
Others, who don't wear it but see it, do.
He's pale, like a big desert, but you can find flowers.
No, not entirely pale:
Between shin and ankle the twin sun marks;
And where his shirt (now draped from a chair back)
Was, he contrasts with dark hands

And neck/face
Like a rained-on street where a car has just been driven
Away.
Don't picture a beer paunch.
And he is a smooth animal, or soft where he isn't smooth,
Down to his toadskin testicles.
He lies prone on clean bedsheets.
There is a single light in the room.
Now run your hand down his back, it's small, and up
The hips and over. Their sheen's like that
On blue metal music boxes made to hold powder.
But the rest of him is sprouted with black down-going hair,
His whiskers in so many foxholes,
Eager to out.
Are they in any order?
Age has so far
Remained locked inside.
I'm not a doctor
And glad not to have a doctor's viewpoint.
I'm glad I haven't the petite,
Overwhelmed sight of an antibody.
And yet I'm not just anybody perusing his body—
I have a reason to like it better than I like other bodies.
Someone else can praise those,
Each lonely and earthly, wanting to be celestial.

VERN RUTSALA

Washrags

In Long Valley the Finns
Brought the old country with them
Brought it in the 'nineties
In steerage in their ragged luggage
They lugged it with them
It was a millstone and the knives in their boots
It was the way they stood around
The store in town
Eyes down shoulders hunched

28

Waiting for everyone else to buy
They packed it with them in gunny sacks
They took it to dances
Condensed and distilled
In pint bottles
They beat each other with it
Behind Finn Hall
Its weight pulled
Them out of school at fourteen
It ruined their teeth with hardtack
And filled their mouths
With strange accents
No soap would wash loose
It was the broken axle and the bad crop
It was the huge tree
They knew would fall
They smiled grimly
Knowing 1929 by its real name
It let the travelling dentist
Pull all my grandfather's teeth
The year he died
It was in the washrag I buried
For my father
To cure a wart

Fame

Our names burn in the air.
Great reputations descend from the trees
like thousands of caterpillars.
Everyone is famous!

Each house has a marquee!
And no one wears the dark
coat of obscurity
any more. We've thrown away

the sad gloves of failure.
The newspaper is enormous—
all page one, filled with everyone's
picture. The seedy dives

of drift and solace
are closed. No one's name is secret.
Every phone book
is a *Who's Who*

and the movie credits never end—
they list all of us! O never again
will anyone be anonymous and all our graves
will be national shrines!

Words

We had more than
we could use.
They embarrassed us,
our talk fuller than our
rooms. They named
nothing we could see—
*dining room, study,
mantel piece, lobster
thermidor*. They named
things you only
saw in movies—
the thin flicker Friday
nights that made us
feel empty in the cold
as we walked home
through our only great
abundance, snow.
This is why we said "ain't"
and "he don't."
We wanted words to fit
our cold linoleum,
our oil lamps, our
outhouse. We knew
better but it was wrong
to use a language
that named ghosts
nothing you could touch.
We left such words at school
locked in books
where they belonged.
It was the vocabulary

of our lives that was
so thin. We knew this
and grew to hate
all the words that named
the vacancy of our rooms—
looking here we said
studio couch and saw cot;
looking there we said
venetian blinds and saw only the yard;
brick meant tarpaper,
fireplace meant wood stove.
And this is why we came to love
the double negative.

KNUTE SKINNER

Blackheads

Now in the after play
I press my fingers against
these blemishes on your
warm and beautiful back
—these little, worm-like, fatty
masses in your follicles—
where I have just held your flesh
in the grip of passion.

What are they made of? They leap
forth, the black tips followed
by the sinuous tails like
miniature streams of toothpaste
but a sickly white.

Can dirt be so white? Are they made
of soap? Who would dare
analyze them for taste?
Though I have run my tongue
lovingly over your body,
I would lack such courage.

Some are so deep they take
seconds to empty, if
indeed they do empty.
Has no one squeezed them before me?
Were they there all the time,
gathering, deepening,
waiting for the touch of my fingers,
secret imperfections
kept virginal for a lover?

Imagine Grass

The planet that we plant upon
rolls through its orbit of the sun,
bending our grass upon the breeze.
While far away the galaxies
in a decelerating pace
reach for the outer edge of space.

Imagine in that final sky
("Give me deceleration; I
will give you mass and curvature.")
at journey's end a far-flung star
of an unnumbered magnitude
Mount Palomar has never viewed.

In that expanded universe
the furthest star will be the first,
poised at the end of everywhere,
on the edge of nothing, like a prayer,
to turn from nothing and retrace,
pulsating through the curve of space.

So many billion light years since
the particle horizon densed,
conceive the universe defined
within the orbit of the mind,
and somewhere in the measured mass
of everything, imagine grass.

Organ Solo

When passion makes me discontent
because my swollen frame is bent,
caught in my master's underclothes,
his wife's neglect would whet my woes.
From hairy root to touchy tip
I'd yearn to hear a zipper zip.
I'd push against my master's fly,
hoping that I might catch her eye,
hoping that she would understand
and take me quickly into hand.

WILLIAM STAFFORD

Passing Remark

In scenery I like flat country.
In life I don't like much to happen.

In personalities I like mild colorless people.
And in colors I prefer gray and brown.

My wife, a vivid girl from the mountains,
says, "Then why did you choose me?"

Mildly I lower my brown eyes—
there are so many things admirable people
    do not understand.

Bess

Ours are the streets where Bess first met her
cancer. She went to work every day past the
secure houses. At her job in the library
she arranged better and better flowers, and when
students asked for books her hand went out
to help. In the last year of her life
she had to keep her friends from knowing

how happy they were. She listened while they
complained about food or work or the weather.
And the great national events danced
their grotesque, fake importance. Always

Pain moved where she moved. She walked
ahead; it came. She hid; it found her.
No one ever served another so truly;
no enemy ever meant so strong a hate.
It was almost as if there was no room
left for her on earth. But she remembered
where joy used to live. She straightened its flowers;
she did not weep when she passed its houses;
and when finally she pulled into a tiny corner
and slipped from pain, her hand opened
again, and the streets opened, and she wished all well.

People Who Went By in Winter

The morning man came in to report
that something had crossed the field
in the night during the storm. He heard
ribbons of wind snap at their tether
and a sound like some rider saying
the ritual for help, a chant or a song.
When we went out all we found
were deep, slow tracks in freezing mud
and some sticks tied together hanging
from the lowest branch of the oldest
tree by the river.

While beginning snow eddied and curtained
thicker and thicker on, we looked.
The grass hurried by, seething, then silent,
brown, all the way to the west, a little
touch-by-touch trail to the mountains.
Our boss turned back: "No.
We can't help them. They sing till
they find a place to winter. They have
tents. They make it, somehow." He
looked off that long way, where
the grass tossed.

Riding home, he told us:
"My people were like them,
over around Grand Prairie—slaves once,
then landowners. Now they pass like
this, and I hear them, because
I wake up and am partly theirs."
He looked at every man, and
he put his hand on the neck of his horse:
"They are our people, yours and mine,
all of us," he said.
"In every storm I hear them pass."

The Swerve

Halfway across a bridge one night
my father's car went blind. He guided
it on by no star but a light he kept in mind.

Halfway to here, my father died.
He looked at me. He closed his eyes.
The world stayed still. Today I hold in mind

The things he said, my children's lives—
any light. Oh, any light.

Father and Son

No sound—a spell—on, on out
where the wind went, our kite sent back
its thrill along the string that
sagged but sang and said, "I'm here!
I'm here!"—till broke somewhere,
gone years ago, but sailed forever clear
of earth. I hold—whatever tugs
the other end—I hold that string.

EVE TRIEM

Gerda, My Husband's Wife

Seldom named,
are you a guilty secret?
I found your snapshot:
a plain woman with eye-glasses
caressing a dog.

In my girl-bride time
there was Danny your son
grudging my very heartbeat.
Not like your kindness,

your ashes transformed
a tall white shadow
you came again and again
to cover my baby from harm.

In the midmark of marriage
despairing of the graces of love
I cried to fireflies
lighting up the raindrops
Gerda! keep what is yours,
he is not my husband.

Wailing what you knew—
the love of a stranger
a trapped fox grinning.

Bordello, Revisited

(for Agnes Thompson)

The note from my dying sister stirs up
reminiscence: his "sabbatical year," a joke
retold in the family how it ended,
when I came home from school and found
the dropout father in the connubial bed.
A man of the moment, never asked how did we eat
or pay rent; and thrilled us with his tales.

36

I remember our dainty mother too proud to tell
troubles scrubbed floors in the house of a madam
on Kearny Street, San Francisco; she was paid
   partly
that we children came there for dinners. The
   eldest,
I could read the dropped kimono, the woman
snubbling the sailor naked, emptying his pockets.

It was cheerful, after skimpy meals, to sit on
   beds
where people were hugging and Oriental waiters
   brought in
heavy silver trays. The glistening green onions,
   red radishes,
the meat dishes—I was a thin, hungry child.

And observant: the sex-tingled men willing to pay
for everything knew they had no price could buy
the beautiful vexing puritan our mother,
wiping floors with her silk hair. Yet they
   urged us to eat.

The madam, a distant cousin of our wayward
   father, had a lion mane.
Too thrifty to go to a beauty salon—too
   busy, perhaps.
One of her lovers, a Hungarian, washed it
   every Saturday.
That sticks in the mind. Makes me like the
   gypsy name.
And I love her ghost that she said to her
   patrons:
Give—
the children need Prang paints, tablets,
   spelling books.

Misdemeanor

On a day of grief
I wandered, sandals on grass,
through a park to a museum,
the memory of hyacinths
remaining to me
                   in fistfuls of honey.

And looked again
at the "girl":
marble head broken off
from a cemetery-stele.

By dew and the pure sun
ripened 2000 years
to a creamy glow.
The budding curls
browned, here and there,
by a sparse earth
the fragment fell into.

To the porous stone
of her smiling-compassionate mouth
I pressed my aching mouth.

In late visits
the lipstick stain
I could not wipe away
tells me and tells
joy of the marble
is in the waiting.

DAVID WAGONER

Lost

Stand still. The trees ahead and bushes beside you
Are not lost. Wherever you are is called Here,
And you must treat it as a powerful stranger,
Must ask permission to know it and be known.
The forest breathes. Listen. It answers,
I have made this place around you.
If you leave it, you may come back again, saying Here.
No two trees are the same to Raven.
No two branches are the same to Wren.
If what a tree or a bush does is lost on you,
You are surely lost. Stand still. The forest knows
Where you are. You must let it find you.

The Labors of Thor

Stiff as the icicles in their beards, the Ice Kings
Sat in the great cold hall and stared at Thor
Who had lumbered this far north to stagger them
With his gifts, which (back at home) seemed scarcely
   human.

"Immodesty forbids," his sideman Loki
Proclaimed throughout the preliminary bragging
And reeled off Thor's accomplishments, fit for Sagas
Or a seat on the bench of the gods. With a sliver of beard

An Ice King picked his teeth: "Is he a drinker?"
And Loki boasted of challengers laid out
As cold as pickled herring. The Ice King offered
A horn-cup long as a harp's neck, full of mead.

Thor braced himself for elbow and belly room
And tipped the cup and drank as deep as mackerel,
Then deeper, reaching down for the halibut
Till his broad belt buckled. He had quaffed one inch.

"Maybe he's better at something else," an Ice King
Muttered, yawning. Remembering the boulders
He'd seen Thor heave and toss in the pitch of anger,
Loki proposed a bout of lifting weights.

"You men have been humping rocks from here to there
For ages," an Ice King said. "They cut no ice.
Lift something harder." And he whistled out
A gray-green cat with cold, mouseholey eyes.

Thor gave it a pat, then thrust both heavy hands
Under it, stooped and heisted, heisted again,
Turned red in the face and bit his lip and heisted
From the bottom of his heart—and lifted one limp forepaw.

Now pink in the face himself, Loki said quickly
That heroes can have bad days, like bards and beggars,
But Thor of all mortals was the grossest wrestler
And would stake his demigodhood on one fall.

Seeming too bored to bother, an Ice King waved
His chilly fingers around the mead-hall, saying,
"Does anyone need some trifling exercise
Before we go glacier-calving in the morning?"

An old crone hobbled in, foul-faced and gamy,
As bent in the back as any bitch of burden,
As gray as water, as feeble as an oyster.
An Ice King said, "She's thrown some boys in her time."

Thor would have left, insulted, but Loki whispered,
"When the word gets south, she'll be at least an ogress."
Thor reached out sullenly and grabbed her elbow,
But she quicksilvered him and grinned her gums.

Thor tried his patented hammerlock takedown,
But she melted away like steam from a leaky sauna.
He tried a whole Nelson: it shrank to half, to a quarter,
Then nothing. He stood there, panting at the ceiling,

"Who got me into this demigoddiness?"
As flashy as lightning, the woman belted him
With her bony fist and boomed him to one knee,
But fell to a knee herself, as pale as moonlight.

Bawling for shame, Thor left by the back door,
Refusing to be consoled by Loki's plans
For a quick revision of the Northodox Version
Of the evening's deeds, including Thor's translation

From vulnerable flesh and sinew into a dish
Fit for the gods and a full apotheosis
With catches and special effects by the sharpest gleemen
Available in an otherwise flat season.

He went back south, tasting his bitter lesson
Moment by moment for the rest of his life,
Believing himself a pushover faking greatness
Along a tawdry strain of misadventures.

Meanwhile, the Ice Kings trembled in their chairs
But not from the cold: they'd seen a man hoist high
The Great Horn-Cup that ends deep in the ocean
And lower all Seven Seas by his own stature;

They'd seen him budge the Cat of the World and heft
The pillar of one paw, the whole north corner;
They'd seen a mere man wrestle with Death herself
And match her knee for knee, grunting like thunder.

Snake Hunt

On sloping, shattered granite, the snake man
From the zoo bent over the half-shaded crannies
Where rattlesnakes take turns out of the sun,
Stared hard, nodded at me, then lunged
With his thick gloves and yanked one up like a root.

And the whole hillside sprang to death with a hissing
Metallic chattering rattle: they came out writhing
In his fists, uncoiling from daydreams,
Pale bellies looping out of darker diamonds
In the shredded sunlight, dropping into his sack.

As I knelt on rocks, my blood went cold as theirs.
One snake coughed up a mouse. I saw what a mouse
Knows, as well as anyone: there, beside me,
In a cleft a foot away from my braced fingers,
Still in its coils, a rattler stirred from sleep.

It moved the wedge of its head back into shadow
And stared at me, harder than I could answer,
Till the gloves came down between us. In the sack,
Like the disembodied muscles of a torso,
It and the others searched among themselves

For the lost good place. I saw them later
Behind plate-glass, wearing their last skins.
They held their venom behind wide-open eyes.

JAMES WELCH

The Man from Washington

The end came easy for most of us.
Packed away in our crude beginnings
in some far corner of a flat world,
we didn't expect much more
than firewood and buffalo robes
to keep us warm. The man came down,

a slouching dwarf with rainwater eyes,
and spoke to us. He promised
that life would go on as usual,
that treaties would be signed, and everyone—
man, woman and child—would be inoculated
against a world in which we had no part,
a world of money, promise and disease.

Harlem, Montana: Just Off the Reservation

We need no runners here. Booze is law
and all the Indians drink in the best tavern.
Money is free if you're poor enough.
Disgusted, busted whites are running
for office in this town. The constable,
a local farmer, plants the jail with wild
raven-haired stiffs who beg just one more drink.
One drunk, a former Methodist, becomes a saint
in the Indian church, bugs the plaster man
on the cross with snakes. If his knuckles broke,
he'd see those women wail the graves goodbye.

Goodbye, goodbye, Harlem on the rocks,
so bigoted, you forget the latest joke,
so lonely, you'd welcome a battalion of Turks
to rule your women. What you don't know,
what you will never know or want to learn—
Turks aren't white. Turks are olive, unwelcome
alive in any town. Turks would use
your one dingy park to declare a need for loot.
Turks say bring it, step quickly, lay down and
    dead.

Here we are when men were nice. This photo,
    hung
in the New England Hotel lobby, shows them
    nicer
than pie, agreeable to the warring bands of redskins
who demanded protection money for the price of
    food.
Now, only Hutterites out north are nice. We hate
them. They are tough and their crops are always
    good.
We accuse them of idiocy and believe their belief
    all wrong.

Harlem, your hotel is overnamed, your children
are raggedy-assed but you go on, survive
the bad food from the two cafes and peddle
your hate for the wild who bring you money.
When you die, if you die, will you remember
the three young bucks who shot the grocery up,
locked themselves in and cried for days, we're rich,
help us, oh God, we're rich.

Christmas Comes to Moccasin Flat

Christmas comes like this: Wise men
unhurried, candles bought on credit (poor price
for calves), warriors face down in wine sleep.
Winds cheat to pull heat from smoke.

Friends sit in chinked cabins, stare out
plastic windows and wait for commodities.
Charlie Blackbird, twenty miles from church
and bar, stabs his fire with flint.

When drunks drain radiators for love
or need, chiefs eat snow and talk of change,
an urge to laugh pounding their ribs.
Elk play games in high country.

Medicine Woman, clay pipe and twist tobacco,
calls each blizzard by name and predicts
five o'clock by spitting at her television.
Children lean into her breath to beg a story:

Something about honor and passion,
warriors back with meat and song,
a peculiar evening star, quick vision of birth.
Blackbird feeds his fire. Outside, a quick 30
    below.

San Francisco and Northern California

ALTA

I Never Saw a Man in a Negligee

i'm frigid when I wear see thru negligees
my almost good figure looks good half hidden,
nipples the only hard bumps on my body & men
are sposed to sigh and go ooh & rub their hands
all over the filmy thing recalling norman mailer
& raquel welch & god knows who.
it never occurred to me to dress that way for women.
we'd pull off our cotton pants & go to it. so i figured,
if women can want the Real Me, men have to too. 2 times
i wore special fucky gowns, you know the type, one look
& he turns off the football game (but they never do)
& i was so busy being dainty & smelling fresh i couldnt
hump, couldnt wiggle, couldnt sweat, couldnt scream & you
   know
damn well i couldnt come.
but when i romp ass in a wrinkly blue shirt smelling like
   printers ink
or slightly soggy slacks after playing with babies,
then the happy human of me wants lovins, & rolls around
   with glee
rolling up, under, over&over o whee.

I Don't Have No Bunny Tail
on My Behind

i don't have no bunny tail on my behind.
i'm a sister of the blood taboo.

my throat's too tight to swallow.
must be because i'm scared to death. i'm scared to live.
how do i get thru the day? the night?
guts, fella. that's how

what are your perversions to me?
what do i care you want sadistic broads in black boots,
cigarettes up your asshole?
what do i care?
that's our child sleeping in that blue crib

how did it feel:
that cigarette up my nose?
how did it feel?
you grimacing "does it hurt, baby? does it hurt?"
how did it feel to curse your pretty smile,
pray blindness strike your ice blue eyes?
how did it feel to curse: may you never know joy.
i hate your very soul.

i swore to avenge all the wasted dead, the caged wives.
what vengeance could answer our pain, our fury?
i hope i find out before i die.
in my cunt is blood & i always want it to be your blood.
i hope you bleed 5 days every month. i hope your strength
    drains down the toilet.

you're afraid of me.
you laugh. you hit me.
you're running scared, man.
our voodoo dolls are all worn out.

yes i hate you.
yes i want your cock

off.
yes i want your blood & balls to spill
like my monthly payment in blood.
yes i want you to beat off in shame,
afraid to call me.
yes i want you dead.
when i was married i prayed to be a widow.
there are still wives. they are still praying.

yes i want you to flinch when i laugh
flinch when i laugh
my teeth tearing your heart, knowing your love is poisoned,
you cannot wash clean,
knowing the earth & i will outlive you.
you are a dying breed, you & your penis guns,

your joyless fucks, you are dying,
you are dying,
the curse of every wicked witch be upon your heart.
i could not hate you more if hatred were my bones.

The Art of Enforced Deprivation

i remember back in hi school
corliss & i were practicing dancing
i was the boy: my hand was round
her waist & the other hand holding her
hand. (that was how we danced back in those days)
her breast was poking me right there & i thot
"wow! boys sure get the good part!"

i looked at her face to see
if it felt as good to her as it did to me
but she wouldnt look at me.
i still dont know.

Hunger for Me

hunger for me hunger hunger for me
hunger i am right here you
can touch me if you reach you
can kiss my opening lips you
can feel my waters burst hunger
for me hunger hunger for me
you will never forget me your
dreams will remind you ignore me
& your dreams will cause you to
cry out my name i will visit you
as you have visited me i will
cause you to
hunger

Daily Courage Doesnt Count

daily courage doesnt count
we dont get diplomas for it.
i worked hard for 5 years with one man,
then had 3 years graduate training with another.

but people called me a divorcee, & acted as if
i had done something wrong.
no one was happy for me,
no one gave me a coming out party.
but i tell you, i came out of those marriages
one smart bitch.

He Said, Lying There

he said, lying there, looking
at me, his voice deep in my ear,
"i love you, alta" his voice
in my whole body like a blessing.

DAVID BARKER

Packard

Once, new, you rolled easy and maroon
down a dry Arizona highway.

Somehow, like me, you came to Oregon. Picking up
a couple of coats of cream enamel along the way. I
too have turned a lighter shade.

That was when someone still cared enough
to fix a bashed fender and lead in a dented trunk.
But you moved to the deep woods and
fell on hard times.

I shall not rub salt in fresh wounds
telling sad stories of the sea air. Unwanted, you were
hauled by trailer from the coast to Salem
to turn over a quick buck.

But I, like some silly old lover, have
plucked the rotted cotton from your springs. I
bear you tender gifts of fiberglass, Rustoleum,
WD-40. I shall patch you up and make you anew,
my darling.

Together we shall travel very far indeed.

50

View from the Planetarium

On these sunny steps
they stabbed Sal Mineo. That makes it
something of a cultural shrine.

We are in our Sunday finery. My
underwear is stuck up my crack
from the long hot ride up the mountain.

The city below
stretches out in an endless column of
glinting windshields. Ant people in ant cars.

In the souvenir shop, a pamphlet I bought:
THE HEAVENS ABOVE. A boy, like myself,
gazes reverently up
at a cumulus clouded sky.

In the domed room house lights dim
creating effects on the walls
of city at sunset, red rays, thin sad cloud,
a lone cactus
stuck up from the darkening foothills.

Admirable scientist, balding technician,
enters the arena. From a million pinholes
the giant steel ant machine
pours forth galaxies.

matisse tits

I know those tits. They are
white halfmoons. A cupped palm
of cool jiggle.

hanging with admirable
detachment on a firm chest. Her
arms are over her head, exposing
armpits erotic with black hairs.

Which doubly make up
for her fully skirted hips.

Her hair is pulled back tight
eyebrows drawn to a thin point
sophisticated as hell.

51

Zoo Dream

The silly Zebras don't know
that they could easily break out
thru this flimsy fence
of sticks and twine.

Because they don't know this
it has the tensile strength of steel.

Stupid me!
I have accidentally strayed
into this diminutive wilderness.

Here come the Zebras.

I two-step it double time
thru the fence. Seeing me do this
effortless thing puts
ideas into their heads.

They are bringing
the Bisons and Elephants and Giraffes
with them.

Gamey snorting of hot breath
on the back of my neck.

Lispy Bails Out

Here in the open cockpit
faceful of breeze
I sniff the winds of change.

Wooden wing struts and guy wires
lend a tentative support. You
look so brave out there, wind
whipped white frock and Florence
Nightingale cape.

Below, the dizzy patchwork map. I
can still hear your courageous last words,
a soft mixture of lisp and postnasal drip

as you step into the nearest available space,
a cloudbank of high hopes
one hand clutching your little nursebag
and the other the ripcord.

52

CHANA BLOCH

Exile

What happened to the ten lost tribes
is no great mystery:
they found work, married, grew smaller,
started to look like the natives
in a landscape nobody chose.
Soon you couldn't have picked them out of a crowd.

And if they'd stayed where they were,
what happiness
would they have endured?
We can't believe in it.

The face of the cities scares us,
day and night empty us, suddenly
we are no longer
God's chosen.

                We salvage

a pewter dish cross-hatched as a bubba's face,
a bent spoon. But the naked
dance of the mouth and the eyes before
we knew we were smiling,

                  promises

of that land . . .

For a while we camp out under the strange trees,
complaining, planning a return.
But we have taken out papers and will become citizens.

Furniture

Last night we talked about God
as metaphor, like
the head of the table
the leg of the chair
God of the Universe.

I haven't got a God to stand on, I said.
And flinched.
No thunder.

Shame on you,
God will punish you, my mother would say,
if you write on Shabbos.
When I wrote, I pulled down the shade.

In those days there was thunder like furniture moved in
     heaven.
God came down from the mountain.
My heart ticked evenly as a clock at the head of the bed.
On Sabbath the candles stood lit on the table,
and four chairs, one at each side,
squaring the round world.

There were crumbs on the tablecloth
and hot wax dripped from the candles
so quietly

we never heard them go out.

JAMES BROUGHTON

It Was the Worm

It was the Worm who said to me,
Do you seek the ultimate mystery
of where the Inmost Light may dwell?
I'm never asked, but I could tell.

Men search for it in starry places,
in cloistered cells, in pretty faces.
But they go looking with eyelids shut.
I tell you Glory lives in the gut.

Within that dark metamorphic maze
Heaven and Hell conjointly blaze.
What else gives light to Eternity?
the Worm, smiling, said to me.

Those Old Zen Blues
or, After the Seminar

> *It's not because it is.*
> *It's not because it isn't.*
> *It is because it is*
> *because it's not at all.*

In Zen you can't yen for anything
since nothing can be had.
When nothing is real in reality
nothing is good or bad.

There's nothing in heaven, nothing in hell,
and nothing is what I am.
Something is where it always was
but it doesn't give a damn.

> *It's not because it is.*
> *It is because it isn't.*
> *It isn't because it's not.*
> *It's not because at all.*

The life I think I ought to live
is just a thought in my head.
I ought to throw my thoughts away
and believe in nothing instead.

There's nothing where I start from
and nothing I comprehend.
Unless I get enlightenment
I'll be nothing in the end.

> *It isn't there because it's there.*
> *It's there because it isn't.*
> *It's where it is because it is*
> *and not because it isn't.*

Afterword: Song of Song

Do you ever hear it?
Do you know
what your voice is
always singing?

Listen!
        It sings
                (like everything)
as if no song
              were ever sung before like this

It
   is the song you have been singing
                          all your life

ROBERT CREELEY

The Tiger

Today we saw a tiger
with two heads come
bounding out of the

forest by the corner of
Main and Bailey. We
were not afraid. The

war had stopped fifteen
minutes previous, we
had stopped in a bar

to celebrate, but now
stood, transfixed,
by another fear.

The Act of Love

     for Bobbie

Whatever constitutes
the act of love,
save physical

encounter, you are
dear to me,
not value as

with banks—
but a meaning self-
sufficient, dry

at times as sand,
or else the trees,
dripping with

rain. How shall
one, this so-
called person,

say it? He
loves, his mind
is occupied, his

hands move
writing words
which come

into his head.
Now here,
the day surrounds

this man
and woman
sitting a small

distance apart.
Love will not
solve it—but

draws closer,
always, makes
the moisture of their

mouths and bodies
actively
engage. If I

wanted
a dirty picture,
would it always

be of a
woman straddled?
Yes

and no, these
are true opposites,
a you and me

of non-
sense,
for our love.

Now, one
says, the wind
lifts, the sky

is very blue, the
water just
beyond me makes

its lovely sounds.
How *dear*
you are

to me, how love-
ly all your
body *is,* how

all these
senses do
commingle, so

that in your very
arms I still
can think of you.

Sounds

Some awful
grating sound
as if some monstrous
nose were being blown.

*

Yuketeh, yuketeh—
moves slow through the water.

*

58

Velvet purr,
resting—

*

Slosh, slush,
longer wash
of it. Con-
verses.

*

Tseet, tseet—
then chatter,
all the way home.

January 12–22, 1970

WILLIAM DICKEY

The Poet's Farewell to His Teeth

Now you are going, what can I do but wish you
(as my wife used to say) "every success
in your chosen field."

What we have seen together! Doctor X,
having gagged us, hurling his forceps to the floor
and denouncing our adolescent politics,

or the time we had caught trench-mouth in Iowa City
and had to drive west slowly and haltingly,
spitting in all the branches of the Missouri.

Cigar-stained and tired of cavities, you leave.
It is time to go back to the pure world of teeth
and rest, and compose yourselves for the last eruption.

As to those things in a glass by the bathroom sink
they will never communicate with me as you have done,
fragile and paranoid, sensing the world around you

as wild drills and destructive caramel, getting even
for neglect by waking me into the pain of dawn,
that empty and intimate world of our bitter sharing.

Go, under that cool light. I will remember you:
the paper reports that people may still feel pain
in their missing teeth, as with any amputation.

I hope you relax by the shadowy root canals,
and thinking of me with kindness, but not regret,
toast me just once in the local anaesthetic.

For Every Last Batch When the
Next One Comes Along

Next door they've finally brought home the new baby.
Well, my wife says, carrying him over carefully
for a tour of inspection, would you look at that for two
    weeks!

It's true he's a good baby, big, fine head of hair.
Look, says my wife, his navel's healed up already
and his you-know-what's bigger than the two-year-old's.

I don't hear much from this baby late at night.
He's too big to be fretful; fill him up with milk
and he just hams comfortably on through till morning

while his two-year-old brother cries, deliberately
wets, goes babyish, tries to crawl into bed with
mother and daddy, get back into their flesh,

all of which is anathema to the pediatrician
who knows how the two-year-old statistically
can't be allowed to slide. Up, two-year-old!

Let's get you back on your feet while there's still time.
The world's no raisin bun aimed straight at you.
There's always a new contender for the playpen.

Though I still feel sympathy for you. Who ever wanted
that excessive baby? Who wanted him to arrive
with that vulgar head of hair? Who wanted him to be

carried around the neighborhood, the mothers saying:
Big babies are good babies; would you look at that perfect
    navel!
Would you ever believe the size of his you-know-what!

DIANE DI PRIMA

from **Revolutionary Letters**

4

Left to themselves people
grow their hair.
Left to themselves they
take off their shoes.
Left to themselves they make love
sleep easily
share blankets, dope & children
they are not lazy or afraid
they plant seeds, they smile, they
speak to one another. The word
coming into its own: touch of love
on the brain, the ear.

We return with the sea, the tides
we return as often as leaves, as numerous
as grass, gentle, insistent, we remember
the way
our babes toddle barefoot thru the cities of the universe.

29

beware of those
who say we are the beautiful losers
who stand in their long hair and wait to be punished
who weep on beaches for our isolation

we are not alone: we have brothers in all the hills
we have sisters in the jungles and in the ozarks
we even have brothers on the frozen tundra
they sit by their fires, they sing, they gather arms
they multiply: they will reclaim the earth

nowhere we can go but they are waiting for us
no exile where we will not hear welcome home
"goodmorning sister, let me work with you
good morning brother, let me
fight by your side"

who is the we, who is
the they in this thing, did
we or they kill the indians, not me
my people brought here, cheap labor to exploit
a continent for them, did we
or they exploit it? do you
admit complicity, say "*we*
have to get out of Vietnam, *we* really should
stop poisoning the water, etc." look closer, look again,
secede, declare your independence, don't accept
a share of the guilt *they* want to lay on *us*
MAN IS INNOCENT & BEAUTIFUL & born
to perfect bliss they envy, heavy deeds
make heavy hearts and to *them*
life is suffering. stand clear.

if the power of the word is anything, America, your oil
    fields burning
your cities in ruins, smouldering, pillaged by children
your cars broken down, at a standstill, choking the roads
your citizens standing beside them, bewildered, or choosing
a packload of objects (what they can carry away) if the
power of the word lives, America, your power lines down
eagle-eyed lines of electric, of telephone, towers
of radio transmission
toppled & rankling in the fields, setting the hay ablaze
your newspapers useless, your populace illiterate
wiping their asses with them, IF THE WORD HAS
    THE POWER YOU SHALL NOT STAND
AMERICA, the wilderness is spreading from the parks
    you have fenced it into, already
desert blows through Las Vegas, the sea licks its chops
at the oily edges of Lost Angeles, the camels are breeding,
    the bears, the elk are increasing
so are the indians and the very poor
do you stir in your sleep, America, do you dream of your
    power
pastel colored oil tanks from sea to shining sea?
sleep well, America, we stand by your bedside,
the word has power, the chant is going up

ROBERT DUNCAN

The Torso: Passages 18

Most beautiful!   the red-flowering eucalyptus,
the madrone, the yew

Is he . . .

So thou wouldst smile, and take me in thine arms
The sight of London to my exiled eyes
Is as Elysium to a new-come soul

If he be Truth
I would dwell in the illusion of him

His hands unlocking from chambers of my male body

such an idea in man's image

rising tides that sweep me towards him

. . . homosexual?

and at the treasure of his mouth

pour forth my soul

his soul   commingling

I thought a Being more than vast, His body leading
into Paradise,   his eyes
quickening a fire in me,   a trembling

hieroglyph: At the root of the neck

the clavicle, for the neck is the stem of the great
artery
upward into his head that is beautiful

At the rise of the pectoral
muscles

the nipples, for the breasts are like sleeping
fountains
of feeling in man, waiting above the beat of his
heart, shielding the rise and fall of his breath,
to be awakened

At the axis of his mid riff

the navel, for in the pit of his stomach the chord
from
which first he was fed has its temple

At the root of the groin

the pubic hair, for the torso is the stem in which
the man flowers forth and leads to the stamen
of flesh in which his seed rises

a wave of need and desire over   taking me

cried out my name

(This was long ago.   It was another life)

and said,

What do you want of me?

I do not know, I said.   I have fallen in love.   He
has brought me into heights and depths my heart
would fear   without him.   His look

pierces my side   •   fire eyes   •

I have been waiting for you, he said:
I know what you desire

you do not yet know   but through me   •

And I am with you everywhere.   In your falling

I have fallen from a high place.   I have raised myself

from darkness in your   rising

wherever you are

my hand in your hand   seeking   the locks, the keys

I am there.   Gathering me, you gather

your Self   •

For my Other is not a woman but a man

the King upon whose bosom let me lie.

64

Sonnet I

Now there is a Love of which Dante does not speak
   unkindly,
Tho it grieves his heart to think upon men
       who lust after men and run
          —his beloved Master, Brunetto Latini, among
           them—
Where the roaring waters of hell's rivers
Come, heard as if muted in the distance,
       like the hum of bees in the hot sun.

Scorcht in whose rays and peeld, these would-be lovers
Turn their faces, peering in the fire-fall,
       to look to one another
As men searching for an other
       in the light of a new moon look.

Sharpening their vision, Dante says, like a man
       seeking to thread a needle,
They try the eyes of other men
Towards that eye of the needle
       Love has appointed there
For a joining that is not easy.

WILLIAM EVERSON

The Gash

To covet and resist for years, and then
To succumb, is a fearsome thing. All you craved and denied
At last possesses you. You give yourself
Wholly to its power; and its presence,
Invading your soul, stupefies
With its solace and its terror.

There is nothing so humbling as acceptance.

I sense the mushrooms in the night,
Tearing their way up through loose soil,
Brutal as all birth.

And I bend my head,
And cup my mouth on the gash of everything I craved,
And am ravaged with joy.

LAWRENCE FERLINGHETTI

Wild Dreams of a New Beginning

There's a breathless hush on the freeway tonight
Beyond the ledges of concrete
restaurants fall into dreams
with candlelight couples
Lost Alexandria still burns
in a billion lightbulbs
Lives cross lives
idling at stoplights
Beyond the cloverleaf turnoffs
"Souls eat souls in the general emptiness"
A piano concerto comes out a kitchen window
A yogi speaks at Ojai
"It's all taking place in one mind"
On the lawn among the trees
lovers are listening
for the master to tell them they are one
with the universe
Eyes smell flowers and become them
There's a deathless hush
on the freeway tonight
as a Pacific tidal wave a mile high
                                        sweeps in
Los Angeles breathes its last gas
and sinks into the sea like the *Titanic* all lights lit
Nine minutes later Willa Cather's Nebraska
                                        sinks with it
The seas come in over Utah
Mormon tabernacles washed away like barnacles
Coyotes are confounded & swim nowhere
An orchestra onstage in Omaha
keeps on playing Handel's *Water Music*

Horns fill with water
and bass players float away on their instruments
clutching them like lovers horizontal
Chicago's Loop becomes a rollercoaster
Skyscrapers filled like water glasses
Great Lakes mixed with Buddhist brine
Great Books watered down in Evanston
Milwaukee beer topped with sea foam
Beau Fleuve of Buffalo suddenly become salt
Manhattan Island swept clean in sixteen seconds
buried masts of Amsterdam arise
as the great wave sweeps on Eastward
to wash away over-age Camembert Europe
Mannahatta steaming in sea-vines
the washed land awakes again to wilderness
the only sound a vast thrumming of crickets
a cry of seabirds high over
in empty eternity
as the Hudson retakes its thickets
and Indians reclaim their canoes

Lost Parents

It takes a fast car
               to lead a double life
in these days of short-distance love affairs
   when he has far-out lovers in
                   three different locations
   and a date with each one
                at least twice a week
  a little simple arithmetic shows
       what a workout he's engaged in
crossing & recrossing the city
     from bedroom to patio to swimming pool
the ignition key hot
     and the backseat a jumble of clothes
               for different life-styles
 a surfboard on the roof
   and a copy of Kahlil Gibran or Rod McKuen
             under the dashboard
    next to the Indian music casettes
   packs of Tarot and the I-Ching
            crammed into the glove compartment

along with old traffic tickets
and hardpacks of Kents
dents attesting to the passion
of his last lover
And his answering service
catching him on the freeway
between two calls or two encounter groups
and the urgent message left
with an unlisted number to call Carol
about the bottle of fine wine
he forgot to pick up
and deliver to the gallery
for the reception at nine
While she shuttles to her gynecologist
and will meet him later
between two other numbers
male or female
including his wife
who also called twice
wanting to know where he's been
and what he's done
with their throw-away children
who
left to their own devices
in a beach house at Malibu
grew up and dropped out into Nothing
in a Jungian search
for lost parents
their own age

JUDY GRAHN

Asking for Ruthie

you know her hustle
you know her white legs
flicker among headlights
and her eyes pick up the wind
while the fast hassle of living

ticks off her days
you know her ways

you know her hustle
you know her lonely pockets
lined with tricks
turned and forgotten
the men like mice hide
under her mind
lumpy, bigeyed
you know her pride

you know her blonde arms cut
by broken nickels in
hotelrooms and by razors of
summer lightning on the road
but you know the wizard
highway, no resisting so
she moves, she is forever missing

get her a stopping place
before the night slides dirty
fingers under her eyelids and
the weight of much bad kissing
breaks that ricepaper face

sun cover her, earth
make love to Ruthie
stake her to hot lunches in the wheat fields
make bunches of purple ravens
fly out in formation, over her eyes
and let her newest lovers
be gentle as women
and longer lasting

from The Common Woman

VI. Margaret, Seen Through a Picture Window

After she finished her first abortion
she stood for hours and watched it spinning in the
toilet, like a pale stool.
Some distortion of the rubber
doctors with their simple tubes and
complicated prices,

still makes her feel guilty.
White and yeasty.
All her broken bubbles push her down
into a shifting tide, where her own face
floats about her like the whole globe.
She lets her life go off and on
in a slow strobe.
At her last job she was fired for making
strikes, and talking out of turn;
now she stays home, a little blue around the edges.
Counting calories and staring at the empty
magazine pages, she hates her shape
and calls herself overweight.
Her husband calls her a big baboon.
Lusting for changes, she laughs through her
teeth, and wanders from room to room.
The common woman is as solemn as a monkey
or a new moon.

VII. Vera, from My Childhood

Solemnly swearing, to swear as an oath to you
who have somehow gotten to be a pale old woman;
swearing, as if an oath could be wrapped around your
    shoulders
like a new coat:
For your 28 dollars a week and the bastard boss
you never let yourself hate;
and the work, all the work you did at home
where you never got paid;
For your mouth that got thinner and thinner
until it disappeared as if you had choked on it,
watching the hard liquor break your fine husband down
into a dead joke.
For the strange mole, like a third eye
right in the middle of your forehead;
for your religion which insisted that people
are beautiful golden birds and must be preserved;
For your persistent nerve
and plain white talk—
the common woman is as common
as good bread
as common as when you couldnt go on
but did.

For all the world we didnt know we held in common
all along
the common woman is as common as the best of bread
and will rise
and will become strong—I swear it to you
I swear it to you on my own head
I swear it to you on my common
woman's
head

SUSAN GRIFFIN

White Bear

In 1867
White Bear
a Kiowa Indian
known for his courage
and eloquence
said to the United
States Congress,

*"I have heard that you intend to
settle us on a reservation near the
mountains. I don't want to settle.
I love to roam over the prairies.
There I feel free and happy, but
when we settle down we grow
pale and die."*

I read this in a museum
White Bear's medicine bag behind
a glass case and me
on the other side
thinking, it is clear
I do not know how to live
anymore words do not
even come to my mouth,
I want to

forget all I have
learned
if it has
led to this, these
Indians knew how to
ride ponies at age five,
chew porcupine needles,
use river clay and plant dyes,
and I tell you,
they had beautiful songs to sing.

I press my hand to the glass
and read
White Bear
committed suicide
in a prison
in Huntsville Texas, 1878. What
reward is there
for patience, I slide my
hand on the cool glass
the keeper lets me through the door.
What shall I do now?
I ask, pedaling my bicycle
up the street.

At home
my daughter waits,
the innocent jailor,
together
we grow pale
doing dishes
and answering the telephone.
She runs
twice as much
as I, yells
much louder,
and when she's unhappy
she cries.

I teach her
to beware of
electricity and
fire.
What else she learns,
I am afraid to
name.

GEORGE HITCHCOCK

Villa Thermidor

He sits in a deckchair reading Colette
and fanning himself with a pair
of shoelaces. In the rose garden

giant snails copulate in rhythms
undulant and infinitely beguiling.
His ancestors lie snoozing

in the family urns. Fog has lately
attacked the poinsettias. On the pier
by the lake there are adenoidal

swellings—the boathouse no doubt
is ill. Umbrellas are descried
gliding above the local peaks.

Undulant and infinitely beguiling.
Next year, says the Oakland Tribune,
snowshoes may be taxed

for their illicit oils. Stingrays
flap in the sand like wounded moths.
Infinite and undulant.

Cocktails are served from five
to seven at the bottom of the pool.

The Chauffeur of Lilacs

—from an old photo
The bandits leap up to the cab,
their stilettos pressed to the flanks
of firemen; the luminous pistons
idle in baths of steam. The brakemen
disappear into culverts, their caps

full of coal. The trigger-finger
changes seats with the fake marquis,
the salesman leaves the smoker,
his cigar half chewed. One-Eyed Pete
draws curses on the grimy window;

the lady in bombazine conveniently
faints as

El Capitano, man
of moustaches, enters the coach, tips
his prodigious sombrero to the women,
spins a dirty peseta and hawks on the carpet.
The ladies swallow their diamonds.
This train will definitely be late
to North Platte.

So bullets
are bitten, the darkness shot down.
The conductor bows with a belly full
of smoke. Beside the engineer stands
the chauffeur of lilacs, a glowing
flare in his glove. They all,
passengers and crew, the dream
and the artist alike, dissolve
into sepia fractions.

Departure

Through the trees outside small
pieces of darkness fall like grace-
notes. The sorrel, mild ferns
and azalea gather the night to them.

We are alone now, you and I, in
this sighing house beneath the firs.
You nod wisely and begin to unravel
the cloth I'd spent all yesterday

weaving. When the night has eaten
the firs, and the sullen glass
gives back nothing but our ashen
images, you'll go to that other

lover, he who commands your nerve-
ends and lays out a map
of follicles only his fingertips
can follow. Then shall I,

wrapped in the hush of blackness,
kneel and gather those bits of
thread which dropped from your hand
to the bare, bare floor.

CAROLYN KIZER

Postcards from Rotterdam

1.

Came such a long way
To find you—
Over an ocean!
Now only a channel
Separates us.
It is enough.

We are divided by water.
I shed one tear.

2.

Waited for your letter
Until I lost interest.
Then it arrived,
Full of protestations.

Ah no, friend, you woo us with words
Just once.
Then you must lay your body
On the line.
And it isn't here.

3.

I thought
When the moon was full again
I would be in your arms.

But I'm not.

I'm in somebody else's arms.
We don't even glance
At the moon.

4.

Having wonderful time
Coming in from the town.

Having wonderful time
Contemplating the bidet.

Having wonderful time
With the shutters drawn.

Having wonderful time
Converting silver into dross.

Having wonderful time walking around
With a five-pound key in my purse

And a plastic flask full of Holland gin.
I shed one tear.

Wish you were here.
Love,   Carolyn.

The Intruder

My mother—preferring the strange to the tame:
Dove-note, bone marrow, deer dung,
Frog's belly distended with finny young,
Leaf-mould wilderness, hare-bell, toadstool,
Odd, small snakes roving through the leaves,
Metallic beetles rambling over stones: all
Wild and natural!—flashed out her instinctive love,
    and quick, she
Picked up the fluttering, bleeding bat the cat laid at her feet,
And held the little horror to the mirror, where
He gazed on himself, and shrieked like an old screen door
    far off.

Depended from her pinched thumb, each wing
Came clattering down like a small black shutter.
Still tranquil, she began, "It's rather sweet. . . ."
The soft mouse body, the hard feral glint
In the caught eyes. Then we saw,
And recoiled: lice, pallid, yellow,
Nested within the wing-pits, cosily sucked and snoozed.
The thing dropped from her hands, and with its thud,
Swiftly, the cat, with a clean careful mouth
Closed on the soiled webs, growling, took them out
    to the back stoop.

But still, dark blood, a sticky puddle on the floor
Remained, of all my mother's tender, wounding passion
For a whole wild, lost, betrayed and secret life
Among its dens and burrows, its clean stones,
Whose denizens can turn upon the world
With spitting tongue, an odor, talon, claw,
To sting or soil benevolence, alien
As our clumsy traps, our random scatter of shot.
She swept to the kitchen. Turning on the tap,
She washed and washed the pity from her hands.

To Li Po from Tu Fu

Milord, how beautifully you write!
May I sleep with you tonight?
Till I flag, or when thou wilt,
we'll roll up, drunken, in one quilt.

In our poems we forbear
to write of kleenex or long hair
or how the one may fuck the other.
We're serious artists, aren't we, brother?

In our poems, oceans heave
like our stomachs, when we leave
late at night the 14th bar,
I your meteor, you, my star.

When autumn comes, like thistledown
we'll still be floating thru the town,
wildly singing in the haze,
I, past saving, you, past praise.

PHILIP LEVINE

My Son and I

In a coffee house at 3 am
and he believes
I'm dying. Outside the wind
moves along the streets
of New York City picking up
abandoned scraps of newspapers
and tiny messages of hope
no one hears. He's dressed
in worn corduroy pants
and shirts over shirts,
and his hands are stained
as mine once were
with glue, ink, paint.
A brown stocking cap
hides the thick blond hair
so unlike mine. For forty
minutes he's tried not
to cry. How are his brothers?
I tell him I don't know,
they have grown away
from me. We are Americans
and never touch on this
stunned earth where a boy
sees his life fly past
through a car window. His mother?
She is deaf and works
in the earth for days, hearing
the dirt pray and guiding
the worm to its feasts. Why
do I have to die? Why
do I have to sit before him
no longer his father, only
a man? Because the given
must be taken, because
we hunger before we eat,
because each small spark
must turn to darkness.
As we said when we were kids

and knew the names of everything
. . . just because. I reach
across the table and take
his left hand in mine.
I have no blessing. I can
tell him how I found
the plum blossom before
I was thirty, how once
in a rooming house in Alicante
a man younger than I,
an Argentine I barely understood,
sat by me through the night
while my boy Teddy cried out
for help, and how when he slept
at last, my friend wept
with thanks in the cold light.
I can tell him that his hand
sweating in mine can raise
the Lord God of Stones,
bring down the Republic of Lies,
and hold a spoon. Instead
I say it's late, and he pays
and leads me back
through the empty streets
to the Earle Hotel, where
the room sours with the mould
of old Bibles dumped down
the air-shaft. In my coat
I stand alone in the dark
waiting for something,
a flash of light, a song,
a remembered sweetness
from all the lives I've lost.
Next door the TV babbles
on and on, and I give up
and sway toward the bed
in a last chant before dawn.

RON LOEWINSOHN

The Windows

Suddenly they are there as I
turn my head at the other end
of the darkness, the three of them
together, tall, austere, gaunt,
parchment-colored, looming down on me.

If they are openings out onto the world outside
(which now is an austere world of the imagination,
peopled with gaunt, parchment-colored presences
looming down from the other end of the dark)
they are also incursions, brooding urgencies,
insistent, demanding, all night spilling into
the dark house, all night they are there.

Goat Dance

"You inspire me," you said.
You bet.
        I breathe you right down into my blood
engorging the sinuses of my
corpus cavernosum
stiff up as a flagpole, my emblem
these days

               O bright tits of the world!

You are touched by the drooping wing
Aphrodite who hovers

                        over all that hath life
                        bee-like, death-like,
                        a wonder

Now the wind comes up & the clothes on the line
wave to me
        The bodies they did contain

painful, painful to see them jerk
that way, a
locomotor ataxia kootchie dance—Eros,

the glue of the world   a pain
in my chest
              stops my breath.
Inside the skirts is meat
                          calling
to meat—& looking into your eyes I saw
skies of the easiest blue.

                    You bet.

The law of the blood,
like you said, "Infinitely personal."

The Leaves

There was a brightness in the branches
that was a body, a white clarity
I saw in there among a cloud of
apple blossoms & green leaves. Her arms
were a little chubby & her legs dangled
down; she smiled at me a dark-eyed
smile, & her nipples as she sat
on her branch, & the line her legs made
where they met her body, & her dark
pubic hair, made another smile, a rich
heavy body, filled with her own presence &
with the greenness of the leaves, but so white,
& leaving, wherever she smiled, a flowering
longing for that clear, heavy fullness.

MORTON MARCUS

Watching Your Gray Eyes

Watching your gray eyes glaze,
the blond hair piled like a halo around your head,
and hearing you say
you've never known such joy
as you have with me tonight,

I remember all those girls
opening themselves like books
on the back seats of Chevrolets,
and realize that what you have of me
I received from them, outside bars
called *Bloody Bucket, Preacher's, Hanging Loose*:
faces eaten away by fog and rain,
names I sometimes never knew—
the sweat, caught breath,
hands clenched against the night.
And received for thirteen years
from the woman who wears my name.
And before that from anyone I touched,
all the way back to when I was seventeen
and the blond woman old enough to be my mother
with the black numbers branded on her forearm.
Her husband had been gassed at Auschwitz,
and she had served her mourning in a doll's house
learning from the Nazis what she gave to me.
Or even before that: the feels and minute lays,
and my cock proudly circumcised,
a tag for two thousand years
which I bring to you here in the heft of my hips—
tenements full of old men,
the crowded cattleboats,
the aisle opening in the Red Sea:
any passageway—ramp, door, bridge,
even an imagined flight of white birds.
That is what I see now, watching your gray eyes
glaze, hearing your mouth call me beautiful,
and, yes, feeling beautiful,
although the warmth on my back
flares from cities burning in the night.

MICHAEL McCLURE

Ode to Joy

I HAVE INHERITED THE UNIVERSE!
IT CAME FROM THE EARTH
that got it from bodies
that became divine.
Ocean, forest, fog,
are wine
and they drink me.
Nothing bad
can ever happen
—it is part of the constellation
—part of the code.
It is all an ode
written in eagles
and plasm.
The chasm is as drunk
as the dizzy height.
What joy to be in flight.

Baja—Outside Mexicali

AMERICANS PASS BY,
WORLD LORDS,
hauling huge land vans
and campers behind
trucks pulling
dune buggies and power boats
of hallucination.
Great timid Gypsy Lords
of plastic objects
and shining metals
roar at 85 miles per—
out of their secret
walled strongholds
in Orange County
where safe
from commy Blacks
and Chicanos
they pile up

                    mickey mouse
                    treasure.
                  They tear on by
                 the now dry desert
              delta of the Colorado River
                 —which was polished
                  off by Boulder Dam
                   and all her babies
                    to make power
               and give water to thirsty
                     Los Angeles.
                  Mexico was paid off
                   with a diddy bop
                   irrigation project
                and a market for cheap
                     agriculture.
                  The Rio Colorado
                 power is and was used
                   to build the art-
                    ifacts on wheels
                   that thunder by.
                   Mexicans watch
               from dust drenched adobe
                  under palm thatch
                    or sometimes
                       from
              a purple and yellow house
                   and they envy.
              The wind-moved tamarisk
                  trees are beautiful
              as graygreen chinchilla fur.

DAVID MELTZER

from A Midrash

The Rabbi is before me.
Sparks structure his face. Sparks compose his body.
One moment he is King Solomon in gold & red robes
in a movie,
the next a white rooster crowing Voodoo,

84

the next a shrunken Chinese poet-sage rolling down a hill, drunk, outrageous,

the next wheel faces him as dawn's *chazzan* singing factory whistles,

the next toss he's a tumbler, springs in the bottom diamonds of his sneakers,

the next instant pinned against the wheel's center, hands & legs spread apart like Leonardo's technic crucifix, ten colored spheres light-up around the hub.

The Rabbi is tall, fat, small, lean, rat-like, a fox, an owl,

a cloud in space with bloody lips, he inhales night.

He's a sudden hawk

up & over the hill.

Once he said,

"Study each spark, each spark. Do you understand? Each spark."

"But, rebbe," I answered, "they go by so quickly."

"In each spark is a letter of the book you yearn to read."

The Rabbi comes & goes & I become his translation.

A single spark is a letter wed to another letter until a word is formed. A single world is a word I spend days travelling thru.

The grocer isn't appeased.

The phone is taken away because I won't answer it.

"You're not here," says the repair-man. "You're on Cloud 9. I know all about you people."

His truck has 43 letters on its left side, a circle with 2 volts of lightning held within it.

But what time is it?

Uncle Lable Leshinsky may still be alive in Brooklyn, may still let the alarmclock awake him at 7:30 in the morning, may still set off to work at the plant, a small building he is in charge of, making belts & ladies' purses. Assembly-line lunacy he attends to daily. Obedient. A golem like the rest of us, he remains mute to the betrayal.

But once he was a glazier in Safed

or was it Prague or Lublin or Kiev or Bialystok or Yampol

or in a cave in Spain they say walls are mirrors which are doors which are gates in to Heaven

Once he made letters of glass that were prisms

that were secret lenses
to read between lines of a bird song
to capture exaltation's first birth lights.
But what time is it?
Is it not now? I ask the Rebbe.

The Rebbe picks up my grandmother's mandolin &
sings a song in Yiddish about almonds & raisins &, in
that instant, manufactures the form of my grandmother &
sings in her voice & my heart is electrified & turns into
glass & breaks apart into a billion particles which
splinter my soul & I bleed & I cry into the Moldau which
ran thru our block in Brooklyn powering the Church
Avenue trolley.

The Moldau turns into the Red Sea raging against
the Great Wall.

Foam of impact fragments into angels & demons
rising like Dachau smoke into the sky, into Paradise.
Fuel for voices. Context & balance for the souls we
share between us.

But then Grandpa Benny enters into me.

Moscow intellectual, gold-wire glasses, octagonal. An
Old Gold hangs from his lips.

He doesn't have to tell me about USA, the place they
came to from all over Europe. Splendid alchemical
America where it all turns to gold & everything is
possible. Peasants instantly transformed into Midas. The
streets so bright you need special glasses to walk down
them.

He doesn't have to tell me in anything.

In Moscow he sits in a favorite cafe with colleagues.
They talk politics & poetry & dreams & of plans
for an underground city filled with fabulous musicbox
beauties, elegant & available.

Grandfather Benjamin came to America & became a
tailor & struggled with the English language & married
Sarah who bore him three sons.

Grandfather Benjamin became a Jew became his own
father from a small village who saw visions of Heaven's
sections & entered each sphere to see what he could see &
bring the news back to the village.

My grandfather's father told gloriously funny tales.

My grandfather taught them to my father & my
father's brothers.

My father tried to tell them to me. But in each new telling the stories became less & less funny, more meagre in detail.

Now I, last of the line, can not remember any of them. Not even the first words.

Grandpa Benny sits in the livingroom of his son's flat in Brooklyn. I'm seven years old & watch him. He sits in the stuffed chair & pretends to listen to the opera on the radio. Smoke from his cigarette rises into light shafts thru two windows that face an alley. An unread copy of *The Daily Forward* on his lap. He keeps falling asleep. Milton Cross talks about the wonders of Texaco.

Now he is dead. Three times removed from Russia. I had no words for questions I never asked. My father is dead. His brother Jack is dead. My grandmother is gone. I would have asked her about the village life. Uncle Lable, the *gilgul* glazier, was her brother & he would show a slide-show of Pardes. Candle-light shining thru his magic letters.

They are all dead.

Three times removed from source, tradition.

All that is left are the musics & the lights.

All that is left are the books, the book.

All that is left is all that will be.

All that is left is all that was. The mysteries. The words are seeds. The stories re-tell themselves. They are memory & they invent my songs. In my head, I swear, Eden flourishes.

JOSEPHINE MILES

Witness

Gassed going between classes
Students said little,
Huddled their books and ran.
As helicopter crews waved down low at them
They were silent
Yelled and were silent.

Now the trees speak, not running or reading
But with cast leaves tallying
The cost of a gas deterrent.
My throat alive still cries
But how to tell without dying
Is not told by the dying trees.

Family

When you swim in the surf off Seal Rocks, and your family
Sits in the sand
Eating potato salad, and the undertow
Comes which takes you out away down
To loss of breath loss of play and the power of play
Holler, say
Help, help, help. Hello, they will say,
Come back here for some potato salad.

It is then that a seventeen year old cub
Cruising in a helicopter from Antigua,
A jackstraw expert speaking only Swedish
And remote from this area as a camel, says
Look down there, there is somebody drowning.
And it is you. You say, yes, yes,
And he throws you a line.
This is what is called the brotherhood of man.

Away

Never going off, always here, I
Never say goodbye. You may
Leave over and over, for good,
For the weekend, for my life; I
Wave and cry

What is my life but your leaving?
Giving a brief biography of my life, I say
Each year they are off, all of them,
Goodbye, goodbye,
Yet here I stay

As in 1940, 41, 58, 59, 60, 70,
Now again they are going away.

Born yet unlearned in travel,
Each sacramental day
I give over
And they take it away.

Conception

Death did not come to my mother
Like an old friend.
She was a mother, and she must
Conceive him.

Up and down the bed she fought crying
Help me, but death
Was a slow child
Heavy. He

Waited. When he was born
We took and tired him, now he is ready
To do his good in the world.

He has my mother's features.
He can go among strangers
To save lives.

If You Will

Shall I pull the curtains against the coming night?
No, there is still a fine sun in the tree tops; let them be.
All right; now it is darker; shall I now
Close out the dark? You will close out the light.
All right; how quick the dark comes. But see how the moon
Floods as it floods the earth even this room.
Moonlight, it's time to sleep, shall I draw now
Curtains against the cold? It's summer weather.
Shall I? Yes, if you will; the light will pass.
It is your life that stands beyond the glass.

Conservancies

Plums on the ground
Lay with a soft sound
And the sweet sense of dissolution they have.
She used to pick them up

With a scoop, thickened with bees.
She would carry away into bottles what she could save
And the cinnamon worked in the kitchen
Saying *save*.

Now when the lingering fresh breezes
Flurry in the field rows
Some sifts of clear summer air,
She pickles the puffs in clear jars,
Brings them out
In winter scarcity,
Gives everybody on his plate of malathion
A rich spoonful of air.

LEONARD NATHAN

Ellora

I was watching the great God dance
In the stony dusk of a cave
At Ellora, when all the beggars
I ever refused marched in.

They were terrible and endless and true
And they marched right into the stone
And they danced right into the God
And looked from His eyes as they danced.

They did not believe I was real,
Rich, yes, and strange, but not real.
They did not grant me my name,
And knew I could barely feel.

If God and the poor are the same,
Nothing can save the world;
It will go on dancing forever
For stone is always the same.

The poor are always the same—
That is the thing you can feel
Watching God dance in His cave.
It is cruel and hard to be real.

To a Foreign Friend

I come sailing through the Indian Ocean
To reach you, expecting like a boy
A jeweled turban and secrets
I could decode with three box tops
And a little attention,
But you are not at home to children.

Instead, here is a cage to study;
In it, perched on a tree, delicate
Fingers curled to a branch,
Fur so soft it would hurt to touch,
Something nocturnal,
Amber eyes like a lemur's, but larger.

A million years ago, when I lifted
On the thought of my own hind legs, hands
In the dizzy air, banging
My skull on the sky, I felt I was watched
By just such a look—
What haunts us most are the near of kin.

All right—what are the reasons for hope?
Have I improved? Inland, behind you,
A panther screaming opens
The eye of a snake, a rock shifts position,
And nothing happens,
I count the bars of the cage while we wait.

The Likeness

What is it like to have just one shirt,
To have no money forever, to have nothing
Pertaining to men, to begin in dirt
And to end in dirt?

What is it like? Dirt for breakfast,
Breakfast for supper, nothing that does not pertain
To misery, to arrive hungry
And depart hungry?

To have nothing pertaining to love or money,
Nothing not dirty and just one shirt,
To be so cold when the world is cold
That to breathe can hurt.

Nothing, I tell you! And what is it like?
They can never, ever, ever tell.
They squat by the wall; they won't go to school;
They will not rebel.

This is a rock. You can chip away
Till it looks like a man and it can't feel pain
And it will not hope and it doesn't want love
And that's all you can say.

HAROLD NORSE

from You Must Have Been a Sensational Baby

a pair of muscular calves
drove me crazy today.
I studied their size, their shape,
their suntanned hairiness. I spoke
to the owner of them. are you
a dancer? I asked. oh no,
I was born with them, he said.
you must have been a sensational baby,
I said. he went back to his newspaper.
I went back to his calves.
he displayed them mercilessly.
he was absolutely heartless.
men stole secret looks at them.
women pretended he was a table.
they all had a pained expression.

92

he went on reading the Sports Page.
his thighs were even more cruel
thrust brutally from denim shorts.
the whole place trembled with lust.

Island of Giglio

we sailed into the harbor
all the church bells rang
the main street on the crescent shore
hung iridescent silks from windows
stucco housefronts gleamed
rose, pistachio, peach
and a procession sang
behind a surpliced priest
carrying a burnished Christ
when I set foot on shore
a youth emerged from the crowd
barefoot and olive-skinned
and we climbed up rocky slopes
till dusk fell and close to the moon
at the mouth of a cave we made love
as the sea broke wild beneath the cliff

GEORGE OPPEN

Sara in Her Father's Arms

Cell by cell the baby made herself, the cells
Made cells. That is to say
The baby is made largely of milk. Lying in her father's
    arms, the little seed eyes
Moving, trying to see, smiling for us
To see, she will make a household
To her need of these rooms—Sara, little seed,
Little violent, diligent seed. Come let us look at the world

Glittering: this seed will speak,
Max, words! There will be no other words in the world
But those our children speak. What will she make of a world
Do you suppose, Max, of which she is made.

Street

Ah these are the poor,
These are the poor—

Bergen street.

Humiliation,
Hardship . . .

Nor are they very good to each other;
It is not that. I want

An end of poverty
As much as anyone

For the sake of intelligence,
"The conquest of existence"—

It has been said, and is true—

And this is real pain,
Moreover. It is terrible to see the children,

The righteous little girls;
So good, they expect to be so good. . . .

Exodus

Miracle of the children   the brilliant
Children   the word
Liquid as woodlands   Children?

When she was a child I read Exodus
To my daughter   "The children of Israel . . ."

Pillar of fire
Pillar of cloud

We stared at the end
Into each other's eyes   Where
She said hushed

Were the adults   We dreamed to each other
Miracle of the children
The brilliant children   Miracle

Of their brilliance   Miracle
of

The People, the People

For love we all go
To that mountain
Of human flesh
Which exists
And is incapable
Of love and which we saw
In the image
Of a woman—We said once
She was beautiful for she was
Suffering
And beautiful. She was more ambitious
Than we knew
Of wealth
and more ruthless—speaking
Still in that image—we will never be free
Again from the knowledge
Of that hatred
And that huge contempt. Will she not rot
Without us and die
In childbed leaving
Monstrous issue—

SIMON J. ORTIZ

The Significance of a Veteran's Day

I happen to be a veteran
but you can't tell in how many ways
unless I tell you.

A cold morning waking up on concrete;
I never knew that feeling before,
calling for significance,
and no one answered.

Let me explain it this way
so that you may not go away
without knowing a part of me:

that I am a veteran of at least 30,000 years
when I travelled with the monumental yearning
of glaciers, relieving myself by them,
growing, my children seeking shelter
by the roots of pines and mountains.

When it was that time to build,
my grandfather said, "We cut stone and mixed mud
and ate beans and squash and sang
while we moved ourselves. That's what we did."
And I believe him.

And then later on in the ancient and deep story
of all our nights, we contemplated,
contemplated not the completion of our age,
but the continuance of the universe,
the travelling, not the progress,
but the humility of our being there.

Caught now, in the midst of wars
against foreign disease, missionaries,
canned food, Dick & Jane textbooks, IBM cards,
Western philosophies, General Electric,
I am talking about how we have been able
to survive insignificance.

My Mother and My Sisters

My oldest sister wears thick glasses
because she can't see very well.
She makes beautifully formed pottery.
That's the thing about making dhyuuni;
it has to do more with a sense of touching
than with seeing because fingers
have to know the texture of clay
and how the pottery is formed from lines

96

of shale strata and earth movements.
The pottery she makes is thinwalled
and has a fragile but definite balance.
In other words, her pottery has a true ring
when it is tapped with a finger knuckle.

Here, you try it;
you'll know what I mean.

The design that my mother is painting
onto the bowl is done with a yucca stem brush.
My other sister says, "Our mother,
she can always tell when someone else has used
a brush that she is working with," because
she has chewed it and made it into her own way.
She paints with movements whose origin
has only to do with years of knowing
just the right consistency of paint,
the tensile vibrancy of the yucca stem,
and the design that things are supposed to have.

She can always tell.

Washyuma Motor Hotel

Beneath the cement foundations
of the motel, the ancient spirits
of the people conspire sacred tricks.
They tell stories and jokes and laugh
and laugh.

The American passersby
get out of their hot, stuffy cars
at evening, pay their money wordlessly,
and fall asleep without benefit of dreams.
The next morning, they get up,
dress automatically, brush their teeth,
get in their cars and drive away.
They haven't noticed that the cement
foundations of the motor hotel
are crumbling, bit by bit.

The ancient spirits tell stories
and jokes and laugh and laugh.

97

GERDA PENFOLD

The Lust for Murder

and the undecided question
why didn't i do it
(sometimes wisely thinking
good thing i didn't
and yet . . .
and yet sometimes i admit
the clean finality of murder
appeals to my aesthetic
sensibility the very thought
of it satisfies my soul
the way legal
arrangements do not)
times i want a knife
in my hand
a stone dagger
and i will be a priestess
and he will lie on the operating
table and i will bring
my hand down from where
it was fully raised in the air
and i will make an incision
in his chest
and with my hand
remove his red beating heart
and raise it up while
the blood flows down
my arm over my white robes
and then
i will feed it to
the lowest of the animals
that's what i wanted
not what happened in
the courtroom where i signed
my name to the pages
of papers and it was all
over and my left hand had to
hold the right hand by the wrist
so that it would be steady

enough to sign
oh no it was not a pen
i wanted in my hand

La Pesadilla

That enraged and frightened woman of Goya
I can feel the perspiration of fear under
Her forty year old armpits I can taste
The sour saliva from the tongue of the bull on which
She is riding feel his wet nostrils hear her
Shrill screaming
And what is there to do about it?
    Her naked thighs where her dress has come apart
    Are not attractive
    Nor the teeth in her wide mouth
    She is not the least attractive
The mindless bull plunging her forward
Does not care where he is taking her

Once when she was young
She was beautiful
He came to her
Disguised as a prince with the
Rose colored gifts of promises
Once when she was young they made long journeys
   together
Through imaginary countries that now have come to this

She cannot stop him
And she does not want to
And she can think of nothing else to do

EUGENE B. REDMOND

Main Man Blues

Do you know my
Slap-a-hand, lend-a-hand main man?

Dirt-deep podner,
Quick-reeling, nigger-feeling friend, then?

Knife-blocker,
Vagina stopper,
Wit-knitted—not-to-be-shitted—bad man?

Have you ever had the *main man blues*?
Have you ever re-dug or coat-tailed
That cleanfully nasty harbinger of corner cuss?

Brothergone/Brother-coming?

Spitfire well digger
Who never got no bigger?
That ghetto-phonic nigger?

In the streets, on the sheets—where we sopped up our own
    blood;
In the churches—where we prayed, preyed, squinting
At fat old sisters or plumb-luscious classmates?

Brothergone/Brother-coming?

Hot rags macker, righteous!
Hot cock tracker, righteous!
Bigdaddy, uncle of mercy in the git-down times:
Slap-a-hand, lend-a-hand, main man?

Midway in the Night: Blackman

Blackman
            /midway in the night/
In the Beulahland of cabarets
            /bronco-busting the moon/
Silent is the howl, hung & mouth-held—
Your penis wrapped, rope-like,
Round your neck:
Your penis clotted, knot-like,
At your throat:

Your manhood dog-loosed
On the auction block
Of an American whim:
Your love cluttered with white fear

100

Your womanview hazed by the rat-tat-tat
Of assassins who snipe your mind
And ambush your history:
Black man,
Lover man:
Man of much-dick
Night-fuck hero
Quick-love artist
Dashman—
Don't let your penis protrude, goat-horn-like,
Through your skull:
Butting its way through
The tender muscular enclosures of your woman:
So anxious you cannot take the last shirt
Off the back of your mind:
So driven you cannot
Utter, in low register / in timed-tone,
The special name of your love.

TOM SCHMIDT

Waking Up

I am not surprised
to find a long wet seal
in my arms,
although there is

something about the darkness.
It nuzzles its cold nose
at my throat as if pleased.
I realize we are

sinking in her element. I know
there are green and yellow fishes
all around in the black water,
the salt in her fur

turns my tongue to smoke.
Our bodies are lazy
until the barking begins
deep in her throat

and we rise,
scattering the striped fishes
with our shoulders.
We burst the surface

into the first daylight,
your brown and butter hair
drenching my face like
summer rain.

Broccoli

Is my favorite vegetable.
Often I sit at home alone
eating broccoli.

Once in a dream
I took this Italian girl
to a large outdoor market
with broccoli filling every stall.
I bought her bouquets of broccoli
everywhere until she disappeared
behind a lovely green pillar
of broccoli.

Later we met in a park,
kissed in secret thickets,
in the warm rocks
beside the blinding river,
until she disappeared
behind a lovely green pillar
of broccoli.

Sometimes in the morning
I look in the mirror
and see my straight brown hair
gone to tight green knots.
My limbs grow oddly sinuous,
even crunchy.

102

My broccoli love
grows larger than the world.
My budding heart swells,
ready to burst clusters
of yellow flame against
the clear sky.

KARL SHAPIRO

Manhole Covers

The beauty of manhole covers—what of that?
Like medals struck by a great savage khan,
Like Mayan calendar stones, unliftable, indecipherable,
Not like the old electrum, chased and scored,
Mottoed and sculptured to a turn,
But notched and whelked and pocked and smashed
With the great company names
(Gentle Bethlehem, smiling United States).
This rustproof artifact of my street,
Long after roads are melted away will lie
Sidewise in the grave of the iron-old world,
Bitten at the edges,
Strong with its cryptic American,
Its dated beauty.

Aubade

What dawn is it?
The morning star stands at the end of your street as you
    watch me turn to laugh a kind of goodbye, with love-
    crazed head like a white satyr moving through wet
    bushes.
The morning star bursts in my eye like a hemorrhage as I
    enter my car in a dream surrounded by your heavenly-
    earthly smell.
The steering wheel is sticky with dew,

The golf course is empty, husbands stir in their sleep
   desiring, and though no cocks crow in suburbia, the birds
   are making a hell of a racket.
Into the newspaper dawn as sweet as your arms that hold
   the old new world, dawn of green lights that smear the
   empty streets with come and go.
It is always dawn when I say goodnight to you,
Dawn of wrecked hair and devastated beds,
Dawn when protective blackness turns to blue and lovers
   drive sunward with peripheral vision.
To improvise a little on Villon
Dawn is the end for which we are together.

My house of loaded ashtrays and unwashed glasses, tulip
   petals and columbine that spill on the table and
   splash on the floor,
My house full of your dawns,
My house where your absence is presence,
My slum that loves you, my bedroom of dustmice and
   cobwebs, of local paintings and eclectic posters, my
   bedroom of rust neckties and divorced mattresses, and
   of two of your postcards, *Pierrot with Flowers* and
   Young Girl with Cat,
My bed where you have thrown your body down like a
   king's ransom or a boa constrictor.

But I forgot to say: May passed away last night,
May died in her sleep,
That May that blessed and kept our love in fields and
   motels.
I erect a priapic statue to that May for lovers to kiss as long
   as I'm in print, and polish as smooth as the Pope's toe.
This morning came June of spirea and platitudes,
This morning came June discreetly dressed in gray,
June of terrific promises and lawsuits.

And where are the poems that got lost in the shuffle of
   spring?
Where is the poem about the eleventh of March, when we
   raised the battleflag of dawn?
Where is the poem about the coral necklace that whipped
   your naked breasts in leaps of love?
The poem concerning the ancient lover we followed
   through your beautiful sleeping head?

The fire-fountain of your earthquake thighs and your
    electric mouth?
Where is the poem about the little one who says my name
    and watches us almost kissing in the sun?
The vellum stretchmarks of your learned belly,
Your rosy-fingered nightgown of nylon and popcorn,
Your razor that caresses your calves like my hands?
Where are the poems that are already obsolete, leaves of
    last month, a very historical month?
Maybe I'll write them, maybe I won't, no matter,
And this is the end for which we are together.
Et c'est la fin pour quoy sommes ensemble.

GARY SNYDER

The Bath

Washing Kai in the sauna,
The kerosene lantern set on a box
    outside the ground-level window,
Lights up the edge of the iron stove and the
    washtub down on the slab
Steaming air and crackle of waterdrops
    brushed by on the pile of rocks on top
He stands in warm water
Soap all over the smooth of his thigh and stomach
    "Gary don't soap my hair!"
    —his eye-sting fear—
    the soapy hand feeling
    through and around the globes and curves of his body
    up in the crotch,
And washing-tickling out the scrotum, little anus,
    his penis curving up and getting hard
    as I pull back skin and try to wash it
Laughing and jumping, flinging arms around,
    I squat all naked too,
                    is this our body?

Sweating and panting in the stove-steam hot-stone
 cedar-planking wooden bucket water-splashing
 kerosene lantern-flicker wind-in-the-pines-out
 sierra forest ridges night—
Masa comes in, letting fresh cool air
 sweep down from the door
 a deep sweet breath
And she tips him over gripping neatly, one knee down
 her hair falling hiding one whole side of
 shoulder, breast, and belly,
Washes deftly Kai's head-hair
 as he gets mad and yells—
The body of my lady, the winding valley spine,
 the space between the thighs I reach through,
 cup her curving vulva arch and hold it from behind,
 a soapy tickle   a hand of grail
The gates of Awe
That open back a turning double-mirror world of
 wombs in wombs, in rings,
 that start in music,
                    is this our body?

The hidden place of seed
The veins net flow across the ribs, that gathers
 milk and peaks up in a nipple—fits
 our mouth—
The sucking milk from this our body sends through
 jolts of light; the son, the father,
 sharing mother's joy
That brings a softness to the flower of the awesome
 open curling lotus gate I cup and kiss
As Kai laughs at his mother's breast he now is weaned
 from, we
 wash each other,
                    this our body

Kai's little scrotum up close to his groin,
 the seed still tucked away, that moved from us to him
In flows that lifted with the same joys forces
 as his nursing Masa later,
 playing with her breast,
Or me within her,
Or him emerging,
                    this is our body:

106

Clean, and rinsed, and sweating more, we stretch
   out on the redwood benches hearts all beating
Quiet to the simmer of the stove,
   the scent of cedar
And then turn over,
   murmuring gossip of the grasses,
   talking firewood,
Wondering how Gen's napping, how to bring him in
   soon wash him too—
These boys who love their mother
   who loves men, who passes on
   her sons to other women;

The cloud across the sky. The windy pines.
   the trickle gurgle in the swampy meadow

   this is our body.

Fire inside and boiling water on the stove
We sigh and slide ourselves down from the benches
   wrap the babies, step outside,

black night & all the stars.

Pour cold water on the back and thighs
Go in the house—stand steaming by the center fire
Kai scampers on the sheepskin
Gen standing hanging on and shouting,

"Bao! bao! bao! bao! bao!"

This is our body. Drawn up crosslegged by the flames
   drinking icy water
   hugging babies, kissing bellies,

Laughing on the Great Earth

Come out from the bath.

AL YOUNG

Not Her, She Aint No Gypsy

Fifteen years up & her tongue's still flapping
She lives in the calcium of her bones
She lives in the toughness of her liver
She lives in the memory of men she's made happy by
    surprise
That's her salvation for now, for the weekend

She raised a son this way but she wont get to heaven
Her heaven's got jukeboxes anyway
Lots of jukeboxes & well-peppered shot glasses, a little bush
    on the side, coin telephones
Her son's a nice kid, digs cars & girls & unh-hunh the North
    Pole, collects books & articles on it & secretly hopes to
    visit it
Just another almost American boy with a mixed-up sisterly
    mom

She was beautiful once, a wild way-out kid (as they said in
    those days) who'd try anything once, twice if it was nice
    enough
She's still beautiful in another kind of way
But she dont know this just yet
All she know is she still got ice & a lotta drink left & the
    happy-headed dude across the table say he just sold a
    tune to some rock band & they threw in a little coke to
    boot so drink up love there's plenny more where this is
    coming from baby

She gets high to connect with ecstasy & pretty soon before
    she know it everything gets to be all elemental
Even as she pulls her panties up & kisses old hairy what's-
    his-name good morning she still dont know just what it is
    that's been bugging her all this time & how come her boy
    turned out so straight

But that's how it go
That's just how it go
She wouldnt change now, she couldnt come down for all the
    pills in Beverly Hills, for all the booze in Veracruz

She aint sold out yet & her tongue's still flapping

Ho

She coulda been somethin
like the Supremes or somebody
Her folks give her everything she need
I use to know her family pretty good
They dont have that much but they
    aint on relief
She call herself in love

Her money it go for that stuff, I guess,
    & for strong mouthwash, I know
I see her buyin Baby Ruths & Twinkies too
    down at the liquor store

Every night she start her day
right under my window when the lights
    come on
She aint bad-lookin neither, just little

She just a skinny little sister
bout big as my fist
but even she done slipped & found out
heaven aint the only H in the dictionary

A Poem for Players

Yes, theyll let you play,
let you play third base or fender bass,
let you play Harrah's Club or Shea Stadium

Theyll let you play
in a play anyway: Shakespeare,
Ionesco, Bullins, Baraka, or Genet,
only dont get down *too* much
& dont go gettin too uppity

Theyll let you play,
oh yes, on the radio, stereo,
even on the video, Ojays,
O. J. Simpson, only please dont stray
too far from your ghetto rodeo

Theyll let you be Satchmo,
theyll let you be Diz,

theyll let you be Romeo,
   or star in *The Wiz*
but you gots to remember that
   that's all there is

Oh, you can be a lawyer or a medico,
a well-briefcased executive with Texaco;
you can even get yourself hired, man,
to go teach *Ulysses* in Dublin, Ireland

Theyll let you play
so long as you dont play around,
so long as you play it hot or cool,

so long as you dont play down the blues
theyll let you play in *Playboy*, *Playgirl*,
   or the *Amsterdam News*

Finally theyll let you play
politics if you dont get in the way
the way some of us did and had to be
iced by conspiracy, international mystery

Theyll let you play anybody but you,
that's pretty much what they will do

Southern California

CHARLES BUKOWSKI

hell hath no fury . . .

she was in her orange Volks waiting
as I walked up the street
with 2 six packs and a pint of scotch
and she jumped out
and began grabbing the beerbottles and
smashing them on the pavement
and she got the pint of scotch and
smashed that too,
saying: ho! so you were going to get her
drunk on this and fuck her!
I walked in the doorway where the other woman
stood halfway up the stairs,
then *she* ran in from the street
and up the stairs and hit the other woman
with her purse, saying:
he's my man! he's my man!
and then she ran out and
jumped into her orange Volks
and drove away.
I came out with a broom
and began sweeping up the glass
when I heard a sound
and there was the orange Volks
running on the sidewalk
and on me—
I managed to leap up against a wall
as it went by.
then I took the broom and began sweeping up
the glass again,
and suddenly she was standing there;
she took the broom and broke it into three
pieces,
then she found an unbroken beerbottle
and threw it at the glass window of the door.

it made a clean round hole
and the other woman shouted down from the
stairway: for God's sake, Bukowski, go with
her!

I got into the orange Volks and we
drove off together.

letters

she sits on the floor
going through a cardboard box
reading me love letters I have written her
while her 4 year old daughter lies on the floor
wrapped in a pink blanket and
three-quarters asleep

we have gotten together after a split
I sit in her house on a
Sunday night

the cars go up and down the hill outside
when we sleep together tonight
we will hear the crickets

where are the fools who don't live as
well as I?

I love her walls
I love her children
I love her dog

we will listen to the crickets
my arm curled about her hip
my fingers against her belly

one night like this beats life,
the overflow takes care of death

I like my love letters
they are true

ah, she has such a beautiful ass!
ah, she has such a beautiful soul!

eddie and eve

you know
I sat on the same barstool in Philadelphia for
5 years

I drank canned heat and the cheapest wine
I was beaten in alleys by well-fed truck drivers
for the amusement of the
ladies and gentlemen of the night

I won't tell you of my life as a child
it's too sickening
unreal

but what I mean
I finally went to see my friend Eddie
after 30 years

he was still in the same house
with the same wife

you guessed it:
he looked worse than I did

he couldn't get out of his chair

a cane
arthritis

what hair he had was
white

my god, Eddie, I said.

I know, he said, I've had it, I
can't breathe.

then his wife came out. the once slim
Eve I used to flirt with.

210 pounds
squinting at me.

my god, Eve, I said.
I know, she said.

we got drunk together. it was several hours later
Eddie said to me,
take her to bed, do her some good,
I can't do her any good any
more.

Eve giggled.

I can't Eddie, I said, you're my
buddy.

we drank some more.
endless quarts of
beer.

Eddie began to vomit.
Eve brought him a dishpan
and he vomited into the
dishpan
telling me between spasms
that we were men
real men
we knew what it was all about
by god
these young punks
didn't have it.

we carried him to bed
undressed him
and he was soon out,
snoring.

I said goodbye to Eve.
I got out and got into my car
and sat there staring at the house.
then I drove off.
it was all I had left to do.

3:16 and One Half . . .

here I'm supposed to be a great poet
and I'm sleepy in the afternoon
here I am aware of death like a giant bull
charging at me
and I'm sleepy in the afternoon
here I'm aware of wars and men fighting in the ring

116

and I'm aware of good food and wine and good women
and I'm sleepy in the afternoon
I'm aware of a woman's love
and I'm sleepy in the afternoon,
I lean into the sunlight behind a yellow curtain
I wonder where the summer flies have gone
I remember the most bloody death of Hemingway
and I'm sleepy in the afternoon.

some day I won't be sleepy in the afternoon
some day I'll write a poem that will bring volcanoes
to the hills out there
but right now I'm sleepy in the afternoon
and somebody asks me, "Bukowski, what time is it?"
and I say, "3:16 and a half."
I feel very guilty, I feel obnoxious, useless,
demented, I feel
sleepy in the afternoon,
they are bombing the churches, o.k., that's o.k.,
the children ride ponies in the park, o.k., that's o.k.,
the libraries are filled with thousands of books of
    knowledge,
great music sits inside the nearby radio
and I am sleepy in the afternoon,
I have this tomb within myself that says,
ah, let the others do it, let them win,
let me sleep,
the wisdom is in the dark
sweeping through the dark like brooms,
I'm going where the summer flies have gone,
try to catch me.

ELLIOT FRIED

Daily I Fall in Love with Waitresses

Daily I fall in love with waitresses
with their bouncing name tags
KATHY MARGIE HONEY SUE
and white rubber shoes.

I love how they bend over tables
pouring coffee.
Their stiff hips nudge green formica,
calf muscles crimp,
forming soft curved shadows.
Their perky breasts hover above potatoes
as jets coming in to LAX
hang above the suburbs
like shades of broken stars.
I feel their fingers
roughened by cube steaks softened with grease
slide over me.
Their hands and lean long bodies
keep moving so
fumbling and clattering so harmoniously
that I am left overwhelmed, quivering.
Daily I fall in love with waitresses
with their cream-cheese cool.
They tell secrets in the kitchen
and I want them
    I know them
they press buttons creases burgers buns
    their legs are menu smooth
they have boyfriends or husbands or children
    or all
they are french dressing worldly—
they know how ice cubes clink.
Their chipped teeth form chipped beef
and muffin syllabics.
Daily I fall in love with waitresses
They are thousand island dreams
but they never stand still long enough
as they serve serve serve.

Mental Health

I used to see her daily, we would lie
upon my water bed and make the current
fly but then she said "I must go.
I'm starting up in a group."
    What for? There's nothing wrong.
"I know, but all my friends are going.
There must be something there."

And so she went. Encountered
once a week, and it was still all
right. Though she often asked me what I
meant . . . she never did before. I'm OK
AND YOU'RE OK, she'd greet me at the door.

The current wasn't quite as strong,
we weren't quite the same
and the more that she explained herself
the lesser we became.
To help us out she joined more groups:
the Isolates, the Outcasts,
the Fetishists, the Infactracides,
the troubled Existentialists,
the high-potential Suicides.
They clung together all the time,
had parties, meetings, brunch and T.
I saw her less, then not at all,
for now she had no time for me.

The moral of the story, friends,
if morals still exist today . . .
Be screwed up or warped or sick
but don't explain yourself away.

WILLIAM J. HARRIS

Modern Romance

One: The Wife

The reason
we got rid
of the robot
was
she was an
absolute slut.
You must
understand,
my Mortimor

is a strong
man
but how long
can even a good
man resist
temptation?
The way
she used to
look at him
and rub
against
him
every chance
she got. She
was a tramp,
that fancy
vacuum cleaner
with tits.

Two: The Husband

My wife never understood Doris.
I mean, the domestic robot.
She was a delight.
Intelligent yet submissive.
Sexy but didn't mind housework.
And she knew her place.
The perfect woman.
Must have been designed by a man.

Of course, a flesh and blood woman
is preferable to a machine
no
matter how perfect
and beautiful
and understanding
and responsive.

Poor Annie was so upset
by this whole mess.
I think a vacation would do her
a world of good.
The Grand Canyon? That's the place . . .

Three: The Robot

Imagine me, marrying
a man like Mortimor.
Why this is the
happiest day of
my life & a true
advancement for
my people. I am
the first robot
in history
to marry a man
of Mortimor's stature.
Oh, he's so
brave to withstand
public opinion
and so strong
to
overcome that
tragedy
of last weekend
when his wife accidentally
fell to her death
from a great height
in Arizona.

Hey Fella Would You Mind Holding This Piano a Moment

for Reg & Susie

As you are walking
down the street
this guy asks you
to hold his violin.
It's a Stradivarius.
Soon as it falls
into your hands
you start playing like crazy.
The violin
almost plays itself.
Your powerful hands
nearly break the instrument

but the music is gentle and sweet.
You sweep your long artistic hair
out of your face.
Everybody
in the room,
in the bull ring, in the
audience, in the Coliseum
starts clapping
and shouting "Encore & Wow."
Everybody whoever
thot you were
dumb & untalented
goes apeshit
over your hidden genius.
"Gee, I never knew you
played," says your astonished high school
principal.

ELOISE KLEIN HEALY

My Love Wants to Park

My love wants to park
in front of your house.

Thank God.
It's been driving me crazy,
going around and around the block.

It's started breaking laws,
obsessively rolls through boulevard stops,
changes lanes without looking back.

It's taken over the transmission,
drops into second
when I try to drive by,
unrolls its own windows.
I had to pull the horn wires
after it learned to "a-uugah"
at the sight of your address.

So just come out here, please.

Please, just look under the hood
and kick the tires.

Try to stay away from the back seat.

9/14/76

What Is Being Forgotten

Quickly. What is being forgotten? Shirts
on a line with stiff arms. Dampening bottles
with cork-rimmed lids. Rain water heated
and sprinkled on white shirts. The wooden
legs of the ironing board and the iron heating.
Air like hot bread. Shirts flattening
under the iron. That every shirt needed
ironing is being forgotten.

Los Angeles

Like an older sister who wasn't quite as pretty
you were never expected to become much,
only to settle your larger body into the practicality
of middle age.
You were never expected to be charming
like the younger one
who could enchant.
There was something about your proportions
that was indelicate—your more abundant waist.
She always had the poetic suitors who
came to visit.
You always answered the door.

Nobody expected it
and you never told about
the lover who met you
loose and large
in the late afternoon
and loved you all night,
completely out of proportion.

123

RONALD KOERTGE

Please

Hollywood Park Race Track is thirty miles
by tangled freeway from Los Alamitos Race
Track, but lately I find myself at one of
them all afternoon and at the other most

of the night. It is because I am lonely and
have nothing else to do. By now, of course,
I am poor as a church mouse because I do
not really care how the horses run. Against

the print of my program I always see your
ugly face and hear, behind me, the yakkity-
yak of your Lucy Ricardo mouth. It distracts
me and though I like one horse, I bet another.

But I have lost before, that does not confuse
me. The thing that I cannot understand is
this: what happened to all those dreamed-for
nights in front of the fire with a bottle

of brandy and a woman in a red dress? Poor
me, that was how I thought it would be when
you were gone, I really did. But it wasn't:
the brandy gave me a headache and the hotsy

turned out to be just another girl with a can
of hair spray in her purse. Surprisingly
enough, I miss you: your noise, stink and
bother. And I have an almost shocking

request to make—stop talking please and
listen. Come back, bitch. Eat me alive.

What She Wanted

was my bones. As I gave them
to her one at a time she put
them in a bag from Saks.

124

As long as I didn't hesitate
she collected scapula and
vertebrae with a smile.

If I grew reluctant she pouted.
Then I would come across with
rib cage or pelvis.

Eventually I lay in a puddle
at her feet, only the boneless
penis waving as an anemone.

"Look at yourself," she said.
"You're disgusting."

Harelip Mary

wasn't popular in high school for
one
    hundred reasons or another.

Oh, a lot of guys took her out
alright
but they always left her lying on
her back
    out in the corn fields.

So there she was—
           a drain on
her parents and a liability to
her pretty friend—standing
outside the Chevron station one
night when

the greasiest boy in town picked
her up
    on a modified Harley.

Two years later and they're still
together. She
rides
    everywhere with him, back
against the pussy bar.

as close to the O.B. position
as she ever wants to get.

And sure Bardhal Bob lays her
down
     in the cornfields all the time
but
  he always picks her up
when he's through.

12 Photographs of Yellowstone

1.   This is Cherry running for her life.
2.   This is the bear that ate up baby.
3.   Here I am complaining to a ranger.
4.   Here we are at dinner compliments of the Forest
     Service.
5.   This is a close-up of my penis on a bed of ferns.
6.   Here are two 13 yr. old girls peeing in the stream.
7.   This is their livid father being soothed by large bills.
8.   This is a time exposure, Cherry in the arms of a
     stranger.
9.   Here we see an unidentified boy masturbating near
     Window Rock.
10. This is the girl who sells film at the lodge sniffing her
     uniform.
11. This is the geyser that scalded all those nuns.
12. These are homosexual elk cruising each other in
     Angel's Meadow.

For My Daughter

She often lies with her hands behind her head
in a San Quentin pose, arms forming a pair
of small empty wings.

She does not slip from the bath in a loose
towel, affording Follies' glimpses
of rump and thigh. She does lumber by
in a robe of immense dunciness.

Her dates are fixed up or blind
often, like specimens, behind thick glass.
She leaves late, returns by 12:00 afraid
perhaps that she will turn into
something worse.

She comes to me and wants to know what to do.
I say I do not know.
She comes to me and wants to know if it will
ever be alright.
I say yes but it will take a long time.

Refusing What Would Bind
You to Me Irrevocably

My wife comes home
smug

because she has spared me so much
pain, ending the affair before
it could begin.

I shove her under the bed where I
have stashed

the man she desires and his brother
who is even better looking.

They are lying there in the lint
and the *TV Guides* and I can see all
those teeth

from across the room.

Tonto

He didn't know why he nursed the white man back to
life instead of lifting his hair because a Texan's
scalp is supposed to look particularly good hanging from
a lodge-pole. But Tonto was tired of living alone,

tired of coming home to a couple of curs, a deer-burger
and a bag of buffalo chips, so he dragged the guy off
to one side and fixed him up as well as he could. For
days the lawman lay between life and death while the
    Indian

sponged his white, spare body and watched. As the firelight
played on those alabaster cheeks, Tonto thought his new
friend was as beautiful as 100 squaws and before he knew
it he was head over heels in love. When his buddy got well

127

he didn't want to run away to Mexico like Tonto planned.
For some reason he wanted to give aid to the oppressed
    every-
where and call himself the Lone Ranger. Tonto told him
    how
they could live on 35¢ a day but it just seemed to push them

farther apart, and he had about talked himself into
going it alone when the Lone Ranger came out in his new
    mask
and tight white pants. He blew the red man's mind: every
night for weeks his head had been full of albinos cavorting

in fantastic costumes and all of a sudden his dreams came
true. After that he didn't have any choice, he followed the
Lone Ranger everywhere. At night they slept side by side on
the prairie and Tonto burned with desire from dusk til
    dawn;

he lived for that moment at the end of each humanitarian
escapade where they crept away unnoticed, for at that time
the white man always touched his burnished arm and he
    never
washed the spot. Furthermore Tonto had a plan. Secretly

he was trying to improve himself in order to be worthy of a
    man
with such great personal beauty, so he sent away for books
and read them in secret. In only a few months he built an
amazing vocabulary; and when he practiced his
    pronunciation

in the resonant badlands and would hear his words bounce
    back,
often he would weep at his own eloquence. By the time the
    Ghost
Mt. case came up Tonto figured he was ready. Sure enough,
    he
solved the murder before the Lone Ranger could figure out
    who

was dead. Then he climbed onto a wagon and delivered
    such an
impassioned address on crime prevention that the sheriff
    actually

bought him a drink and invited him around to the house for
dinner.
Not long after that on their way to new adventures the
Lone Ranger

turned in his saddle. "Tonto," he said. "It's about that Ghost
Mt. business. It don't look good for a dumb redskin to show
up a white man like that. Now I don't know where you
picked
up all that horseshit about community spirit and what-not
but

I want you to forget it. Think of the partnership, if nothing
else. We need each other, buddyroo. And remember white is
white and red is red, kiddo." So Tonto went back to his
little
words but that last sentence stuck in his mind. He thought
about

it for awhile then burned his books and went down to a
near-by
creek. There he scrubbed his copper skin with such
loathing that
he was all scars for weeks. When the white man finally
noticed
he said, "What's up injun? Cut yourself shavin'. Yuk. Yuk."

Tonto just looked into those beautiful blue eyes and shook
his head. And because he could not say I Love You he
said the silliest thing that he could think of. "Ugh," he
muttered to his black and white horse. "Get um up, Scout."

GERALD LOCKLIN

The Dwarf

She went away from us upon a snow-white
steed, that forest virgin scented with
the rain of evergreen, to wile the mythic
hours in a prince's castle. Was it right

of her to take away her apple
innocence from seven dappled
dwarves, to arbitrarily
absent us from felicity?

She went away to share a snow-white bed
with some tall aqua velva future king
who'll never know the pleasure wrested
from a woman willing, yet unwilling,

know how bigly bad a simple tree
appears to a tiny man, nor will they ever
either of them know the human thing
is not to be snow-white but to be ugly.

The Toad

"Do you love me?" I asked.
"Love you? How could I love a toad?"

That made a lot of sense,
so I asked her, "How's about
if we just kind of sleep together?"
Naturally she had to think that one over at some length:

"And never turn on the lights?"
"All right," I said.
"And you are gone before the sun comes up?"
"All right," I said.
She lowered her voice: "But you will
love me toad-style, not like humans?"
"Of course," I said.

"Well, then," she said, "we'll try it
for a week, but let's not ask for miracles."

I came to her each night for half a year,
returning with the sun to quarry
in the steaming, mud-caked bean fields.
Did she ever think about me at her gay
martini luncheons, dinners for two
at Scandia?
To think that I, a humble toad,
had given my heart to a fashion designer.

In May I lost her to a troll,
a recent arrival from Brooklyn.

bobbie's cat

is chasing its tail again.
the damn thing won't stop twitching.
is it possessed of a demon
or just a bent nerve?

perhaps it's all in the head.
sure, that's it,
the cat is driving itself crazy.
no, no, cats don't go crazy.

i go crazy
but it's not *my* tail that twitches,
it's bobbie's.
i circle it incessantly.

women are so destructive,
even the best of them.
the worst mistake a man can make
is to be nice to a woman.

the bible has it all wrong:
eve came first
and God created man
to distract her vile temperament from Himself.

ashamed, contrite,
God then created bourbon
without which
He knew man simply could not stand it.

"are you still mad?"
"no, i'm not mad."
"why aren't you talking to me?"
"what am i supposed to say?"

"maybe we could go out to a movie."
"if you'd like."
"would *you* like?"
"if you'd like."

bobbie, you spoiled little bitch,
don't you know how bad i need you?
i am going broke and writing badly.
they are charging me again with unprofessional conduct.

last night someone smashed a window in my car.
my wives and kids are calling out to me.
i'm drinking every waking hour
and sleeping badly.

now, out of nowheres, hemorrhoids.
at last, a literal, physical pain in the ass.
up to now
i've had to make do with you.

pedagogy

in the sixth grade they gave us a belgian nun.
she was just learning the language, and she often
had to ask the english word for something.
little things, like doorknobs, blackboard, chalk.

we were a rotten and sadistic bunch.
we gloried in sabotage.
our previous teacher was now in r-wing of the local hospital,
which is where you went when you couldn't stop screaming.

one day sister bonita asked us what you call
an electric outlet—you know, the thing on the wall
that you plug the plug into.
we told her it was called a cunt.

she left the room to find the janitor, to explain
what it was of hers that needed fixing, what it was
exactly that she couldn't fit the plug into.
she returned to class a tearful but a wiser woman.

which reminds me of a piece of profound advice
imparted to me by a young professor upon the occasion
of my going forth from graduate school:
"remember, locklin," he said, his hand upon my tweedy
    shoulder,
"in teaching you are always dealing with the criminal
    mentality."

132

don't answer the phone for me the same

don't answer the phone for me the same
as for your ex-boyfriends, dig?
eschew that little cry of surprise
which suggests: someone else is here with me.

save it for pete, who writes such
execrable verses and who pretends
to be your friend, but who really wants
to get into your pants, *we* know it, don't *you?*

save it for the guy who calls from fresno,
who only met you half an hour in vegas:
i believed it when you told me that;
i believe everything you tell me.

and save it for your mommy and daddy
who only call when we're making love.
save it for your girlfriends, who are
always looking for a fourth for an orgy.

since, however, i call or come
to visit you every single day,
there is something supererogatory
and degrading about being greeted with surprise.

please, therefore, cut that shit out.

nila northSun

little red riding hood

laying in the hospital
after a heart attack
gramma called as many of
her eight sons she could find
she didn't call
her only daughter
babe age 34
gramma never knew where

she'd be
jail on the streets
in a bar in klamath falls
or shacking up with one of
her chicano or indian dyke lovers
in LA

babe left home at 16
married a regular capt. hook
complete with a patch over his eye
a damn good poker player but
she left him a year later

in & out of jail
car theft robbery
narcotics bad checks
she went from 120 to 180 lbs.
cut her long black hair into
short bleached chunks
got her face bitten & chewed
by her jealous girlfriend
started talking like a black pimp

gramma didn't call her
but she showed up at the hospital
a bottle of whiskey in one hand
a can of beer in the other
freshly beaten up
oozing cigarette burns on her arms
slobbering & crying
"momma, momma"
babe was the only one
who came to visit gramma

the way & the way things are

gramma thinks about her grandchildren
they're losing the ways
don't know how to talk indian
don't understand me when
i ask for tobacco
don't know how to skin a rabbit
sad sad
they're losing the ways

but gramma
you told your daughters
marry white men
told them they would have
nicer houses
fancy cars
pretty clothes
could live in the city

gramma your daughters did
they couldn't speak indian anymore
how could we grandchildren learn
there are no rabbits to skin
in the city
we have no gramma there to
teach us the ways

you were still on the reservation
asking somebody anybody
please
get me tobacco

ROBERT PETERS

The Beach

And now,
wherever I walk
heel and soleprint
(saltdrenched)
stir the
rotted eyestalks
of lobsters, crunch
marooned shells . . .
Look! There is a
creature on the beach,
brine gone forever.
There are purple arms,

six at least. Furious,
it sets each limb
and hoists its body,
blue bulb, above
its arms flared out,
defies lethal air,
element, and for a
moment, swells
then bursts, shoots
forth ink, curls in its
tentacles, rests,
becomes a glob
which the sun will
bleach, erase: it
grows extinct,
is not.

Claremont

Ann was astounded when
she saw her brothers
doff their clothes and then
chase Claremont through
the wheat and thistles.
Miss *C* was fearsome!

Caught, she fondled the
splendid laughing boys
as if they were unicorns
or spindles. Each one
she took by mouth
gesturing for Ann to
look and follow. It
would not hurt, she said,
and was not bestial.

Ann ran, heard Claremont
squeal and saw her weird
position: one brother pumped
betwixt her legs, another
breached her chest. At home
Ann sat beside the fire
unable to eat her dinner.

Allen Ginsberg Blesses a Bride and Groom:
A Wedding Night Poem

I enter, jingling hindu temple bells, deodorant ears
   laughing and happiness-fulfillment lips breathing
towards stretched-out nakedbody sandwich, happy bride
   and
   mayonnaise bridegroom on hot cupcake sheets
cool icecream pillows, shuddering alpha and omega lips and
   eyes glinting holy messages, spuming from holes (ascetic
orifices of general love), myself garbed simply, pilgrim
   almost,
   alphabet soup of virtues, pubic albatrosses, sweetbutter
hairy tangles—all under a loving overhead lightbulb
   as these lovers avoiding me grind glorious thickpressure
fuckskins, forcing me, outcast, St. Anthony giggles
   assaulting
   my crayfish loins, tender vinegar crabs unhouseled, weird
seaweed veins, to do it myself this time, onanistic, choking
   it off, caressing, archer-shooting, spurting, draft of
moistured weeping nightbreeze, nude ghost, erectile, from
   shuddering Blakean cockspaces, hungering, till I point
forefinger at tormented Christian bed tossing, endlessly
   rocking
   itching from head to asshole. The bride wails, sheets
   swirl,
bridegroom in pinkcream chambered nautilus rocking,
   hard honeyself not yet flaccid, sees me in fluorescent
   shadow
gaiety of fat neck above and below, cock waving,
   going over, depositing armlets, hairbraids & anklets
on the floor, I crawl in between sexy nutrient sandwich,
   elephant happiness tears flow, crocodile-snapping
   muskmists,
intricate practiced lovegestures from me, me, itinerant
   epithalamium-maker, as the redundant bride unsheathes
   her
turpentine claws, rakes bleeding trail of sexhatred down my
   anus-shuddering spine.

KENNETH REXROTH

from **On Flower Wreath Hill**

I

An aging pilgrim on a
Darkening path walks through the
Fallen and falling leaves, through
A forest grown over the
Hilltop tumulus of a
Long dead princess, as the
Moonlight grows and the daylight
Fades and the Western Hills turn
Dim in the distance and the
Lights come on, pale green
In the streets of the hazy city.

II

Who was this princess under
This mound overgrown with trees
Now almost bare of leaves?
Only the pine and cypress
Are still green. Scattered through the
Dusk are orange wild kaki on
Bare branches. Darkness, an owl
Answers the temple bell. The
Sun has passed the crossroads of
Heaven.
      There are more leaves on
The ground than grew on the trees.
I can no longer see the
Path; I find my way without
Stumbling; my heavy heart has
Gone this way before. Until
Life goes out memory will
Not vanish, but grow stronger
Night by night.
         Aching nostalgia—
In the darkness every moment
Grows longer and longer, and
I feel as timeless as the
Two thousand year old cypress.

VI

Clustered in the forest around
The royal tumulus are
Tumbled and shattered gravestones
Of people no one left in
The world remembers. For the
New Year the newer ones have all been cleaned
And straightened and each has
Flowers or at least a spray
Of bamboo and pine.
It is a great pleasure to
Walk through fallen leaves, but
Remember, you are alive,
As they were two months ago.

* * *

Do there still rest in the broken
Tumulus ashes and charred
Bones thrown in a corner by
Grave robbers, now just as dead?
She was once a shining flower
With eyebrows like the first night's moon,
Her white face, her brocaded
Robes perfumed with cypress and
Sandalwood; she sang in the Court
Before the Emperor, songs
Of China and Turkestan.
She served him wine in a cup
Of silver and pearls, that gleamed
Like the moonlight on her sleeves.
A young girl with black hair
Longer than her white body—
Who never grew old. Now owls
And nightjars sing in a mist
Of silver and pearls.

VIII

* * *

Mist drenched, moonlit, the sculpture
Of an orb spider glitters
Across the path. I walk around
Through the bamboo grass. The mist

Dissolves everything else, the
Living and the dead, except
This occult mathematics of light.
Nothing moves. The wind that blows
Down the mountain slope from
The pass and scatters the Spring
Blossoms and the Autumn leaves
Is still tonight. Even the
Spider's net of jewels has ceased
To tremble. I look back at
An architecture of pearls
And silver wire. Each minute
Droplet reflects a moon, as
Once did the waterpails of
Matsukaze and Murasame.
And I realize that this
Transcendent architecture
Lost in the forest where no one passes
Is itself the Net of Indra,
The compound infinities of infinities,
The Flower Wreath,
Each universe reflecting
Every other, reflecting
Itself from every other,
And the moon the single thought
That populates the Void.
The night grows still more still. No
Sound at all, only a flute
Playing soundlessly in the
Circle of dancing gopis.

Parity

My uncle believed he had
A double in another
Universe right here at hand
Whose life was the opposite
Of his in all things—the man
On the other side of zero.
Sometimes they would change places.
Not in dreams, but for a moment

140

In waking, when my uncle
Would smile a certain sly smile
And pause or stagger slightly
And go about his business.

from The City of the Moon

X

Buddha took some Autumn leaves
In his hand and asked
Ananda if these were all
The red leaves there were.
Ananda answered that it
Was Autumn and leaves
Were falling all about them,
More than could ever
Be numbered. So Buddha said,
"I have given you
A handful of truths. Besides
These there are many
Thousands of other truths, more
Than can ever be numbered."

KIRK ROBERTSON

Postcard to a Foetus

i just thought
since you're all curled up
inside there
i'd tell you about it
how it was
when your mother & i
came together
in a moon of cherries
squirrel ran up a tree

wind blew but stopped
when the pipe was lit
& the breath was trapped
in small buckskin pouches
i was told
you will have a tough life
all you can do
is go through it
and that's how small things
survive like grass
pushes up through
cracks in the asphalt

The Clorox Kid

i scrub the floor
occasionally
i get called
on these jobs
like when someone is dying
& it gets to be too much
of a mess
& the mess must simply
be disposed of.

there seems to be
a certain peak out point
at which we all get too much
of dope booze
doctors
or finally life.

at that point
they call me in
the angels of mercy
would rather not soil
those uniforms & somebody
must pick up
the mess.

i'd just gotten back
from a quick beer/sandwich
at duck's market
& was resting up

for the nightly 9 o'clock
cardiac crapout
coupled with overdoses
on this & that
when they wheeled him in.

he had drunken clorox
thinking it was sweet
wine
not just a sip
or two
but a whole fuckin half-gallon

when i got there
to mop up the puke
the whole ward smelled
like clorox & small diamonds
in his eyes
registered clorox.

his liver was gone
the doctor too
nothing to do
nothing that could be done
he sterilized that room
simply
by dying
in it.

i punched out at 11.

in the morning
he was cut into small
4 inch squares
& they scoured the sinks
the walls
the floors with him.

punching in at 3
the next day
even the time clock
exuded a soft clorox hum
as i dipped my mop
in
& started scrubbing.

The Giant Squid of Tsurai

he lives out
there beyond the rock
with the sea
lions in a cave
of bathtubs

surfacing every now & then
to peep
at naked hippie nookie
on the rocky beach

no one
ever swims out
or comes to call

he beats off
a lot
changing tentacles
like a revolving door
on a ten-day cycle
and belching

GARY SOTO

History

Grandma lit the stove.
Morning sunlight
Lengthened in spears
Across the linoleum floor.
Wrapped in a shawl,
Her eyes small
With sleep,
She sliced papas,
Pounded chiles
With a stone
Brought from Guadalajara.
                              After

Grandpa left for work,
She hosed down
The walk her sons paved
And in the shade
Of a chinaberry,
Unearthed her
Secret cigar box
Of bright coins
And bills, counted them
In English,
Then in Spanish,
And buried them elsewhere.
Later, back
From the market,
Where no one saw her,
She pulled out
Pepper and beet, spines
Of asparagus
From her blouse,
Tiny chocolates
From under a paisley bandana,
And smiled.

That was the '50s,
And Grandma in her '50s,
A face streaked
From cutting grapes
And boxing plums.
I remember her insides
Were washed of tapeworm,
Her arms swelled into knobs
Of small growths—
Her second son
Dropped from a ladder
And was dust.
And yet I do not know
The sorrows
That sent her praying
In the dark of a closet,
The tear that fell
At night
When she touched
Loose skin

Of belly and breasts.
I do not know why
Her face shines
Or what goes beyond this shine,
Only the stories
That pulled her
From Taxco to San Joaquin,
Delano to Westside,
The places
In which we all begin.

After Tonight

Because there are avenues
Of traffic lights, a phone book
Of brothers and lawyers,
Why should you think your purse
Will not be tugged from your arm
Or the screen door
Will remain latched
Against the man
Who hugs and kisses
His pillow
In the corridor of loneliness?

There is a window of light
A sprinkler turning
As the earth turns,
And you do not think of the hills
And of the splintered wrists it takes
To give you
The heat rising toward the ceiling.

You expect your daughter
To be at the door any moment
And your husband to arrive
With the night
That is suddenly all around.
You expect the stove to burst
A collar of fire
When you want it,
The siamese cats
To move against your legs, purring.

But remember this:
Because blood revolves from one lung to the next,
Why think it will
After tonight?

ANN STANFORD

Robert Fulton

"Plate the Second": Water Color, 1804

This cross section, here incorrectly titled
"Mechanical Drawing for a Steamboat,"
is not a steamboat at all.
This is part of a submarine.

Note how at Valve A the water
is pouring in. The deck just skims
above the water line outside.
Inside, the water surrounds

A cylinder. This is the core
of the boat. Its sides, one inch thick,
can stand pressures to one hundred
perpendicular feet of water.

Six men can enter the core
through the hatch at the top.
And men, turning a handle,
turn the screw that drives the vessel.

Between Deck B and the upper deck
on both sides of the boat the inventor
has neatly spelled out its purpose.
It has "Chambers for Submarine Bombs."

This ship can surface by day. By night
it can submerge and enter a harbor
and its bombs, left anchored or floating,
will destroy whatever passes.

147

This plate depicts a practical
submersible ship. Robert Fulton
praised it as an instrument
for true liberty and peace.

Before

When I lay in my mother's womb
Her heart boomed in the chamber above me
The great clock.
Since then I have been enamored of time
And rivers too and seas
Like the sea in which I floated.

Going Away

The horses are going away
The tall mare and the four-year-old.
Their bridles lie by the drive,
And their gear and what is left of the oats.

They do not know. They are out there sleeping.
Over them the tin roof bangs in the wind.

They will wade into acres of grass
And hear the new sound of a sea
That breaks past the hill and the steady branches of oaks
In a place where the roads have not come yet.

How they will run in the big pasture
Or stand, flicking their tails in the sunlight
Those high beasts that looked over our shoulders
Or stood silent, nuzzling, blocking the way.

They called to us when we were slow at evening.
The young one was born here.

We will go back into our houses
We will forget how large the world was once.

The Gift

It was round, orb being most nearly perfect,
And warm perhaps, though hardly of any color,
Smelling of spring, faintly, of hyacinth.
It was not fruit, though on those trees first planted
Eastward, of life and knowledge, it may have grown.
There were many trees in Eden. And this not eaten.
Yet flower neither, though soft as petals
Yet harder perhaps, like pearls hunted
Through dark shore-caves, or rubies hidden,
Precious as those, glanced at and not seen.
Transparent, then, and gone like water
Floating off, yet here; and single, out of many,
And not illusion, though it may have been.
Solid and constant, ephemeral and shaken,
Fruit, flower, or stone, or given or taken.

CHARLES STETLER

A Toast

here's to nick and nora charles,
pioneer hedonists who brightened the way
out of our grim cotton mather past.

they won where many stout revelers succumbed:
f. scott, zelda, hemingway, and crews gallantly
pursued the gin-filled grail until
john calvin, not john barleycorn, completely broke them.

but the pox of collective guilt and depraved man
could not daunt the thin man and his wife.
she, in genuine liberation, poured as they drank
for breakfast, lunch, and supper
without a single belch of shame.
nor did they ever start the day
stabbed with remorse or headache pledges.
nick usually set the morning tone:
"how about a drop to cut the phlegm?"

they loved life, each other, all the pleasures
of the flesh, despite Salem's fire and brimstone,
and Asta stands as wagging proof that
they were just alive, and not rebelling.
nora always slept with nick, not the dog,
and all three remained completely non-neurotic.

Jeep

Lee Handley's dead. Age 52. Heart attack at home
in Pittsburgh. The obit stretched out across 20
years and 3,000 miles like a Proust madeleine cake.

You ask, who was Lee Handley? He was called
Jeep and finished a few thousand hits
short of Stan the Man, Paul Waner, or DiMag
but well up there in miscues off the field.

My first Idol. The hot corner was your spot
and you were often on the griddle. There you were
when I saw my first major league game
in a doubleheader going six for nine
and sealing off left field like a leper colony.

From then on I fawned over your career
the way Eddie Fisher tagged after Liz.
Once I even coaxed your average up to .350
in July although it sagged in September to
your all time high .284.
All through the war I languished at the turnstile
til you and all the other stars came home.

But it was the things you did without
the ball that made for bolder headlines.
Picked up for molesting little girls. Arrested
for showing dirty movies in your home.

Those foul tips taught me what I needed
to know about sports. All the playing that's
important doesn't happen on the field. I'll bet
Mother Handley flicked your hand off your tool
and replaced it with a fielder's mitt.
Then you didn't get laid enough in high school
so you ran around the bases more instead.

We had a lot in common, my first fallen idol.
Let others learn from you
the secret of spring training.
Forbes Field will soon go the way of all
old ballparks but your many busts will
always have a place in my Hall of Fame.

World's Fare

from dollars to T-shirts
we're living in a world
where all things shrink.

it's vital that you buy
every item two sizes too big:
reputation, sausage, honor,
beef rib eye, incredulity.

unfortunately we're all stuck
with what's between our legs.

The Graduate

Nick could hardly wait. He was now eligible
to attend his first convention
having emerged from his 5-year apprenticeship
a card-carrying con man.

Sent in $100 reservation fee,
got his party paraphernalia ready:
pigeon drop kit, gigolo eyebrows,
Roman Holiday loafers, deposed prince cummerbund.
He would show the pros he had learned the trade.

All the legends of con would be there:
Loretta Young, World War II, John Denver,
The Meek who will inherit the earth,
an un-cockeyed optimist, the ventriloquist
who threw his voice 8 years for Eisenhower.
Dick Nixon was the scheduled chairman.
Nick was anxious to find out
what they all really looked like.

A note was waiting for him
at Chicago's Palmer Hotel:
"Dear Member,
Every year we're surprised
how this old chestnut still grabs
a couple squirrels."

Free Enterprise

then there was the guy
                    with Conrad Hilton know-how
who realized the only way
                    to compete with Jack LaLanne
was to open up a string
                    of yoga body shops
guaranteeing in sex sedentary weeks
                              to graduate one and all
with biceps like Carol Burnett
                         a chest out of Buchenwald
Himalayan haircut, mystical
                    complexion and halting speech
plus a giggle that sounds like
                    "Maraheesh-hee-hee-hee."

The diploma is a 7-cornered Springmaid sheet
with rope belt cut from drapery pulls
that once hung in San Simeon.
The eternally wilting daisy and sandals are extra.

Policy of the House

karl, my friend, caught the crabs.
such a scrappy bunch, he admired,
then grew accustomed to their ways.
he enjoys a nip himself;
they seemed to thrive on Kwell shampoo.

however, this new relationship
appeared potentially bad for business.
a bar owner, he shakes many hands.
during one prolongish clasp,
he spied one cosmopolitan little devil
do a Fosberry Flop, from forearm to forearm.

152

karl's first thought: miniature rat guards.
then he found the perfect cure,
strapped a flea collar on each wrist.
business is back to normal.

ADRIEN STOUTENBURG

Ivory Paper Weight

Elephants are born with so much clothing,
wrinkled and folded,
and such a cargo of bones, cartilage, nerves—
only their brains being small, gray jewels—
and everyone a Cyrano,
noses curled like vines,
but tuskless, the sucking mouths open.

The cow has two breasts only,
a kind of mountainous woman
on tree trunk legs,
and a body wide enough
to create shade without leaves.
The young one stands there
as under a parasol or rock.

Bulls keep to themselves
after rutting;
sometimes go mad
from a strange gland in the forehead,
or an abscessed wound;
are massive, always,
twice-ponderous in rage or lust

That one I held in my thought . . .
that one, older than the hunters who stung him,
forever walking backward to keep the wind
from his bullet-silvered eyes . . .

I searched for him through circuses and dream,
held his knobbed head
(a dying mountain, nerve-crossed as a leaf),
then touched a brittle tusk.
It shattered, traveled, and rolled down
to this blind figurine
that holds—at times—
the papers on my blowing desk,
and my beast-haunted mind.

V.D. Clinic

How bald that microscope was,
   eye without lashes
   except for my student gaze
   fringed at the peephole
   where pale, swimming commas arrived
   on the stage,
   trapped on a slide
   as naked as a mirror.

A woman had been surprised,
the smear alive
with the richness of a recent lover.
   Positive Wasserman; positive guilt.
   My starch coat creaked and turned.

Her legs were thin.
Her stockings hung.
Her eyes were not,
had never been her own.

A sting of medicines,
   a scent as from the mouth
     of someone chewing herbs—
      and something clanged:

the waste can's lid
above the swabs . . .
   and then the noiseless skid
     of beasts or angels skating down
       into their nameless, cotton graves.

Dogskin Rug

Second grade mornings
it held some warmth for my waking feet
in its deep, collie-colored hair,
even when the rainspout froze
to a cataract gray
and winter gasped beneath
the December floor.

Only he, sprawled headless,
was a carpet there,
with a short flash of tail;
bright white it wagged
on a backyard line
when my grandmother's rug-beater throbbed
dust back into an antic life.

He had been a playmate of my infancy,
she said, and too much loved
to toss back to the bone-heaped world.

Beneath the fur
there was the skin
lean as parchment
with a leaf-map of veins.
At times I dreamed a heart
still drumming there,
or a crib of teeth
around an indolent, summer bone;
as under a buffalo robe
in the old, flapping car,
I thought of windy beards
and hoofs.
          Coonskin or pony's pelt,
we borrowed their warmth
for days when cold creaked
like a ship, the world as bare
as their lost skeletons.

I was content
on those sharp days and night,
alone,
to have that speechless collie there.

JOHN THOMAS

The Last Frontier

In the portraits he sits cross-legged on a mat,
fierce eyes glaring from under shaggy brows,
and his right fist clenched in his lap
(always reminding me of Jersey Joe Walcott,
how he could catch them coming in, the young eager ones,
with that stiff right).
Rinzai, the old giant-killer—came up the hard way:
hung around Vulture Peak for years
and every time he opened his mouth to ask a question,
Huang-Po hit him again;
ran off finally to Ta-yü, who said,
"Don't cry on my shoulder, boy;
git on back where you belong and be grateful
for Huang's grandmotherly kindness!"
It is said that these words enlightened Rinzai
and he walked all the way back to Vulture Peak
and punched Huang-Po in the nose, saying:
"Your Buddhism ain't so much after all, you old buzzard!"
So when Huang died Rinzai sat in his place
and he was a holy terror, catching them coming in,
the young eager ones, with that sledgehammer right.

They were a hard and desperate bunch,
real mountain men, half horse and half alligator,
hanging by their toes from foggy cliffs,
yodelling obscenities across the river gorges.
Live up there long enough, wild garlic for breakfast and
tiger tracks in the back yard,
and you just naturally get disrespectful
—the Emperor T'ai Chung came up one year,
travelling light and hiking twenty days to get there,
hoping for some answers;
asked some innocent question and Huang-Po
slapped him twice and ran the Son of Heaven clear off the
    mountain.
Or as Rinzai said to the monks,
"If you want to make it, kill anyone who gets in your way!
If you encounter the Buddha, slay him;
if you encounter the Patriarch, slay him;

156

if you encounter the Arhat or the parent or the relative,
slay them all without hesitation: that's the only way.
I tell you, no Buddhas, no holy teachings, no discipling, no
    testifying.
What do you seek in a neighbor's house?
Why put another head above your own?
You're all crazy, biting into every pile of shit in your path!
I tell you, don't get hung up on anything,
but stand above, pass on, and be free."
Rinzai, the old giant-killer, the old hatchet man!

It's a long way to Rinzai's roost—
the gorges are steep, the trails are choked with bramble
    bushes;
broken-down bridges over roaring mountain creeks,
bitter cold at night and the air thin, like a knife at your
    windpipe;
your pack gets heavy so you're dropping things all along
    the way;
if you make it at all, you'll be empty-handed,
big blisters on your heels and skinned knees.
When you get there, don't be surprised if he sets the dogs
    on you.
This is the last frontier, boy,
too steep for horses and a thousand miles from the nearest
    Sunday school.
Nobody comes out here unless he's crazy or wanted for
    murder.
This is the last frontier, boy:
think twice before you start
and never say I didn't warn you.

CHARLES WRIGHT

from **Firstborn**

—Omnia quae sunt, lumina sunt—

The sugar dripping into your vein;
The jaundice rising upon your face like a blush;
The glass box they keep you in—

The bandage over your eyes;
The curdled milk on your lips;
The plastic tube in your throat—

The unseen hands that linger against your skin;
The name, like a new scar, at your wrist;
The glass box they keep you in—

We bring what we have to bring;
We give what we have to give;
Welcome, sweet Luke, to your life.

from **Tattoos**

3. Snake-Handling Religious Service, East Tennessee
1951

Body fat as my forearm, blunt-arrowed head
And motionless, eyes
Sequin and hammer and nail
In the torchlight, he hangs there,
Color of dead leaves, color of dust,

Dumbbell and hourglass—copperhead.
Color of bread dough, color of pain, the hand
That takes it, that handles it
—The snake now limp as a cat—
Is halfway to heaven, and in time.

Then Yellow Shirt, twitching and dancing,
Gathers it home, handclap and heartstring,
His habit in ecstasy.
Current and godhead, hot coil,
Grains through the hourglass glint and spring.

13. The Janitor; Kindergarten; Corinth, Mississippi
1940

What I remember is fire, orange fire,
And his huge cock in his hand,
Touching my tiny one; the smell
Of coal dust, the smell of heat,
Banked flames through the furnace door.

Of him I remember little, if anything:
Black, overalls splotched with soot,
His voice, *honey, O, honey* . . .
And then he came, his left hand
On my back, holding me close.

Nothing was said, of course—one
Terrible admonition, and that was all . . .
And if that hand, like loosed lumber, fell
From grace, and stayed there? We give,
And we take it back. We give again . . .

The Southwest

MEI-MEI BERSSENBRUGGE

Chronicle

I was born the year of the loon
in a great commotion. My mother—
who used to pack $500 cash
in the shoulders of her fur gambling coat,
who had always considered herself
the family's "First Son"—
took one look at me
and lit out again
for a vacation to Sumatra.
Her brother purchased my baby clothes;
I've seen them, little clown suits
of silk and color.

Each day
my Chinese grandmother bathed me
with elaboration in an iron tub;
amahs waiting in lines
with sterilized water and towels
clucked and smiled
and rushed about the tall stone room
in tiny slippers.

After my grandfather
accustomed himself
to this betrayal by First Son,
he would take me in his arms,
walk with me
by the plum trees, cherries, persimmons;
he showed me the stiff robes
of my ancestors and their drafty hall,
the long beards of his learned old friends,
and his crickets.

Grandfather talked to me, taught me.
At two months, my mother tells me,
I could sniff for flowers,
stab my small hand upwards to moon.
Even today I get proud
when I remember
this all took place in Chinese.

Book of the Dead, Prayer 14

Good-bye,
try to stay awake now you're dead.
Look hard at those demons
and don't be afraid.
All the bright lights and bells
are yourself returning
from wandering.
Try to look at them.
What terrifies
you must be beautiful.
I won' cry, make you sad.
If you embrace
these assaults you'll be free.
But of course you are frightened.
Hair stiffens
all over you. So you'll fall
back down to us, back
into another dying body.
So I'll see you again.
Maybe without knowing you,
also knowing.
I tell you so you won't worry.
Try to stay awake.

RICK CASILLAS

Yaqui Women: Three Generations

Rita

Behind her, mesquite and caliche dirt
Before her, mesquite and caliche dirt;
Rita would have laughed had anyone been there
to tell her she'd crossed a boundary.
She'd have lifted her scarf painted
with Our Lady of Guadaloupe
and uncovered her ammunition belt;
she'd have lifted her medicine pouch
of a hundred pockets
and said,
"These are things that people have made,
and people may make them
in as many pieces as they please.
No people made the earth;
no people can divide it.
The muscles of this place flex
across a skeleton of mountains
and if anyone were fool enough
to cut the earth
it would spit blood
the way a horned toad does
the way the earth does when it splits itself
and spurts a shelf of rock to scab a wounded hillside.
Can I fail to find my home
wherever rocks fall down mountains
to remind me of the blood
that washes my own bones?
You might as well say that the Yaqui words
could be cut from my tongue
or my soul cut from me before I die.
You might as well say that the wind
could push me from my home."

Elena

If there was dirt, Rita's daughter
could force corn and squash from it;
if there were stones, she could make them

into metates to grind her meal.
Elena gripped the land until it sweated out her harvest
and she'd have snorted had her mother been there
to deny that she'd put the caliche and mesquite
behind her, between her and the days
when Rita had walked among the Yaqui
and spoken the tongue Elena never used.
"It cost enough to send your bones
back to your land," Elena would have said,
"So don't tell me that nothing separates it from mine.
When the man came to take my picture
—cut a piece of my soul from me,
as you'd have said,
to put on a piece of paper—
didn't I insist on standing in front of the fields
whose dirt I carry in my nails
and whose pebbles hobble my step?
Could I find a home
where I could not hear the mission bells,
where I could not walk to the top of the mountain
and see the roofs of the town?
You might as well say
that the wind could push me from my home."

Ernestina

At the word of a man she'd never see,
Elena left her land.
Her bones lie under the town,
where her daughter lives now.
Ernestina has followed her husbands
when they went to join armies
at the bidding of this same unseen man.
The women did not even feel the wind of his voice
as it pushed them from their homes.
So little does Ernestina know the place she lives
that when she looks at the ground she sees dirt
and does not recognize oncoming life,
cannot feel the compelling pulse of earth
that her grandmother saw in rock
thrust through a mountainside,
that her mother saw in sprouting plants
that cheated smothering stillbirth,

pushing away a caul of pebbles
to gasp in open air.
Ernestina knows no Yaqui to speak to her sons,
and the sons of her sons
will let the metate grow cold on the porch.

MICHAEL HOGAN

Prison Break

Free, free, I would run until
air burned like a sulphur match in my throat.
Stop, the willow would say. Stop!
Only the wind would encourage me.

Free, there would be a whole day
just for the grass and its restful growing.
I'd lie and survey a single stalk
or any suspicious bug beside it.

Free, before I left these parts for good
I would have my revenge on the wall.
I'd pull away bricks and crumbling mortar
with angry liberated hands.

Free, free, the winds would rush
through the broken places my hands made.
Dragons blazing like Northern Lights
would leap out and frighten the stars.

Food Strike

After the fifth day
they turned off the water
and I lay there on the bottom bunk
scratching my hog bristle beard
smelling the fearsweat of my body

seeing my rib cage stark and white
like the week old remains
of some small animal.

They turned off the water
and immediately
though I'd just drank a cupful
my tongue became swollen with imaginings
my throat closed
and heat rose from the catwalk
in a visible aura
coming to claim my emaciated life.

TURN ON THE WATER YOU BASTARDS
and fresh like an ocean breeze
the cell block sounded its solidarity
bellowing like a hurricane
against the seawall of indifference
TURN ON THE WATER we yelled together
and a thousand steel bars rattled with thunder.

We suspected then that their ploy
was futile
that all our voices could together prick
even the tough hided souls
of those desert havalinas
who held us captive.

still
it was glorious
exceeding all our expectations
when
the water
spitting rust flecks like blood
on the cellblock floor
finally came back on.

Fish

The kid's packed the last five months
of his old lady's letters
in a Cherry Tyme box rolled up
in his mattress along with a towel

and now he's moving from the tank
to A-run scared and winking
at some big dude.
Tonight he'll tell his whole life story
to someone sitting on the bottom bunk
and the dude
(maybe the same one he winked at)
will watch the way the kid's hair
falls gently down over one eye,
trying to catch a swish in the voice.
In a month the kid will have
a locker full of tailormades, new shoes,
special-pressed blues,
and no room at all for a Cherry Tyme box
with letters from a face he can't remember.

Parting

We keep going, we keep going
and we think: just beyond this rise
just across this bridge we will come
to a place that is right for us.

Go on without me friend, I am stopping here.
I am stopping here to try a new posture
to determine whether it is the place
or the way we fit ourselves to it that counts.

If I am right, you may never know.
You might think: what he could have done
had he found his place.
Maybe you will say: we received his signals.
They will flicker out in time
like candles after a High Mass
but if I am right, if I am right
the rich smell of celebration will remain.

I will make this temporary altar my cathedral.
You will say: what a Mass it could have been
if held in Notre Dame.
You will continue looking for Notre Dame
or some newer place that is right for you.

If you ever get there, think of me.

Shaman

He lived apart, sometimes in a cave in the mountain,
sometimes in a hogan at the edge of the village.
He would come speak to the tribespeople, but often
they heard him with only one ear.
     The bravest among them said:
He lives alone,
he takes men as well as women, even youths,
he examines water tracks and entrails and exposed
    roots, veins in stone, wind in grass, blood stains,
    cactus skeletons, sudden birds, clouds, dung—
what can such an one know of people?
What can he tell us of our ways, of our future?
If he wants to guide us, let him be of us.
     The most fearful among them said:
He knows secrets, he can
harm us if we do not pretend to harken to him,
he will work spells against us, he'll poison our
    children,
he will dry up the brooks and springs, he will
keep away the rains, he will bring disease:
we must respect him even if we do not like him.
     The wisest of them (but they were few) said:
He looks at us out of different eyes, he
can distinguish our pace when it has taken us
    too fast, too slow,
he is like an arrow into the tree trunk of our life—
he can tell us of ourselves what we are too close to
    perceive.
He is present at our beginning and at our end
    at the same time.
He is not against us but he suffers distance
to tell us the meaning of our closeness, our lostness:
he is a blister, a thorn, a cockleburr, a scorpion,
rattlesnake, mountain, gopher hole—
he's beargrease, wet tongue, touch, laugh,
a song, a rainfall, a smooth path: when we need him,
he's there to hold us back, to push us forward.
     The young said:

He has taught us not to be afraid of our bodies,
to be tender in our passion, to love all of ourselves
and even the snake in the path—as part of the
    Great Spirit.

Still he lived apart.
Still they heard him often only with one ear.
Still, when they found out what he had said was true,
    it was in their own entrails that truth awoke.

He was a buzzard and an eagle
a horned toad and a wren
a dry arroyo and a mountain freshet.
In his eyes wild mustard bloomed in winter;
in his mouth, acacia spoke red thru thorns.

I did not ask him his name.
He planted his seed in my throat. I sing his life!
His life sings me!

from 108 Tales of a Po'Buckra

No. 106

the dark brother touches me
with my own wanting:
I am all over
risen with his fingertips.

I ask him if he loves me:
he looks and says me nothing.
I frown . . . I command him to tell me
he loves me.
Mildly, as one looks at a child,
he looks at me
and says me nothing.

Ten years pass.
He is married now, his wife
has returned him to himself
with a girlchild
and a boychild.

It is Thanksgiving Day: we
have shared dinner.

We ride in his car
side by side.
I have asked him nothing, but
quietly he affirms me:
"I told my wife
that, besides marriage
and the mystery of children,
I have one friend."

("Buckra" is an American corruption of an African
word, "Mbakara," meaning "boss man." A "Po'Buckra"
is a poor white.)

LINDA KING

I Wasn't No Mary Ellen

They were the Thompsons
and they were fat and dirty
and their little girl Mary Ellen
said her mother, big fat Ellen
and her Dad had sex because she
heard them at night and I knew
my mother and Dad never
had sex and I never heard them

I didn't like to go to her house
because her house stank and our
house didn't stink and Mary Ellen
always wanted to play nasty and
she even wanted to play it with
her big brother and I didn't like
him because everybody knew he
played nasty with the Coalman girls

My sisters had told me about a
little girl nine years old in Mexico
who had had a baby and I for sure

172

didn't want to have a baby with
one of those dirty Thompsons
who didn't mop where the separator
had run milk on the floor and even
let chickens and pigs in their house

I went on home and I played with my dog
and I didn't think there was anything
wrong with playing with my dog, you
know that way, because I loved my dog
I really and truly loved my dog and we
loved and kissed every day, but even with
him, on those rare times, I was cautious
to make sure he went in the back way
I didn't want no litter on my hands

Hooked on the Magic Muscle

I like a man around
they are smart and a comfort
I suppose they were made
for women's pleasure
the way they're
put together . . . that muscle

And it is a pleasure
to make them mad
using words like red capes
and here they come
charging, snorting, puffing
it gives you a kick somehow

The reason why women
don't feel the urge
to fight bull, wrestle, box
play football and tear each
other up like men do
is because she has man as her sport
and she'll spend hours
practicing her skills
naturally becoming superior

her only danger lies
in outwitting herself

Men realize they are playing
a sport of somekind, but
believing he is superior
he hardly takes the time to
understand the rules
as this game is so complex
it is nothing like football
wrestling, ice hockey or even chess

The playing becomes so
easy when men get drunk or stoned
which they consider manly
women are almost forced to
join them from boredom
rather than wait the hours
until they get their minds back

Most women will agree
that it is almost impossible
to find a man who doesn't
spend half of his time watching
football, basketball, playing horses
drinking, drugging or both

But, I will admit
his teeny weeny wiggling sperm
does help produce a child
in some small way
and if you get hooked on
the magic muscle
the color of his eyes
or even how his beard grows in
you've got to make do
and hope they will
stop using the same old
women are bitches song
to argument they can't answer
and eventually get around
to a better showing

174

Whore

"if I were a woman, he said
I'd be the biggest whore in town
why not? I just say, why not? . . . ha, ha . . ."
and he explains how a girl
can make $65,000 a year tax free

"it's a sticky business, I said
I wouldn't want that many men's
vibes in me or on me
my aura would turn purple
my soul would get sick
my brain turn to dollars
my backache
my cunt turn shapeless
my mother image destroyed
not to mention disease . . ."

"come on, . . . ha, ha . . . now tell me
really tell me why you wouldn't
consider that kind of money?"

"whoring is a business
you serve whomever comes
I like to pick and choose
and who knows someone
like you might arrive . . ."

The Great Poet

For C. B. (Charles Bukowski)

he lumbers from the bed like a
three hundred pound orangoutang
he can't find his glasses
he can't find his shorts
he can't find his stockings
skinny arms
skin hanging at the elbows
belly bulging
he throws bed sheets and quilts
in the air bellowing
farts noisely
scratches his ass with pleasure

he can't find his shirt
he can't find his wallet
he can't find his shoes
hair and beard unkept
he eats apples and oranges
by the dozens
makes strange noises to himself
expects other to understand
his hand signs and grunts
belches loudly in restaurants
announces he's going to *take a crap*

the only ape in town who
uses yards and yards of
pink flowered toilet paper

KARL KOPP

Manly Diversion

Buying wood from Mrs. Lalo Roybal
stove-length chunks of piñon
I help an old Indian throw them
into the bed of my pick-up

He's lived in California
  picked apricots
had twelve men under him
  had it good
and doesn't like working for a woman

          so when Mrs. Roybal comes
to double-check the weight and count my money
behind her back he throws on more wood

          and shows me
  winking
by his shack a group of stumps chain-sawed
to look like crotches
  penis-branches
in the center

but most like women's asses
thighs and cunts
   and we laugh together
while my son looks on

      no different
   years ago
when I swam bare-ass in the Sudbury
getting there on a girl's bike wrenched
from the rack at school
   swam
with Charlie Totman and Brian Kelly
until Miss Lena B. Cushing principal
came in her car to roust us

       just the top of it showing
black through the trees
and going beep beep beep beep beep beep
Miss Lena B. looking straight ahead

       even when we ran towards her
our little balls and cocks flapping
singing Lenalenalenalenalenalena
her face stayed in profile stiff
to the bun of her iron-grey hair

so why think now of that girl raped
in Raton
   beaten
   then run over by his car
her neck and back broken
   pancreas crushed
until it would digest itself

why feel that horror
here among these silly totems
my son puzzled by the grown-up fun
beyond the ken of Mrs. Roybal

STEVE ORLEN

Bar Mitzvah

This morning of my birthday, rain is starting to fall.
A little old man greets me, hair bristling from his ears.
He takes me by the hand, I to become a member of his
    house,
And he a member of mine. My father leans in the doorway,
A bridge of polished shoes, and has forgotten how to pray.

My grandfather twirls his talis fringe, the kind of man
Who does everything twice just to make sure. He sailed
Here from Odessa where everyone was Jewish, where plain
Events, like morning prayer and the rain, had meaning.
I love his paper face and his gruff tones in God's House.

In God's House I can't hear the rain. I might be anyone,
Anywhere, praying or waiting his turn. The letters
In the Torah wait like baby teeth under a pillow. I finger
The sheepskin scroll and wait for a sign, but the words
Go backwards; no one sings in unison, each at his own pace.

This is a house divided, healthy with argument. The wonder
In these voices tries to conjure a face: a great-grandfather
Asleep in the Ark, Russian, sad, so small only a child
Could find it. All I have to guide me leans in the blood.
Today I must learn to weep in a foreign tongue.

In Praise of Beverly

When you walked down the stairs
to touch my root
God knows what brought you.
Barely fourteen, already known
as the town pump and proud
of your clear attributes.
I imagine you in that narrow bed
close to your parents' drunk
lungless breathing, plotting love.
I don't think we ever kissed,

but once we lay in a ditch
in summer, roasting apples,
careless for hours. When the fire
caught the weeds, you held my root
and grinned and said "Let's wait
and see the fire engines come!"

You got sent up early
to The House of Good Shepherd.
The mothers were jealous,
forgive them. When the friendly
leering cop told me,
"I hear you been dipping the wick
in Beverly," I blushed and stammered,
proud. Then lied, forgive us all,
to save my skin.
The night they took you away
I dreamt your face, your hands
that pulled away the dark, were mine,
and groaned to share your misery.
I found my own in my good time.

ROBERT PETERSON

The Young Conquistador, 15

The young conquistador, 15, is growing:
wears amulets of ivory, has given up shoes,
& smokes everything.
Begging to be kissed, girls introduce themselves

in stores. And men make proposals
when he dozes in parks.
He yearns for Tokyo or France
but won't fly kites
or dance in the dark.
His only hero talks to God in public on the telephone.

Happily in debt, nearsighted
& born shameless

He sleeps on the beach, preferably alone.
"Love," he says, "is an ordeal for two."

The Young Conquistador

The young conquistador arrives at odd hours
without an appointment. Striking piratical poses.
Demanding spice, opium, salve, banknotes
& liqueurs . . .

Or displaying lurid chapters of his life
written in green ink
on torn pages of his clothes.
We speak of naked nymphs & huge sums of gold.

I suggest he throw out his good suits
& alibis, pedal south in the off-season
to study ancient games of the Aztecs.

But he's not keen on sports
& his bicycle is falling apart. His mother's
last hope: that he'll give up vice for art.

LEROY V. QUINTANA

Legacy II

Grandfather never went to school
spoke only a few words of English,
a quiet man; when he talked
talked about simple things

planting corn or about the weather
sometimes about herding sheep as a child.
One day pointed to the four directions
taught me their names

El Norte

Poniente   Oriente

El Sur

He spoke their names as if they were
one of only a handful of things
a man needed to know

Now I look back
only two generations removed
realize I am nothing but a poor fool
who went to college

trying to find my way back
to the center of the world
where Grandfather stood
that day

Last Night There Was a Cricket in Our Closet

I got out of bed twice, took down boxes and
suitcases in a search and destroy mission
but couldn't find him.

Then, we were crickets.
You, rubbing your legs against mine
and vice versa

trying to find me
trying to find you
that cricket in the other's closet.

A. A. RIOS

Cortes

When the sun whipped our skins
and blood ran from every scream
we could not stop slaving;
we worked for the Coming happily,
until the blood dried, turned brown,
and we were Indian.

Soon it happened, the sun grew legs
and walked on the earth and water.
His rays of light and warmth
turned hot, to real whip-tails,
but we took comfort in the Truth,
the Mystery of Quetzalcoatl.

Here was the sun with a face, returned,
his body polished and shining, his voice
speaking Great Brilliance.
We believed and rejoiced and prepared
to welcome the greatest of Indians.
We gave him lives.

We gave him Malinche, and sons.
It would all soon be good.
If He dimmed, we blinded ourselves
staring at the sun, and we were rewarded.
The trees bore skulls as fruit
and we feasted.

Nani

Sitting at her table, she serves
the sopa de arroz to me
instinctively, and I watch her,
the absolute mamá, and eat words
I might have had to say more
out of embarrassment. To speak,
now-foreign words I used to speak,

too, dribble down her mouth as she serves
me albóndigas. No more
than a third are easy to me.
By the stove she does something with words
and looks at me only with her
back. I am full. I tell her
I taste the mint, and watch her speak
smiles at the stove. All my words
make her smile. Nani never serves
herself, she only watches me
with her skin, her hair. I ask for more.

I watch the mamá warming more
tortillas for me. I watch her
fingers in the flame for me.
Near her mouth, I see a wrinkle speak
of a man whose body serves
the ants like she serves me, then more words
from more wrinkles about children, words
about this and that, flowing more
easily from these other mouths. Each serves
as a tremendous string around her,
holding her together. They speak
nani was this and that to me
and I wonder just how much of me
will die with her, what were the words
I could have been, was. Her insides speak
through a hundred wrinkles, now, more
than she can bear, steel around her,
shouting, then, What is this thing she serves?

She asks me if I want more.
I own no words to stop her.
Even before I speak, she serves.

Cinco de Mayo, 1862

We loved them, so we only crushed the skulls
of those who slept content. The restless were
immune; we called them "the invisibles."
Of them, we told our eyes "be unaware."

We loved them now as dead men. We forgave
the sleepless, who were whiter now than when
they came, and let them help us dig the grave
of strangers, dig the grave of ugly men.

There were no cries of killing. Those who slept
had called each one of us amigos. We
had laughed, and drank the pulque with them, kept
the money, used their language frequently.

A ghost picked up a skull; from underneath
we watched the cancer, spewing through the teeth.

REG SANER

How the Laws of Physics Love Chocolate!

This dumbbell bee must be working
the half-dozen highest buttercups on earth.
Low alpine sun, bright enough to hurt.
Under my feet a 7-acre snowbank gargles
like gangster summer, riddled with kitchen taps.
Folding the map to a hat I squint under its brim
at the bee that can't get enough.
Corollas needlepoint moss. Way above
timberline and the tundra still corny
with blossom. Each cliff face, the same
machine of prey, able to wipe my brains
on its next stone. I come because
the useless is pure Greek.
At the back of each columbine's head,
a consort of blue trombones.

Passing It On

I was three and already
my world shook with you.
Now I'm what's left. The eyes
I have are yours, your mouth.
That trick of your upper lip—
and those slurred l-syllables
you still slide
into a few of my words.

Now in my dreams again
and again your lacquered
casket sinks, becomes your door
into the grass. To one side
the clay heap waits to fall
a shovelful at a time.

I walk up close. I heft a clod,
then eat. Gnawing, I taste
the darkness between us
you suddenly died in. For years
it's been the red fist
of your heart that I've chewed
and gagged on, till I'm bled out
and odd of it.

And your small, thick hands.
Their anger has made my own hand
tremble, passing it on.

Already I'm hurt
by my son's look—the way
his eyes beat and grow secret
under this strange love
shaken into me.

The Space Eater Camps at Fifth Lake

To make this scene I climb miles
upgrade on my knees
taking things in. The downhill water
bright at the seams, tossed salad swatches

of trail, deer dung gumballing
the ground. Each sawn trunk of windfall,
a birthday surrounded, its bull's-eye
rippling from seed
like a stone in the lake. At ponds
whose tundra edges seem rich
I put my hand on Miss America's muff.

Packing in, I've time to think
how silly I look, lugging all this metaphor,
but make camp. My thoughts squat
their twig fire like city wolves,
as under these great magma winds
we play Rousseau
lounging his garden bench at Versailles,
prying the lid of primitive time
rational as topiary. There can be
no real loneliness here; I marrow it
into each crag.

Towards midnight I crawl from the tent
to watch a moon nearly at full
pulled from my own sublime,
its grand gesture
stuffing the mountain's ark
with shadows. Further up, this galaxy
I forgot gives my eyes
both barrels.

Under the rosy foreskin of dawn,
turned for a parting glance, I leave
and take all I can. The mountain's huge
bite of glacial cirque
hovers a small glass square
pressed to the shape of a tent,
with, still slightly warm,
a sleep-print. All summer I'll come
and go, eating spaces like these
to make sure.
My death must be a simply enormous death.

Flag

Up from the bottom
of a thick green light
he rises, wearing
his crocodile skin
like a difficult lesson
the river has taught him.

Overhead the cautious
staff members circle.
From time to time
they alight,
picking bits of experience
from his teeth.

As he levels squarely
into the nation's great
glass eye
he is saddened
by the malice of others
but he forgives them,
weeping thumbtacks.

On his right hand
and behind
the flag of his office hangs,
a wet 4th of July,
refusing to burn.

RICHARD SHELTON

Excerpts from the Notebook of
the Poet of Santo Tomas

If you live where I come from
and you want to be rich
and beautiful, first get rich.

Then we'll tell you
you are beautiful.
Hell! Settle for that.
You can't have everything.

*

Walk down Main Street at midnight
when the only places open
are two bars in the same block.
Turn the corner and walk past
the homes of the good people
of Santo Tomas. Everybody
will be doing one of three things
rather well: sleeping, drinking,
or the thing we all think we would
do better with somebody else's
husband or wife. And maybe
an angel, like a huge white moth,
will be hovering over each of us.

*

Years ago some desperate
farmer took this land away
from the desert, and every summer
the desert wants it back.
In the heat, everything
stops moving, even the dogs.
All night cicadas drill our teeth.
Water gets scarce
and what little there is
is warm and bitter, but we learn
to drink our liquor straight.

*

New people come here
sometimes, but don't stay long.
I'd like to know what attracts them.
Maybe the need to suffer;
we all have it, like a bird
pecking away inside us

as if inside an egg.
Some people think that if you
suffer enough you'll get to be
better, even noble, but I've lived
here forty years and I get
meaner every day.

*

I have nothing to recommend me
except longevity. And hell,
what good is that?
Show me an old man who doesn't
envy every stud he sees
and I'll show you a body
with the undertaker's fingerprints
all over it.

*

Because of the way they dress
it's getting hard to tell
the whores from the female
schoolteachers, which probably
means that whoring isn't
as well paid a profession
as it used to be, what with
all the enthusiastic
amateurs around here.

*

I used to think this bar
was the center of the community
and if I sat here long enough
I'd learn everything worth knowing
about the people of Santo Tomas.
But this afternoon I went
to the funeral of the richest
man in town and watched his two
widows fighting over which of them
would follow his coffin to the grave.
Now I realize that all

significant social events
still take place in church.

*

The earth is moving several ways
at once, but sometimes I wonder
if we are going with it.
And when the drive-in movie
shuts down for the night,
the stars remain over Santo Tomas
like holes in the darkness
through which we see
a cold, enormous light.

*

I don't think death will be
much use to us,
since we've grown accustomed
to using pain for our purposes,
and even love, when we have to.
I think death will arrive
when we have nothing left to use
to get what we want,
or when we no longer want anything,
whichever comes first.

I've learned to wait. Nothing
we want is ever worth
what we go through to get it,
and the difference between what
little we have to offer
and how much we're asked to pay
is life, a kind of debt
we always owe somebody.
I'm in no hurry to pay it.

One More Time

with my hat on backwards
to salute the sun
which rises behind me

with my incredible consistencies
a shoebox full of cloves and absences
and an anguished letter from my friend
the misunderstood flute
I am moving on

wearing time thin on my shoulders
a little naked hope and not enough
hair to cover my head

I am moving on
with the dentist's bill in my mouth
my teeth in my pocket
and my ticket
in the coat I left in the closet

with the pain in my hip
like a splintered leg I have walked on
so long I know every tooth
in the bone
with my bottle of whiskey and the pain
like a baby I drug and rock
in its cradle all night
saying for God's sake
go to sleep

with the ghost of the father I loved
who could not love me
now holding my hand

and a good woman who was foolish enough
to take me and keep me
not out of charity
but out of her still unsatisfied need
I have survived

191

I trusted the blind possibilities
and we groped our way
expecting no miracles no
undeserved spittle of Christ

but if it were offered
I would take the journey again
out of darkness through darkness
into darkness
if it were offered
I would take the same journey again

Letter to a Dead Father

Five years since you died and I am
better than I was when you were living.
The years have not been wasted.
I have heard the harsh voices
of desert birds who cannot sing.
Sometimes I touched the membrane
between violence and desire
and watched it vibrate.
I learned that a man
who travels in circles
never arrives at exactly the same place.

If you could see me now
side-stepping triumph and disaster,

still waiting for you to say *my son*
my beloved son. If you could only see
me now, you would know I am stronger.

Death was the poorest subterfuge
you ever managed, but it was permanent.
Do you see now that fathers
who cannot love their sons
have sons who cannot love?
It was not your fault
and it was not mine. I needed
your love but I recovered without it.
Now I no longer need anything.

NAOMI SHIHAB

My Father & The Figtree

For other fruits my father was indifferent.
He'd point at the cherry trees and say,
"See those? I wish they were figs."
In the evenings he sat by my bed
weaving folktales like vivid little scarves.
They always involved a figtree.
Even when it didn't fit, he'd stick it in.
Once Joha was walking down the road & he saw a figtree.
Or, he tied his camel to a figtree & went to sleep.
Or, later when they caught & arrested him,
his pockets were full of figs.

At age six I ate a dried fig & shrugged.
"That's not what I'm talking about!" he said,
"I'm talking about a fig straight from the earth,
gift of Allah!—on a branch so heavy it touches the
    ground."
"I'm talking about picking the largest fattest sweetest fig
in the world & putting it in my mouth."
(Here he'd stop and close his eyes.)

Years passed, we lived in many houses, none had figtrees.
We had lima beans, zucchini, parsley, beets.
Plant one! my mother said, but my father never did.
He tended garden halfheartedly, forgot to water,
let the okra get too big.
"What a dreamer he is. Look how many things he starts
and doesn't finish."

The last time he moved, I got a phonecall.
My father, in Arabic, chanting a song I'd never heard.
"What's that?" I said.
"Wait till you see."

He took me out back to the new yard.
There, in the middle of Dallas, Texas,
a tree with the largest, fattest, sweetest figs in the world.
"It's a figtree song!" he said,

plucking his fruits like ripe tokens,
emblems, assurance
of a world that was always his own.

Night Shift

At 2 a.m. the world is populated
by a mysterious breed.
Pale-skinned, the creatures
shake, sweep, & dust.
You see them in the doorways
of theaters, wearing T-shirts & aprons,
solitary under restaurant neon.
Children live for years
without knowing they exist.

Tonight, driving down San Pedro,
I see these voiceless bodies
preparing my familiar world
& realize I have always been
on a night shift.
I have always been doing something
quiet, tedious, a cleansing below the surface.

So many nights I have stripped away
the cigarette butts & peanut shells
with a new deliberation.
This is why I have not married.
Why my friends have babies & I have none.
I polish the counter,
fill each tin canister with sugar & tea,
stack the tickets on a neat metal spear.

And I know, wherever I appear to be in the world,
I will always be here first.
This dark task is tattooed on my heart,
pure & necessary,
I will do it over & over
as long as it needs to be done.

Snakes

The rattlesnakes have begun to come out,
                    into the gardens,
            out of the mountains,
                    from the parched fields,
        after water it is said,
            after mice;
the papers have announced it,
    we find warnings
            tacked to our doors—
I think one gardener,
            a faithful servant,
        has been bit, stooping
to tend a marigold,
            and a child reported
        her hand horribly mangled—
the citizens have been armed,
                    mothers keep their
            brooms by the door,
                    police carrying shotguns . . .
I have seen none. walking
        barefoot through the beds,
    checking the mulch
                behind lattices,
            even rabbit burrows . . .
I have never been harmed;
but last night fidgeting
        I awoke dizzy to sweet music;
outside on the lawn, the road,
    the housetops, our flowerbeds
                were full of them, almost erect,
their thin necks

swaying toward the moon,
        humming, smiling,
                    sensuously
    drinking in the light;
while others sped
                back and forth on great
                        rice-paper wings,
        carrying messages
            across the cloudless night. . . .

Gooseberries

On his deathbed my Grandfather
sang about meeting his wife in heaven.
he, a weaver, who as a young man had
yodelled across the Alps to his sheep,
and on Saturdays wheeled a lawnmower
through town to care for relatives in the cemetery,
spent Saturday nights drinking
a glass of beer with his violin,
at last succumbed, a skeleton
floating in the sea of the sheets.
beneath his chin he saw the ribs
opening and through the skin the fine webs
of his hands making their final gestures
past his face. he nodded at the fiery
wolves that snorted around his bed as they had
around the bed of his mother gone crazy. at the last
he remarked our bodies were clothed in heat wavering
from the floor to points at the tops of our heads.
in that inland house with its widow's walk
                            higher than the maples
he went hungering up the chimney
all in one piece, and his little wife
who baked for him ran out
            and tore up the gooseberries.

Dog Hospital

Riding by there every day
surrounded by eucalyptuses and palms
I hear them barking behind the whitewashed adobe fence,
see from my bicycle the ladies going in carrying
the loved ones in their arms—
in fact have been there myself
met the receptionist smiling beneath her cap,
read the magazines on training waiting
for the nodding Japanese man
who tries to pet her as he gives her shots,
gets bitten on the hand. nevertheless
days later she comes out smiling, refreshed
as she jumps into my arms and he almost
bowing winks. though riding by now
there are stories of those others calling
over the walls, that they are left to starve,
given other brains, arms
sewn to their necks, and
some are locked in cannisters,
lowered down polished tubes
into caves where there is no light
except the candle in their heads,
and the shadows around them that they
seeing now bark at.

Variation

(cántelo con tristeza)

across the alley from the alamo
          live an old paint pony
   and a Navajo,
whose head is like a lump
          of black chewing gum;
   the horse
      has never brushed his teeth.

they stand there giving an Indian
      "howdy" to all that pass by,
a grunt, looking at the sky;
   the horse chews on the Indian's shoulder . . .

they used to wash their frijoles
                            in the creek
        and pick their teeth around the fire;
get a little drunk once a week—
    until one day, looking at the sky
                    they went away
down the railroad track,
            wishing, not looking:
toot, toot, they never came back.

KEITH WILSON

The Arrival of My Mother

—New Mexico, 1906

She got off, according to the diary,
dressed in a lovely beaded gown, fresh
from Washington with sixteen trunks of ballgowns,
chemises, blouses (4 Middie), shoes and assorted
lingerie. She was at that time about 25, old
for an unmarried woman. Her stiff mother was at
her side, she also wildly overdressed for New Mexico
sun and wind.

What must she have thought, seeing my uncle standing,
hat in hand in the dust of that lonely train house,
cracked yellow paint, faded letters of welcome
for passengers that rarely come?

The buckboard was waiting and they rode out into
the darkness of evening toward the tent, the half
built frame homestead house, wind dying as the sun
sank, birdcries stilled.

I see her now outshooting my father and me, laughing
at our pride and embarrassment. My sister as good a
shot, waiting her turn. Or that picture of her

on horseback, in Eastern riding clothes beside the Pecos.
A picnic when I was small and how my father lifted me up
to her and she carefully walked the horse around rock
and sand.

I suppose she finally arrived in New Mexico
in the April of one year when my sister and I sat beside
a rented bed, each holding one of her hands and watched
her eyes grow childlike, unmasked as a *kachina*
entering the final *kiva* of this Dance. The graceful
the slim laughing woman of my childhood. The old mother
heavy with her years slipped away and the woods of New
England dimmed as these dry hills ripened and caught
her last breath, drums, drums should have beaten
for the arrival of my mother.

On Drinking & a New Moon
Through the Window

If I needed brandy alone
there would be no problem.

Swirl of golden lies in a
handcut glass, foolish fakeries.

What I need is a new brain.
A head clear, ready for dawns.

Instead I have this bent body
haunted by a thousand lives.

The Celt in Me

In a museum here I saw a Celtic swordblade,
rusted, bent in combat. No handle.
These men who built what now are shadowed ruins,

my ancestors; from deathmasks, carvings
I see similar features. Gaiety, defiance,
Lost causes, futile wars. Indians of Europe.

Always the High Goddess, Moon Lady of White
streaming with light with eyes that touch
as the breeze moves through the Holy Tree.

199

From ancient barrows, dim men with old robes
walk gravely through the Danube mists
their arms outstretched for me.

The Lake Above Santos

And there it was once, on the banks
of the slow Canadian. A small town,
with people, charged with the event
the small beauties of their days.

Now the boat passes over,
walls of stone houses clear
beneath the water, windows,
doors, fish swimming through

      —the sinker pulls my line
down, hook bouncing on a fireplace,
water so translucent one can see
a red coffeepot, homely things.

Below our boat, a whole universe
of fishes, minnows, hurtling
bumping, turning silver
one great shining ball:

        moving, orbited,
        each one tiny, perfect
        each with his own teeth
        own hunger nudging his belly along.

They pass, a silver globe over
buried houses, conquistador dreams
of ancestors, quiet ghosts
of piñon fires, voices gentle
with evening, still speaking

        —under the fingers of the wind
          a thousand minnows
          catch light on tiny scales

Over buried, drowned Santos, Hill
Town, a moon rises.

The Rancher

Hard old grey eyes, no pity
in him after years branding cattle—
a cruel man with cows & men

he drove both hard & once
when he was 70 tried to kill
a young puncher for smiling at his

old wife, sat down & cried in fury
because his grown sons took his
ivoryhandled .45 away, held

his head in his arms & didn't
ever come back to the dance.
After awhile his wife went slowly

out into the clear night
saying how late it is getting
now isn't it? without

pity for his eyes, him showing
nothing the next morning
barking at the hands to get

popping, the sun already up,
coffee on the fire and him
stifflegged, hard pot hanging

over the saddlehorn, he led
fall's last drive
across the hazy range.

The
Great Plains

MARVIN BELL

The Home Front

German submarines were an idea we watched
off the south shore of Long Island;
two newsmen drove and acted suspiciously
all night to prove two spies could;
I spent afternoons at the Bay
watching for unidentified airplanes;
the Lockheed Lightnings were beautiful
with box tails; nights, I was *on the air*,
mobile. Listening to the news,
I kept track on the flap of a carton
of captured and killed: we were way ahead;
we wanted the war to come closer:
we made up stories for the Coast Guard
in which the Germans were monsters.
But we could never be taken prisoner,
not by a long shot, not while the tide
went out under our care.

A Memory

The first wife floats in memory calmly
who formerly was storm-tossed, who gave
at the edges a whitewash to those rocks
on which she would founder, who founded
the Territory Hysteria, bordering
the knife, the state of the doomed union,

who spent lavishly the genital coin,
who ate up the year's best and its worst,
who was the slaveship that came in,
who wasted the fortune in the hold we
have mentioned, who put out for history
a veil of tears, and a sour milk steam.

Recall, also, how you arrived by that ship,
seasick and blubbering as much as anyone,
and how it took you, for all its wooden groans,
to land, and then let you leave.
You were the dullest coxswain alive.
You were put in the hole for good reason.

Garlic

Russian penicillin—that was the magic
of garlic, a party and cure. Sure,
you'll wrestle the flowers for fixings,
tap roots and saw branch for the ooze
of health, but you'll never get better.
I say you're living a life of leisure,
if life is life and leisure leisure.

The heart's half a prophet; it hurts
with the crabapple floating on top,
it aches just to know of the ocean—
the Old Country split off from the New—
and the acts of scissors inside you.
The heart of the East European,
poor boiler, is always born broken.

The sore heart weighs too much
for its own good. And Jewish health
is like snow in March, sometimes April.
The brothers who took their medicine
with you (garlic!) are dead now too.
The herb that beat back fever and sore
went home to its family: the lilies.

What Is There

When the grass, wet and matted,
is thick as a dry lawn is not,
I think of a kind of printing—
a page at a time, and the thick
paper hung up to dry, its
deep impressions filled and shapely
where ink is held and hardens.

And I wonder then at the underside
of those damp sheets of grass—
the muddy blood of those buried
coming up into the flattened green
as I press it underfoot, and pass,
and the sun drawing moisture
until we accept what is written there.

ROBERT BLY

from **The Teeth Mother Naked at Last**

II

Excellent Roman knives slip along the ribs.

A stronger man starts to jerk up the strips of flesh.

*"Let's hear it again, you believe in the Father, the Son, and
the Holy Ghost?"*

A long scream unrolls.

More.

*"From the political point of view, democratic institutions
are being built in Vietnam, wouldn't you agree?"*

A green parrot shudders under the fingernails.
Blood jumps in the pocket.
The scream lashes like a tail.

*"Let us not be deterred from our task by the voices of
dissent...."*

The whines of the jets
pierce like a long needle.

As soon as the President finishes his press conference, black
wings carry off the words,
bits of flesh still clinging to them.

* * *

The ministers lie, the professors lie, the television lies, the
  priests lie. . . .
These lies mean that the country wants to die.
Lie after lie starts out into the prairie grass,
like enormous caravans of Conestoga wagons. . . .

And a long desire for death flows out, guiding the enormous
  caravans from beneath,
stringing together the vague and foolish words.
It is a desire to eat death,
to gobble it down,
to rush on it like a cobra with mouth open.
It's a desire to take death inside,
to feel it burning inside, pushing out velvety hairs,
like a clothes brush in the intestines—

This is the thrill that leads the President on to lie.

* * *

Now the Chief Executive enters; the press conference
  begins:
First the President lies about the date the Appalachian
  Mountains rose.
Then he lies about the population of Chicago, then he lies
  about the weight of the adult eagle, then about the
  acreage of the Everglades.

He lies about the number of fish taken every year in the
  Arctic, he has private information about which city *is* the
  capital of Wyoming, he lies about the birthplace of
  Attila the Hun.

He lies about the composition of the amniotic fluid, and he
  insists that Luther was never a German, and that only
  the Protestants sold indulgences,

That Pope Leo X *wanted* to reform the church, but the
  "liberal elements" prevented him,
that the Peasants' War was fomented by Italians from the
  North.

And the Attorney General lies about the time the sun sets.

* * *

These lies are only the longing we all feel to die.
It is the longing for someone to come and take you by the
    hand to where they all are sleeping:
where the Egyptian pharaohs are asleep, and your own
    mother,
and all those disappeared children, who used to go around
    with you in the rings at grade school. . . .

Do not be angry at the President—he is longing to take in
    his hand
the locks of death hair—
to meet his own children dead, or unborn. . . .
He is drifting sideways toward the dusty places

Reading in Fall Rain

The fields are black once more.
The old restlessness is going.
I reach out with open arms
to pull in the black fields.

All morning rain has fallen
steadily on the roof.
I feel like a butterfly
joyful in its powerful cocoon.

           *

I break off reading:
one of my bodies is gone!
It's outdoors, walking
swiftly away in the rain!

I get up and look out.
Sure enough, I see
the rooster lifting his legs
high in the wet grass.

Looking at a Dead Wren in My Hand

Forgive the hours spent listening to radios, and the
words of gratitude I did not say to teachers. I love your
tiny rice-like legs, that are bars of music played in an

empty church, and the feminine tail, where no worms of Empire have ever slept, and the intense yellow chest that makes tears come. Your tail feathers open like a picket fence, and your bill is brown, with the sorrow of an old Jew whose daughter has married an athlete. The black spot on your head is your own mourning cap.

A Hollow Tree

I bend over an old hollow cottonwood stump, still standing, waist high, and look inside. Early spring. Its Siamese temple walls are all brown and ancient. The walls have been worked on by the intricate ones. Inside the hollow walls there is privacy and secrecy, dim light. And yet some creature has died here.

On the temple floor feathers, gray feathers, many of them with a fluted white tip. Many feathers. In the silence many feathers.

MICHAEL DENNIS BROWNE

The Plants

1

In my house I keep green books,
whose pages turn without me.

2

You, window-friend, facing south,
you bear the dawn on your leaves
and the day's last blood.
And in that dawn how quickly
the dark's load slides from you.
And the mind more slowly
its bad dreams . . .

Jerusalem Cherry you are called.
And at Easter a tiny
green Christ rose up in your leaves.

3

You, darker friend, facing
your perfect twin in the mirror,
you, rooted but no prisoner,
you are small; but at night
I see myself sitting under you,
while the larger body is sleeping.
Australian Umbrella Tree.
With a wet cloth I wipe your leaves.
It is as if I clean a lens.
You go up into midnights.

4

And I want heart to be
a plant that in a dark house
stays wet, its leaves dripping;

a green book I keep,
whose pages turn without me.

The Man

A man comes in the door
who makes your skin shiver.
He says: *I want the television.*
You say: *Have it.*
He says: *I want the dog.*
The dog, you say, *is more difficult.*

You wrestle; he is a snake,
he is fast, he is all over you,
his nails rip your back.
Darling, you say.
He tears the stocking from his head
& is the girl of your dreams. ·

J. V. BRUMMELS

Jeans

Get them new.

Wash them in a horse tank.
Wash you in them.

Work construction in them,
Or farm. Keep explaining
That better times are on the way.

Go in them.
Come in them.

Don't fray them purposely,
But never cut a worn hem.
And if you must sew,
Hand-stitch with red thread.

Sleep in them for a week.
Live in them for a semester.

Put them on for a hangover.

If they survive,
Pat them and you
On the ass.

They're a one-man dog
And, once broken, will bite another.

VICTOR CONTOSKI

Money

At first it will seem tame,
willing to be domesticated.

It will nest
in your pocket
or curl up in a corner
reciting softly to itself
the names of the presidents.

It will delight your friends,
shake hands with men
like a dog and lick
the legs of women.

But like an amoeba
it makes love
in secret
only to itself.

Fold it frequently;
it needs exercise.

Water it every three days
and it will repay you
with displays of affection.

Then one day when you think
you are its master
it will turn its head
as if for a kiss
and bite you gently
on the hand.

There will be no pain
but in thirty seconds
the poison will reach your heart.

Dream 1971

At 5:10 a.m. Uncle Henry
came back from the dead
still partially bald
his face a round red sun
his fists full of cards.

I thought he had answers
shoving his hands toward me.

He had just one question:
what do you do
with cards like these?

from **Broken Treaties**

Teeth

1

Kiss the one you love.
Behind the lips
teeth are waiting

like a man with a weapon
waits in a dark alley.

2

They are not knives
but clubs.

They come down on meat
like a lead pipe
on the head of a woman.

3

Sometimes in dreams
they wither and turn soft
like rotten cactus.

They curl up and fall out
like men refusing to fight
an unpopular war.

4

If you are beaten long enough and hard enough
your teeth will be knocked out.

Then you can use them as chessmen:
front teeth, pawns;
back teeth, pieces.

5

They line up in the mouth
like soldiers for inspection.

Ever since I can remember
they have surrounded the tongue,

reminding what is soft
of what is hard.

Those I Love

Those I love—
even in my dreams
I see only their backs.

O, let me be there
with them
in a far country

away from the hanging tongues
and the sheep faces
of those that love me.

The Mailman

In the dark of night
he has opened what is mine
looking for money
and copying excerpts
for his novel.

For years he has
burned my mail in secret
trying to make me believe
my friends have forgotten me.

Nocturne for the U.S. Congress

Shadows fall like men
on the steps of the U.S. Senate Building.

The sun goes down over the House of Representatives
like a motion to discuss secret wars in Asia.

The janitor turns out the lights one by one.
He searches the empty washrooms for bombs.

The urine of our elected representatives
disappears like the young. It goes underground
where it mingles with the urine of the poor
and the statesman-like urine of the president
and the pale virtuous urine of the first lady.

Oh, it is night
when taxes ripen like grapes.

It is night for the Department of Commerce.
It is night for the United States Treasury.
It is night for the Ways and Means Committee.

The pure stars march across the heavens
of Washington D.C. like armies.

And darkness descends on the Department of Justice.

PHILIP DACEY

The Black Death

There had been portents:
In Rome, blood poured
From freshly-cut bread;
A fiery column
Hung over Avignon;

And a great dog roamed
The German sky with a drawn
Sword in his paws—
An angel rode his back
And laughed. Then it struck:

Stately manors
And poor hovels
Emptied to fill
Each pit with a hundred
Shovelled dead.

The sure sign was this:
A swelling below
The shoulder, a bubo—
Known in the street
As "shilling in the armpit."

Doctors warned, Move
Slowly, if at all.
Sing but little.
When air comes in,
So does poison.

Men walked outside
With fragrant spices
Raised to their noses:
The perfume of death
Could take away breath.

Some shut all doors
And windows, ate
The most delicate fare.
Sweet music was played
And they listened hard.

Others went out
To meet it square
With a dying whore:
The lifted prick
Mocks the limp sick.

Children whispered how,
At night, one could see
Blue flames leap
Out of the mouths of the dead
And dance, ghostly, overhead,

And their parents couldn't
Keep from dreaming
All night of drinking
From a dying man
His thick, black urine.

So the flagellants
Marched, who whipped
Themselves with sticks
Until blood came
And the good death of orgasm.

But victims need victims:
The plague, all knew,
Was a hellish Jew-
Plot. Rabinowitz
Got a knife in the throat.

Everywhere, Death rushed
And Profit kept pace:
Men hawked dice
With the pips filled in
And prayers painted on:

Oremus. Our Father
Who art in heaven.
Seven and eleven.
Throw the bones. I pass.
Lord, have mercy on us.

The Animals' Christmas

They are always living
in Christmas.
Though they walk years
through a field
they can never step

out of the birth of a god.
In each dark brain
a star
sending light through their sinews
leads their hooves

forward from one miracle
to another,
the gleams
tipping grass
like the bright eyes

of uncountable millions
of babies
a field has borne.
When they rub a tree,
a secret myrrh

descends onto their backs.
They carry and offer it
without even trying.
From their nostrils
they breathe good news.

GARY GILDNER

They Have Turned the Church Where I Ate God

They have turned the church where I ate God
and tried to love Him into a gym

where as an altar boy I poured water and wine
into the pastor's cup, smelling the snuff
under his lip on an empty stomach

where I kept the wafer away from my teeth
thinking I could die straight to the stars
or wherever it was He floated warm and far

where I swung the censer at Benedictions to the Virgin
praying to better my jump shot from the corner
praying to avoid the dark occasions of sin

where on Fridays in cassock and Windsor knot and
    flannel pants
I followed Christ to His dogwood cross
breathing a girl's skin as I passed, and another's
trying less and less to dismiss them

where I confessed my petty thefts and unclean dreams
promising never again, already knowing
I would be back flushed with desire and shame

where I stood before couples scrubbed and stiff
speaking their vows, some so hard at prayer
I doubted they could go naked, some so shiny
I knew they already did it and grinned like a fool

where I stood before caskets flanked by thick candles
handing the priest the holy water
feeling the rain trickle down to my face
hearing the worms gnaw in the satin and grinding my teeth

Geisha

The boxer bitch is pregnant
puffed up like an Oriental wrestler!

The boys stand back,
aloof, embarrassed
or unsure of their hands.

But the girls, their cheeks aflame,
are down on shiny knees
praising all the nipples.

After an All-Night Cackle with Sloth & Co.
I Enter the Mansion & Greet the Dawn

& three baby barn swallows
are being fed on the wing
on the lip of the rain
gutter next to my bathroom window.
There they squat, 1—2—3
little gentlemen dandies
wrapped in their capes,
their necks tucked in
as if nobody loved them.
—Not true! here comes Momma
with a beakful of bug mush
& all three perk into *me-me-me!*
while flapping the air pizzicato!
Ah, the gent on the left gets it quick,
good for him, good for Momma—
& off she flits for another scoop
& they settle down.
                              Dog-fashion

they scratch their heads,
pick in their slick blue
tails for appetizers,
snub a dizzy wasp . . .
Quietly, I take this moment to leak
wishing I too were starting
the day so fresh, & could flap
for something plucked
alive in mid-air, in love,
& drop my chalky crap, my gnats & flies,
in the gutter with such distinction.

TOM HENNEN

Job Hunting

I want a job as a low cloud
Heavy as my wet wool cap
So if I'm hit
By lightning on the hill
I won't have to explain being out so late
Or how my socks got damp.

In the early morning I'll hang
Over evergreen branches
My ear lappers down
As lights go on
In the bedrooms
Alarm clocks ringing like words
Of the first awake.

Almost frozen
I drift sideways
Across the sky
Rain turning to snow.

Woods Night

Primitive man
Tied to a stake
No leg
Breaking free
He is surrounded
Axe blows
Pine trees

He drifts
Overturned, past island
After island
Past midnight
Near my shore
I am still awake
Listening
Toward the lake

The last thing
I want to hear before going to sleep
Is that man
Splashing ashore.

LOUIS JENKINS

My Feet

When I awake and look at my feet
I realize they must have waited all night,
immigrants clutching their papers,
clumsy thick bodied peasants
still heavy with the old soil.
I think how many days they
must have stared at the ocean in dismay,
tried to cling to the pitch and roll,
no talent for swimming.
Now they stand, weary, bewildered,

still waiting, wondering which steps
to take across the snows
of this first long winter
in the new world.

DONALD JUSTICE

Party

    After midnight the charm
    Begins to seem less potent,
And still the little band of initiates

    Stand about in their circle
    Attempting the ancient modes
Lord Bacchus himself must have invented.

    If so far they have failed
    To summon up any but the
Familiar demons of a banal whimsy,

    Let us not imagine
    That the invisible ones
Are either innocent or ignorable.

    Even now as we go on
    Pretending to pay them only
The politer forms of inattention,

    Leer and Pinch Me and their kind
    Are taking possession of
Our crowded rooms, our empty persons.

Men at Forty

Men at forty
Learn to close softly
The doors to rooms they will not be
Coming back to.

At rest on a stair landing,
They feel it moving
Beneath them now like the deck of a ship,
Though the swell is gentle.

And deep in mirrors
They rediscover
The face of the boy as he practices tying
His father's tie there in secret

And the face of that father,
Still warm with the mystery of lather.
They are more fathers than sons themselves now.
Something is filling them, something

That is like the twilight sound
Of the crickets, immense,
Filling the woods at the foot of the slope
Behind their mortgaged houses.

WILLIAM KLOEFKORN

Otoe County in Nebraska

On the run is the Otoe County corn rootworm,
overcome by laboratories:
who have purpled the soil with nuggets enough
to deter the deepest scavenger.
Thus as you drive the plush curvaceous trails
of Otoe County
you can sense the rootworm's grim retreat—
the dirty little no good
crop killing bugger
hightailing it for Kansas and Oklahoma,
for south Texas,
through Mexico
to a tip in Yucatan
from which it can throw itself
for mercy into the sea,
You can imagine it going without breakfast,

halfway now across the Caribbean,
dogpaddling its hundred thousand legs
to maintain a slim distance
between its life's little juice
and the laboratories that,
running at full throttle with periscope up,
cannot unlock their hatches until that
last little juice has been spilled.

Meanwhile, back in Otoe County,
the cornrows rise corpulent as green trees.
In a red Volkswagen you are a snail,
hunched and alien and terribly humble.

from **Loony**

29. The Good Folks at the Camp Meeting

The good folks at the camp meeting
are singing and shouting
and clapping their hands,
and some are crying,
and the right little, tight little
Mendenhall girl
is on her knees at the altar,
praying to the top of the tent.
Last night old Mrs. Carlson
won the victory in
her right ear,
where now, she says,
she can hear a smattering
of the highest parts of the sermon.
The preacher says that he has
never been to college,
but that he has a sheepskin
from the ivory towers at Jerusalem,
and that more than once
he has trod up Calvary,
stepping where Christ himself stepped,
and that he felt His presence there.
The preacher says that
he would rather be just a poor beggar,
and live in a shack
by the side of the road,

and know Jesus,
than to be as rich as Rockefeller,
which the preacher says
is like a boat without a rudder
or a fish without a tail.
And listen:
tomorrow night, for sure,
Junior Ogden's mother
is going to throw away
her crutches.

And the August air is hot and still,
full of tentpoles and ropes,
sweat and sawdust and straw.
And more and more,
as the night wears on,
the good folks at the camp meeting
warm to the hand of loony:
all of us, it seems,
full of wrath and worms and vinegar,
all slightly disconnected in the head
and needing mercy.

51. During the War

During the war
Thelma Hunt's whitewall tires
hit home like a sniper,
according to Mr. Terrell,
and Mr. Terrell himself,
who had not had the privilege
in the first place, he said,
of selling Thelma her Chevrolet
(worse yet, he said,
she bought it twelve miles south, in Kiowa),
said he wouldn't be surprised
if Mrs. Hunt was somehow in cahoots
with the Gestapo.
Just look at her head,
Mr. Terrell says,
how square it is,
how harder than a helmet.
And the way she trims and pampers
her lawn and house and garden every day,

whether or not they need it:
that's strictly from beyond the water,
loony, sir,
and one thing more:
she has an Iron Cross up her ass,
or I'm not Presbyterian!

Mr. Terrell does dress well
and says he tithes,
says he'd rather sell
a brand new car at cost
than be seen in broad daylight
goosestepping the main street,
like Axis Sally herself,
on out of town tires.

·

TED KOOSER

Fort Robinson

When I visited Fort Robinson,
where Dull Knife and his Northern Cheyenne
were held captive that terrible winter,
the grounds crew was killing the magpies.

Two men were going from tree to tree
with sticks and ladders, poking the young birds
down from their nests and beating them to death
as they hopped about in the grass.

Under each tree where the men had worked
were twisted clots of matted feathers,
and above each tree a magpie circled,
crazily calling in all her voices.

We didn't get out of the car.
My little boy hid in the back and cried
as we drove away, into those ragged buttes
the Cheyenne climbed that winter, fleeing.

Abandoned Farmhouse

He was a big man, says the size of his shoes
on a pile of broken dishes by the house;
a tall man too, says the length of the bed
in an upstairs room; and a good, God-fearing man,
says the Bible with a broken back
on the floor below the window, dusty with sun;
but not a man for farming, say the fields
cluttered with boulders and the leaky barn.

A woman lived with him, says the bedroom wall
papered with lilacs and the kitchen shelves
covered with oilcloth, and they had a child,
says the sandbox made from a tractor tire.
Money was scarce, say the jars of plum preserves
and canned tomatoes sealed in the cellar-hole,
and the winters cold, say the rags in the window frames.
It was lonely here, says the narrow gravel road.

Something went wrong, says the empty house
in the weed-choked yard. Stones in the fields
say he was not a farmer; the still-sealed jars
in the cellar say she left in a nervous haste.
And the child? Its toys are strewn in the yard
like branches after a storm—a rubber cow,
a rusty tractor with a broken plow,
a doll in overalls. Something went wrong, they say.

Gates

If a gate stands open long enough,
it can't be closed again. Slowly,
the morning glories tie it fast,
and the strength that kept it flying
over the grass-tops lets it down.

The same thing happens if a gate's
left closed; you lose it to the fence
(that's what a fence wants, after all).
A rule of thumb: if you can't use
your gate enough to keep it swinging,
better to leave it standing wide.

Christmas Eve

Now my father carries his old heart
in its basket of ribs
like a child coming into the room
with an injured bird.
Our ages sit down with a table between them,
eager to talk.
Our common bones are wrapped in new robes.
A common pulse tugs at the ropes
in the backs of our hands.
We are so much alike
we both weep at the end of his stories.

Tom Ball's Barn

for Bill Kloefkorn

The loan that built the barn
just wasn't big enough
to buy the paint, so the barn
went bare and fell apart
at the mortgaged end of twelve
nail-popping, splintering winters.
Besides the Januaries,
the barber says it was
five-and-a-half percent,
three dry years, seven wet,
and two indifferent,
the banker (dead five years),
and the bank (still open
but deaf, or *deef* as it were), *and*
poor iron in the nails that
were all to blame for the barn's collapse
on everything he owned, thus
leading poor Tom's good health
to diabetes and
the swollen leg that threw him
off the silo, probably
dead (the doctor said)
before he hit that board pile.

GREG KUZMA

After Sex

Oh to be moving as we once were
in long swoops over the bare face
of the earth. But now we are wrought
with looseness and disgust.
The world has opened to us disclosing
a canker.
But oh to be moving.
And yet love itself is buried,
as it should be, out of the weather
and our vision.
Blood in our mouths.
Natural like a fish rotting.
But.
No posterity creeping in us.
Only to forget the thighs
and the rudiments, the tug
of war that ends in collapse.
Oh to be moving again
in long swoops over the bare face
of the earth, looking down on each
other's bodies, landmarks,
fictions of will and need.

The Wolfman

has a problem he is too old
to turn
yet still
the strangeness is in him
nights when the moon rises
feels his throat tremble
lift up

sometimes
coming home
his eyes glaze he dreams
of the briars the threshing

of ankles
clip clop in the dark
of the police on horses

seeing horses something in
his blood becomes unfrozen
he would like to be down
on all fours dreams
of the hill top and safety
alone with his paws
licking them
blood in his face

sometimes at his desk over
words he starts at the groaning
that's in them
almost goes into the spaces
where they are white

the double o's like eyes
the double victory of his name
that nearly lifts him
out of the stiff black clothes

at night
cannot sleep cannot bear
where the sheet touches
    cannot
breathe in the strong man
liquor but goes to the window
looks out on the ground
where the moon weaves its
    trails
through the leaves
short hairs on his neck stretch
for the wild wind

and now he is running the
torches behind him are
    squints
in the darkness he hears rifles
open their muzzles to pain
that is flying up past him
he kicks up the dirt with
the bullets he keeps his knees

high in the air
zigs through the snags
of the forest behind in
the field a flutter of gowns
a necklace of starlight
voices and handkerchiefs
the long white throat with its
gash

thinks someday he will write a book
with a white cover
whose pages are edged in red
listing signs of his passing the
tracks in the bushes the
dribbles of blood on the ground
fur snagged on a thorn
a whole chapter devoted to panting
recounting his disappearance
his life among men
quiet walks among women

long Sundays plucking the hair
from his cheeks the fitting
of shoes the perfumes he required
clipping the strong dark nails
combing the streak up his head

moon rising without him
might be its suitable title

MERIDEL LE SUEUR

The Village

The Village has always lain in the path of the conqueror.
The villages of Viet Nam, of Africa, of Peru and Brazil,
of Ireland, Spain, Mexico, Cuba, Haiti, Iowa, New
Mexico, Thailand, look up in anger at the sky filled with
fire, at napalm burning crops and skin, and still
they plunder the Village and the Villagers.

The Puritans plundered villages from coast to coast;
drove the Cherokees on the Trail of Tears, threw smallpox
infected clothes into the Mandan villages, Kit Carson
drove the Navajos off their lands into the concentration
camps; north of Trinidad, Colorado, you can see the
monument over the Black Hole of Ludlow, a tent village
burned by Rockefeller. Cortez marched over the bodies
of the Indian villages, destroyed from Ohio to Tierra del
Fuego; Hearst left a village of skulls at the mines of Potosí.
My family fled the Irish villages taken over for sheep
runs for the mills of Newcastle. My Iowa village is owned
by absentee landlords now. Name Lidice, the villages
of pogroms, Guernica; from the Big Horn to Viet Nam—
the Massacre of Wounded Knee to the Mekong Delta,
the same Village—our Village.

I Light Your Streets

I am a crazy woman with a painted face
On the streets of Gallup.
I invite men into my grave
                for a little wine.
I am a painted grave
Owl woman   hooting for callers in the night.
Black bats over the sun sing to me
The horned toad sleeps in my thighs,
My grandmothers gave me songs to heal
But the white man buys me cheap without song
   or word.
My dead children appear and I play with them.
Ridge of time in my grief—remembering
Who will claim the ruins?
                and the graves?
                the corn maiden violated
As the land?
I am a child in my eroded dust.
I remember feathers of the hummingbird
And the virgin corn laughing on the cob.
Maize defend me
Prairie wheel around me
I run beneath the guns
                and the greedy eye

And hurricanes of white faces knife me.
But like fox and smoke I gleam among the thrushes
And light your streets.

Dead in Bloody Snow

I am an Indian woman
Witness to my earth
Witness for my people.
I am the nocturnal door,
The hidden cave of your sorrow,
Like you hidden deep in furrow
                    and dung
        of the charnel mound,
I heard the craven passing of the
                white soldiers
And saw them shoot at Wounded Knee
                upon the sleeping village,
And ran with the guns at my back
Until we froze in our blood on the snow

I speak from old portages
Where they pursued and shot into the river crossing
All the grandmothers of Black Hawk.
I speak from the smoke of grief,
                from the broken stone,
And cry with the women crying from the marsh
Trail and tears of drouthed women,
            O bitter barren!
            O barren bitter!
I run, homeless,
            I arrive
    in the gun sight,
                    beside the white square houses
    of abundance.
                My people starve
In the time of the bitter moon.
I hear my ghostly people crying
        A hey a hey a hey.

Rising from our dusty dead the sweet grass,
The skull marking the place of loss and flight.

I sing holding my severed head,
   to my dismembered child,
A people's dream that died in bloody snow.

THOMAS MC GRATH

from **Letter to an Imaginary Friend**

      V

    The road outside the window was "our"
road
Once. It is now anybody's road.
       It is the road
On which everyone went away.
      Take it.
        To the coulee
        bottom—
Head south on the ice toward the Indian graves and the
  river.

   * * * * * *

    And what's here—on the little bluff
Over the little river?
    A way station, merely;
A half-way house for the Indian dead—analphabetic
Boneyard . . .
     It was here the Sioux had a camp on the
    long trail
Cutting the loops of the rivers from beyond the Missouri
  and Mandan
East: toward Big Stone Lake and beyond to the Pipestone
  Quarry.
The place of peace.
    A backwoods road of a trail, no tribal
Superhighway; for small bands only. Coming and going
They pitched camp here a blink of an eye ago.

It's all gone now—nothing to show for it.

                                        Skulls
Under the permanent snow of time no wind will lift
Nor shift . . .

                    —these drifting bones have entered the rock
                    forever . . .

And all done in the wink of an eye! Why my grandmother
    saw them—
And saw the last one perhaps: ascending the little river
On the spring high water in a battered canoe.

                                        Stole one of
 .   her chickens
(Herself in the ark of the soddy with the rifle cocked but
    not arguing)
Took the stolen bird and disappeared into history.

And my father, a boy at Fort Ransom, saw them each
    spring and fall—
Teepees strung on the fallow field where he herded cattle.
Made friends and swapped ponies with a boy his own
    age—
And in the last Indian scare spent a week in the old fort:
And the soddies abandoned, then.

                                Wounded Knee—
The last fight—must have been at that time.

                                        And now
All: finished.

            South Dakota has stolen the holy
Bones of Sitting Bull to make a tourist attraction!

3.

And the people?

            "First they broke land that
            should not ha' been broke

                                and they *died*
Broke. Most of 'em. And after the tractor ate the horse—
It ate *them*. Most of 'em. And now, a few lean years,
And the banks will have it again. Most of it. Why, hellfar,
Once a family could live on a quarter and now a hull
    section won't do!
Half of the people gone left the country; the towns dyin';
And this crop uh hayseeds gutless—wouldn't say shit
    and themselves
Kickin' it out their beds. It's hard lines, buddy!"

Bill Dee speaking his piece: hard times
In the country.
                    Bill Dee: last of the old bronc-stompers
From the gone days of Montana mustangs we used on
    the farms
For light work and for riding and the pure hell of having
Outlaws around . . .
                    The same Bill Dee of the famous
                    removable
Eye: which he'd slip in your shot-glass sometimes—
    O blinding and sobering
Sight!
            —"Just take a swally uh *that* and say what yer
            innards
Perdick fer the follyin' winter! Take a *glass* eye view
    of the world 'n
Change your luck!"
                    Not only a glass eye: a gab
Nine miles longer than a telephone wire.
                    A sense of style:
Could roll cigarettes on a bucking horse in a high wind—
But only one-handed of course . . .
                    Was the greatest success
                    I know
Out of the old days alive
                    alone
                    but alive—
Had decided he wanted to be a broncsnapper and cowboy
    and *made* it—
On the last ranch on the hither side of the moon.
                    And lived
                    there
Still: on the Bonesack.
                    (Ranch in the Sand Hills.)
                    And a small cabin
Built there: of elm and cottonwood made: a squatter—
"Ain't a hell of a lot, but it's more 'n some got:
    'n hol' that, Tiger!"
He rattles on as we rattle along in his ancient car,
And that's where we're heading: down to the Hills in the
    late-winter day.

*   *   *   *   *   *

"Old Sheyenne got better fishin' each year," Bill says.
"Them honyocks around here just too *lazy* to fish. They
    druther
Buy them damn *froze* fish in them plastic bags.
Why, hellfar, you remember that place where that spring
    comes in—
Nigh my cabin? Used to take fish out of there with *scoop*
    shovels—
Gunnysacksful! 'n people with pitchforks spearin' the
    big uns!
They don't fish there no more—nobody but me. Why, boy,
We get you some whoppin' Northerns 'n the best-eatin'
    goddam Walleyes—
Takes an illegal net to get illegal fish, 'n I *got* one!"
Illegal fish flesh and fowl—about all that he lives on.

And into the Hills lost places: now, following
The river, and again buckjumping over the iron, faceless
Ranchroads: opening the gates in the fences,
    kittycornering and quartering
The waste . . .

                    Dead houses here in the bottom lands:

                                        an eyeless
Schoolhouse, abandoned, crumbles;

                                undenominational
                                forever,
A church is stumbling into an empty future, lofting
A headless and rotting Christ on the cracked spool of a
    cross:
Unspinning god at a loss in the psalm of the man-eating
    wind.

"Ever'body here got blown out in the last of the dusters.
Should never been farmed no-way. The country's sure
    empty. But me—
I like it this way.

                    And the animals comin' back! Why,
                    hellfar,
They ain't only pheasant and grouse—man, there's
    wild *turkey*.
There's deer, there's foxes, there's—last night I swear I
    heard a coyoot—

Heard it or dreamed it . . . They're comin' back sure—
    the old days."

Dreamed it; no doubt. And dreamed the old days as well:
    doubtless.
Another fast dreamer . . .
                        At last we arrive at the shack.

Here's Uncle Chaos come to meet me halfway!
                                        Seems so:
Near the house an antique car is racing into the ground
And releasing its onetime overpriced atoms into the void
At the speed of rusty light.
                        Over the doorway a splintering
Rack of flinty deer horns starts no fires in this wind.
Hung from the wall, abandoned gear goes into the
    weather:
Worn spurs and rotting saddles and bridles
                                    emblems
Of the gone days.
                Indoors, deerskins cover the floors,
The bed, the few chairs.
                    There's a new shotgun.
                                        A rifle
My father gave him—25–20 Winchester brushgun.
Traps, snares, spears and fishing tackle: the illegal
Net . . .
        Ground zero
                Bill Dee
                        at home on the wind,
Adrift and at home in the universe
                            alone . . .
                                    alive . . .

                                    And the others—
I think of Tiger Good in his shack on the Maple River
Trapping and hunting his way through the big freeze of
    the Thirties;
Of the squatters in Troop Number Nine's log cabin here on
    the Sheyenne;
Of that nameless one who lived as a hermit here in the
    Hills;

And of Moonlight John: his home a de-mounted twodoor
  carbody
Beside route 46.
                        Froze to death there in a three day
                        blizzard:
Winter of the blue snow . . .
                              mavericks
                                    loners
                                          free men

KATHLEEN NORRIS

The Middle of the World

The night is cloudy
A man with a lot on his mind,
A naked woman
Sit in the middle of a field, in the middle of the world.
It is quiet there.

He is like a horse
Making friendly gestures,
His body unexpectedly silky.
Shuddering, he reaches up inside her
Rocking her
On the inland sea.

He shivers, half-clothed.
He will work cattle tomorrow
If the weather holds.
She is naked, creamy.

They give back
The waters of the air
And the moon, descending,
Goes far into their night,
Their faces and their lives:
This night, and the world, unfinished.

Focus

to a cowboy

I don't know what I'm looking at,
What other shape
Is in the room, whether it's male
Or female, close
Or far away,

I don't know anymore.
Say that mares are just like women,
A pain when they're in heat.
They want it, and don't want it,
And kick the hell out of a stallion.

That sounds right.
Corral them, break them
In dust and confusion.
One'll turn out,
Let herself be rid to hell and back.

Rub her down then,
Speaking softly.
It's almost tender,
The way it's done.

CARL RAKOSI

Poetry

Its nature is to look
        both absolute and mortal,
as if a boy had passed through
or the imprint of his foot
        had been preserved
unchanged under the ash of Herculaneum.

Tune

Today I was pleased by the image
                                    of the Japanese wrestler
legs apart
            hair tied in the back
looking like Turkey
                    astride the Anatolian fault

and a voice in me
                    cried
"Let us go down to the river
                            and find Armenia

and listen again to that way of speaking in Vasari:
'It is related that Giorgione
                                in conversation
with certain sculptors
                        at the time
when Andrea del Verrocchio was engaged with his bronze
    horse . . .' "

Being Natural

How hard one has to labor at it.
There are explanations, of course,
and confessions,
but that is not what is meant.

The way is lost.
The character is gone.

Simplicity

o rare circle,
you are not in favor now.
Not much is written about you.
Perhaps not much is known about you.
But when I hear this,

"I am just a widow woman.
What do I know?"

and when I see the father of many children
hurrying to the polls in Saigon
to pick the candidate whose symbol is the plow

and when I hear an eighteen year old tell the judge
"So here is Tom Rodd.
                    I wanted to go to Selma
and Montgomery but I didn't.
I wanted to go to Washington and confront the President
                                        but I didn't.
But this war is too much for me to say I didn't.
So I'm prepared to go to jail.
                    I have no beef against this court.
I want my friends to know that I'm an optimist.
I drink beer and I play the banjo."

O rare simplicity,
            when I hear this,
I know I am in your honest presence.

No One Talks About This

They go in different ways.
One hog is stationed at the far end
of the pen to decoy the others,
the hammer knocks the cow
                        to his knees,
the sheep goes gentle
                    and unsuspecting.
Then the chain is locked
around the hind leg
and the floor descends
                    from under them.
Head down they hang.
The great drum turns
the helpless objects
and conveys them slowly
to the butcher waiting
at his station.

The sheep is stabbed
behind the ear.

Gentle sheep, I am powerless
to mitigate your sorrow.
Men no longer weep
                              by the rivers of Babylon,
but I will speak for you.
If I forget you, may my eyes
lose their Jerusalem.

The Indomitable

copulate
               $<$ *copulare:*
to join,
        to couple;
says nothing
               of lust,
the iron master,
                     sweaty,
breathless,
        fierce.

The Experiment with a Rat

Every time I nudge that spring
                              a bell rings
and a man walks out of a cage
assiduous and sharp like one of us
and brings me cheese.

                    How did he fall
                              into my power?

The Children

Hand in hand, they are marching
along the hallway, looking
for cats and seagulls,
the footprints of the troll,
speaking to rocks
of a new home for angels,
herding butterflies
in far mountain meadows,
teaching skyscrapers how to swim.

And they are watching,
always, like rows of turtles
on a river bank.
Their eyes look out
from deep within their shells,
where we cannot
see them.

In the Heartland

Who can say
why the birds in this country
crash so hopelessly against
the windows of passing cars?
The ditches by the highway
are filled with their broken wings—
the intestines of rotting rabbits,
raccoon fur, a calf trying to rise
from the pulpy mound
that used to be his hindquarters,
three dogs, one without a head,
a cat hanging from a thin wire noose
on a dead elm tree branch . . .

All along the main streets
tv sets are turning off.

The houses look like old men
squatting in long rows,
ready to pitch forward into the earth
as easily as pebbles slipping into still water.

CARY WATERMAN

Pig Poem

The pig's ears blossom and fold
like lush jungle lilies.
It is their only attractive feature
except for the shell shaped feet
that try to escape each night into the creek.

Each pig roots under the Prickly Ash,
undermines the foundation of the sauna,
and buries all underwear left lying around.
They are the fat of my existence;
a greasy black skillet.

The Dani of New Guinea have lived forever
on pigs and sweet potatoes.
They have never been christianized.

Death on the Farm

Half way between the house and the barn
there is a dead Holstein dairy cow,
black and white like a map of the world.
She is big eared and square toothed
and frozen solid.

Who ever said death was fluid
and wore long garments like a wind?
Death is a pile.

The truck from the rendering kitchen
should have been here days ago.
Now it is too late.
The cow is beginning to come back to life.
I can see her breathing from the window.

She looks comfortable there
even though the dogs have begun chewing a dark hole
that will end at the heart.
After they come to take her,
after her fingered milk bag,
her white braced hips are gone,
her breathing will go on in that place;
Up and down against the soft weeds,
in and out,
filling with water the dark space
that goes between us
when we are not even looking.

CHARLES WATERMAN

Neighbor

Morning and evening a heron flies
to and from the fishing of the lake.
It sees the slow wall of the nest you are making
stone by stone,
and that you never leave the ground.
It thinks you have built too far from water
and expects failure for you.
It remembers the camp
of shellfish people two thousand years ago,
whose huts were also interesting,
who sometimes shouted "Neighbor!"
It thinks about them all the way to the lake.
On the way back it would stop to talk,
maybe to advise;
but it has mouths and mouths to feed,
little long necks stretching to the sun.

The New Cows

Like thunder they run out, like Holstein thunder—
These dark females swinging their heavy equipment, these
   barbarous ladies
That slip, fall, run with irregular glances
At us. No one touches them; they keep their separateness,
   in fear.
In a moment we can abandon our proprietary poses for
   the real work,
Which is to get each of the hornless, black and white
Clouds of female energy to a particular stall
And lock her head in it. At first,
It is like being in a mill of giants: each cow's strength,
Multiples of mine, is a sea wave, against which
We skid and shout, and often just
Get out of the way.
                Finally, we outwit them; we
Pick a particular cow, and though she bolts and shoves,
We stanchion her. One by one, cursing, exhilarated, we
   do the same
To all but one huge heifer. She has never
Been in a barn before, and she won't move. We rope her;
   even then we can't hold her;
We tie her to a solid post and watch, dismayed,
As she bucks and falls and bats her head
On concrete. When she gets her wind we winch her,
One step at a time toward food she refuses
To recognize.
             Later, while they eat, we milk them;
By electric light we go among them, washing and talking,
Joking and happy. Two-thirds of the way through milking,
We find a "woman" who will be tonight's favorite:
She stands on two hooves while the machine is on her,
And almost dances.

DON WELCH

Blue Heron

The people south of Gibbon call him
Big Fungus, but a tree can't hold
the parasitic weight an eye does.

But he's big, big enough to carry off
a hog (if it had scales and pooched
its mouth like shad). And he's bigger
than that, big enough to be his own
crane rick.

He's the only high nester I know who's
added to his feet a retractable neck.

All day he sits picking minnows from
behind the clear shades of his smooth
nictating eyes, and dreaming of evening.

When the sun's half a degree to hunger
or a second beyond his circadian clock,
the scales of his feet clamp, his reversed
knees squat, his tail-less anus crumples,
and he's airborne.

He doesn't unroll feathers, he loosens
everything, and for the first ten feet
each bone goes crippled and only his neck
storks.

In the next quarter mile ten thousand
miracles happen, and his neck comes back
in indented satisfaction.

Funeral at Ansley

I write of a cemetery, of the
perpetual care of buffalo grass,
of kingbirds, catbirds, and
cottonwoods;

of wild roses around headstones,
with their high thin stems and tight
tines, their blooms pursed in
the morning.

I write of old faces, of cotton
hose and flowered dresses and
mouths which grew up on
the weather.

And I write of one woman who
lies a last time in the long sun of
August, uncramped by the wind which
autumns each one of us

under catbirds, kingbirds, and
cottonwoods, and the gray-green
leaves of the buffalo
grass.

Bark

Useless to ask what this was
before it crusted. It has the face
of Frost over Auden. But it doesn't
worry. It takes itself in folds.

Ants climb it because it's theirs.
Beetles hide in it because it's fun
to tease beginning peckers. Adult
peckers are something else again.

Aphids know this, and so they sneak
out at dark to dibble in its wounds.
But the only things bark doesn't love
are leaves and lightning.

The goddamned leaves think bark's a scab.
They're always picking at it with their fingers,
thinking if the edge came off they'd feel
a flush of dying into life.

But they just dull their edges, and bark
sends them messages of oriental consolation.
You can always tell when the messages
come through. Leaves' mouths

grow frenetic as they defend
the beauty of their multifoliate existence.
Bark just trunk-chuckles, and occasionally
cuts off their sap.

The
Midwest

AI (FLORENCE OGAWA)

Woman

The adobe walls of the house
clutch the noon heat in tin fists
and while bathing, I fan my breasts,
watching the nipples harden.
I pinch them, feeling nothing, but wanting to,
and shift my weight from left buttock to right,
while the water circling my waist tightens,
as if you had commanded it.
I stand up, spreading my legs apart,
ready to release the next ribbon of blood.

All right. You want me now, this way.
I haven't locked the door.
My swollen belly feels only its heaviness,
you would weigh less than the pain
chipping away at my navel with an ice pick of muscle.
I can carry you.
The blood, halved and thinned, rolls down my legs,
cupping each foot in a red stirrup
and I am riding that invisible horse,
the same one my mother rode.
It's hungry, it has to be fed,
the last man couldn't, can you?

Twenty-Year Marriage

You keep me waiting in a truck
with its one good wheel stuck in the ditch,
while you piss against the south side of a tree.
Hurry. I've got nothing on under my skirt tonight.
That still excites you, but this pickup has no windows
and the seat, one fake leather thigh,
pressed close to mine is cold.

I'm the same size, shape, make as twenty years ago,
but get inside me, start the engine;
you'll have the strength, the will to move.
I'll pull, you push, we'll tear each other in half.
Come on, baby, lay me down on my back.
Pretend you don't owe me a thing
and maybe we'll roll out of here,
leaving the past stacked up behind us;
old newspapers nobody's ever got to read again.

The Anniversary

You raise the ax,
the block of wood screams in half,
while I lift the sack of flour
and carry it into the house.
I'm not afraid of the blade
you've just pointed at my head.
If I were dead, you could take the boy,
hunt, kiss gnats, instead of my moist lips.
Take it easy, squabs are roasting,
corn, still in husks, crackles,
as the boy dances around the table:
old guest at a wedding party for two sad-faced clowns,
who together, never won a round of anything but hard
    times.
Come in, sheets are clean,
fall down on me for one more year
and we can blast another hole in ourselves without a
sound.

Woman to Man

Lightning hits the roof,
shoves the knife, darkness,
deep in the walls.
They bleed light all over us
and your face, the fan, folds up,
so I won't see how afraid
to be with me you are.

We don't mix, even in bed,
where we keep ending up.
There's no need to hide it:
you're snow, I'm coal,
I've got the scars to prove it.
But open your mouth,
I'll give you a taste of black
you won't forget.
For a while, I'll let it make you strong,
make your heart lion,
then I'll take it back.

Why Can't I Leave You?

You stand behind the old black mare,
dressed as always in that red shirt,
stained from sweat, the crying of the armpits,
that will not stop for anything,
stroking her rump, while the barley goes unplanted.
I pick up my suitcase and set it down,
as I try to leave you again.
I smooth the hair back from your forehead.
I think with your laziness and the drought too,
you'll be needing my help more than ever.
You take my hands, I nod
and go to the house to unpack,
having found another reason to stay.

I undress, then put on my white lace slip
for you to take off, because you like that
and when you come in, you pull down the straps
and I unbutton your shirt.
I know we can't give each other any more
or any less than what we have.
There is safety in that, so much
that I can never get past the packing,
the begging you to please, if I can't make you happy,
come close between my thighs
and let me laugh for you from my second mouth.

The Sweet

The man steps in out of the blizzard with his Klootch,
his Eskimo prostitute and the room heats up, as they
cross the floor. I know he is dying and I spin a half
dollar around on the bar, then slide my eyes over the
   woman.
She has a seal's body. Her face is a violet in the center
of the moon. The half dollar falls over, I remind myself
that to love a Klootch is always to be filled with emptiness,
turn and lift my glass.

I shake my head, drink. When I hear retreating footsteps,
I turn. The man stands at the door, facing me. His hand
gropes out, as the woman backs off and I see the Northern
Lights flare up in his eyes, before he stumbles and falls.
The woman leans back against the wall. I pick up the half
dollar, spin it around again and go to her. We walk out
into the darkness and I am cold as I squeeze her buttocks,
her blue, dwarf stars.

GWENDOLYN BROOKS

Horses Graze

Cows graze.
Horses graze.
They
eat
eat
eat.
Their graceful heads
are bowed
bowed
bowed
in majestic oblivion.
They are nobly oblivious
to your follies,
your inflation,
the knocks and nettles of administration.

They
eat
eat
eat.
And at the crest of their brute satisfaction,
with wonderful gentleness, in affirmation,
they lift their clean calm eyes and they lie down
and love the world.
They speak with their companions.
They do not wish that they were otherwhere.
Perhaps they know that creature feet may press
only a few earth inches at a time,
that earth is anywhere earth,
that an eye may see,
wherever it may be,
the Immediate arc, alone, of life, of love.
In Sweden,
China,
Afrika,
in India or Maine
the animals are sane;
they know and know and know
there's ground below
and sky
up high.

Steam Song

Hostilica hears Al Green

That Song it sing the sweetness
like a good Song can,
and make a woman want to
run out and find her man.

Ain got no pretty mansion.
Ain got no ruby ring.
My man is my only
necessary thing.

That Song boil up my blood
like a good Song can.
It make this woman want to
run out and find her man.

The Mother

Abortions will not let you forget.
You remember the children you got that you did not get,
The damp small pulps with a little or with no hair,
The singers and workers that never handled the air.
You will never neglect or beat
Them, or silence or buy with a sweet.
You will never wind up the sucking-thumb
Or scuttle off ghosts that come.
You will never leave them, controlling your luscious sigh,
return for a snack of them, with gobbling mother-eye.

I have heard in the voices of the wind the voices of my dim
        killed children.
I have contracted. I have eased
My dim dears at the breasts they could never suck.

I have said, Sweets, if I sinned, if I seized
Your luck
And your lives from your unfinished reach,
If I stole your births and your names,
Your straight baby tears and your games,
Your stilted or lovely loves, your tumults, your marriages,
        aches, and your deaths,
If I poisoned the beginnings of your breaths,
Believe that even in my deliberateness I was not deliberate.
Though why should I whine,
Whine that the crime was other than mine?—
Since anyhow you are dead.
Or rather, or instead,
You were never made.
But that too, I am afraid,
Is faulty: oh, what shall I say, how is the truth to be said?
You were born, you had body, you died.
It is just that you never giggled or planned or cried.

Believe me, I loved you all.
Believe me, I knew you, though faintly, and I loved,
        I loved you all.

ABBIE HUSTON EVANS

The Wrestling

"Who are you, slim-hipped tussler?"
—All night in the dark,
Like Jacob with his angel,
I wrestle until dawn.

When daybreak comes, it shows me
Who was the Adversary.
I know my topmost worth then,
The touched thew bearing witness.

Primary

Few originals, but mighty,
Waking in the prime—
Pull and release, light, sound, growth, color—
Broke through space and time.

Who but God could have imagined
Cineraria blue,
Or seen scarlet in not-scarlet,
Underived and new?

He alone could call from darkness
Yellow yet unhinted
Where it lay a dreaming splendor
Of the mind, unminted.

Green was easy, given yellow,
One made out of two.
But these tunneled through pit blackness:
Scarlet; yellow; blue.

In Space-Time Aware—

Abysm past thinking on, chill
With menace cutting off words;
Yet yielding toehold to buds
And nooks to the younglings of birds.

Shaken by terror and joy
I see I belong where I am,
Here in the whelming abyss
As it were in the crook of an arm.

DONALD FINKEL

They

are at the end of our street now cutting down trees
a scream like a seven foot locust
they have cut off another
neatly at the pavement
never again will the pin-oak threaten a taxi
will the ash lie in wait to fall on a child

it is a good time for this
the sun is bright
the plane has only just begun
to sprout little shoots from under her fingernails
never again will she dance
her terrible saraband in the tornado
the sweet gum trembles
bristling with tiny mines like brown sea urchins
never again will he drop them on the walk
to menace the sensible shoes of mailmen

they have brought a machine that eats trees
that shits sawdust
they cut off limbs to feed it
snarling it chews the pale green fingers of the plane
the pin-oak's wrinkled elbows and knees
they fill truck after truck with the dust
in the schoolyard now they are cutting down the children
I hear their screams
first at the ankles
it is nothing then to sever

their soles from the asphalt
there is no danger their falling
on the school and crushing it

I have invented a machine that shoots words
I type faster and faster
I cannot keep up with them
in front of the house now they are cutting the rosebush
vainly she scratches their hands like a drowning kitten
they are cutting the grass
scythes in their wheels they race over our lawn
flashing in the sun like the chariots of the barbarians
the grass blades huddle whimpering
there is no place to go
it is spring and the street is alive
with the clamor of motors
the laughter of saws

When I Was Young I Tried to Sing

Whoever I am   the mountains exalt themselves before
    my eyes
and if I do nothing about the mountains but look at them
they are all I am   what fills these trouser legs
what moves the pen across this page   is mountains.

The colts tumble into the field on their implausible legs
wheel and wait for the mares   feinting at the timothy
so my eyes have gone running ahead   they stand
    peacefully
drinking the grass   we are all   the colts   my eyes
these shoes   waiting for the mares.

I catch a glimpse of the man who wears my shoes
before whom the trees line up with their backs to the
    mountain
and the mountain peacefully sets his hair aflame   I tune
    in
on his pleasure   it is pleasure itself to hear his veins
singing   I am moved easily these days.

His pleasure keeps running ahead   my eyes know
    where

263

the colts are hiding behind his shoes　　the timothy
trembles in the windy shadow　　no light but the
mountain's burning hair　　we watch the trees
assemble in the moon　　the grass lift up
her million silver tongues　　　and the mares
the mares drinking it in　　drinking it in.

ROBERT HAYDEN

The Whipping

The old woman across the way
　　is whipping the boy again
and shouting to the neighborhood
　　her goodness and his wrongs.

Wildly he crashes through elephant ears,
　　pleads in dusty zinnias,
while she in spite of crippling fat
　　pursues and corners him.

She strikes and strikes the shrilly circling
　　boy till the stick breaks
in her hand. His tears are rainy weather
　　to woundlike memories:

My head gripped in bony vise
　　of knees, the writhing struggle
to wrench free, the blows, the fear
　　worse than blows that hateful

Words could bring, the face that I
　　no longer knew or loved . . .
Well, it is over now, it is over,
　　and the boy sobs in his room,

And the woman leans muttering against
　　a tree, exhausted, purged—
avenged in part for lifelong hidings
　　she has had to bear.

Those Winter Sundays

Sundays too my father got up early
and put his clothes on in the blueblack cold,
then with cracked hands that ached
from labor in the weekday weather made
banked fires blaze. No one ever thanked him.

I'd wake and hear the cold splintering, breaking.
When the rooms were warm, he'd call,
and slowly I would rise and dress,
fearing the chronic angers of that house,

Speaking indifferently to him,
who had driven out the cold
and polished my good shoes as well.
What did I know, what did I know
of love's austere and lonely offices?

Frederick Douglass

When it is finally ours, this freedom, this liberty, this
    beautiful
and terrible thing, needful to man as air,
usable as earth; when it belongs at last to all,
when it is truly instinct, brain matter, diastole, systole,
reflex action; when it is finally won; when it is more
than the gaudy mumbo jumbo of politicians,
this man, this Douglass, this former slave, this Negro
beaten to his knees, exiled, visioning a world
where none is lonely, none hunted, alien,
this man, superb in love and logic, this man
shall be remembered. Oh, not with statues' rhetoric,
not with legends and poems and wreaths of bronze alone,
but with the lives grown out of his life, the lives
fleshing his dream of the beautiful, needful thing.

DARYL HINE

August 13, 1966

Emerging from the naked labyrinth
Into the golden habit of the day,
Glittering with sweat, a wrestler
With the sun, in his fierce palaestra,

Every drop an angel and a man,
Adept at the being that becomes a man,
You stop before the simple backdrop, look
And listen not to the abstract ocean but to me.

At our backs the breakers serially
Beat a tattoo upon the flat-bellied beach;
In our faces the minutes wait to strike and yawn;
And now the afternoon is nearly gone,
Meanwhile we sit absorbed and precious to each
Other, for the time being where we want to be.

DON L. LEE

The Revolutionary Screw

(for my blacksisters)

brothers,
i
under/overstand
the situation:

i mean—
    u bes hitten the man hard
    all day long.
a stone revolutionary, "a full time revolutionary."
    tellen the man how bad u is
    & what u goin ta do
    & how u goin ta do it.

it must be a bitch
to be able to do all that
talken. (& not one irregular breath fr/yr/mouth)
being so
forceful & all
to the man's face (the courage)
& u not even cracken a smile (realman).

i know,
the sisters just don't
understand the
pressure u is under.

&
when u ask for a piece
of leg/
it's not for yr/self
but for
yr/people————it keeps u going
& anyway u is a revolutionary
& she wd be doin
a revolutionary thing.

that sister dug it
from the beginning,
had an early-eye.
i mean
she really had it together
when she said:
       go fuck yr/self nigger.

now
that was
revolutionary.

HOWARD MC CORD

In Iceland

If there are wild men,
they love gently.

They wash their bodies
in streams we drink
from, and we do not
notice.

They hunt with the skill
of a willow moving to
the wind—one egg, one fowl,
one fish a day, and the sweet root
of angelica, which even
the clumsy may stalk.

If there are wild men,
you will know it
only by the snapped bleat
of a ewe some dawn,
or a bottle of good Polish
vodka gone from your tent.

My Cow

The stones rattle on the hillside
in the fog: the brindle cow is lost,
or drunk again on jimson weed.
She wants to fly, thinks
she is flying, but her hooves
run out of air deep in the heart.
She shakes her head like a dog,
and lows with long, dizzy notes
slipping from her throat, the white
depths groaning under the press of flowers.
She is dreaming, and clambering
toward the moon, or a sunrise
spliced into the night.
The light from her bones blinds her,

the soft edges of stone reach out
like bramble fingers, pluck at her ribs,
pinch her ears. She's speaking Chinese
now: "Wan wu chih mu" she bugles,
calling on The Mother to tame
the stones, melt the snow
that burns in her four bellies, get
her back to earth.

I follow two miles in the fog,
find her the lee side of a watertank
in soft repose, belching,
smiling like an old man.

from Longjaunes His Periplus

My father gave me the freedom of love.
  And with a box of old coins,
    augury by flowers, accounts of the stars
      (Rigel, Algol, Mizar, Aldebaran), a sextant,
        and instruction in the tree of the Sephiroth,
          knowledge that the secrets of Shekinah
            and Tantra are identical, and form
              the full quaternity.
He taught me to walk,
  and rubbed my shins with the fat
    of antelopes.

I knew most what he meant
  when a hundred miles off the coast of China
    I saw the Yellow River still integral,
      holding back the blueness of the sea.

It is for this I walk
  only for this are the many names of birds meaningful.
    Widdershins, the devil's contraries,
      the force of the witch
        exist.
Never believe the law.
  Never obey in conscience: refuse power.

                    Everywhere the solemn
                    malignancy of life
                    is the burden
                    to be carried into the mountains.

The Bear That Came to the Wedding

Epithalamium for Patte and Ralph 7 VI 69

In this poem the Bear shambles in
        like a slightly drunken uncle,
politely hands the Bride
        a tidy knot of Shooting Star, Strawberry
Blossoms, and Violets, nips
        the Groom gently on the left shank
and disappears, humming or snorting
        we are not sure, but dancing
certainly, and we are left alone
        with the enormity of the forest's blessing,
wondering what to make of our lives after this,
        the Bear's visit, thinking it might mean
                                Love.

JOHN N. MORRIS

A Child's Nativity

Struck dumb at arm's length,
The crayon Madonna regards
As if with aversion
Her terrific baby,
A three-foot man
She holds only in her hands.
He stares like guns.

Angels are falling
Under a sharp star,
Alleluias
Issue from their heads.
Enormous thin sheep
Intent as wolves
Surround Him.

Three

Mouth's disfurnished eyes
Distinguish only size.
He often has confessed
The newborn have it best:
Who hangs upon the teat
Has all the world to eat.

When Cock is on his walk
He has no time for talk.
Clenched in his appetites
He trawls the Village nights.
Pacifically he sighs
Between whatever thighs.

And I? My only lusts
This set of thin disgusts,
I find the every other
Is never worth the bother.
My candy on the shelf,
I keep me to myself.

The Fathers

When we shall finally be
The children's simple story,
The story they tell the children,
Then we shall be the fathers

Dead in their terrible clothes
There on the mantel beside us
Looking out of their eyes
With their eyes, looking before us.

Running It Backward

A simple flick of the switch
And his familiar figure
Steps back out of the doorway,
Out of the fond familiar arms

That now drop eagerly to her sides.
Backward he rapidly walks
On the crazy pavement
Into his car whose door
Flies into his hand at a gesture;
Expertly staring ahead, he
Reverses quickly out of the picture.

At first it is mildly funny
Watching him perform
With such cheerful address
These difficult backward
Easy forward things.
So when the whiskey
Arises into the bottle
And, smiling,
He refuses his first job
And returns the diploma
With a firm handshake,
We laugh.
       But suddenly
It is turning serious, we see
That he is going
Where we do not wish to follow.
That smile still on his face
But growing doubtful now,
He is climbing down
Out of his college,
Through algebra and beginning French
Into a taste for Coca-Cola.

Now quickly he falls
Through the grades
Into his shorts
And the birthday parties.
Though a profusion of gifts
Resume their brilliant paper,
There, as the breath returns
To him who gave it
And laughter fades
To pure expectancy,
Before the match withdraws
That seemed to lean

To seem to put them out,
Out of the dark the candles come
At once alight.

Here with a flick of the switch
It is time to be stopping,
For looking ahead
We foresee what is true
But improper to be shown:
How, soon, he is going faster,
How he lapses from language
Into helpless tears,
A rage beneath naming
Shaking him as he dwindles;
How, behind his silent scream,
He disappears
In a fury of flapping and clicking
Into the dark and shining
Whirring tiny mouth of the machine.

LISEL MUELLER

Life of a Queen

1. Childhood

For two days her lineage is in doubt,
then someone deciphers the secret message.
They build a pendulous chamber
for her, and stuff her with sweets.

Workers keep bringing her royal jelly.
She knows nothing of other lives,
about digging in purple crocus
and round dances in the sun.

Poor and frail little rich girl,
she grows immense in her hothouse.
Whenever she tries to stop eating,
they open her mouth and force it down.

2. The Flight

She marries him in midair;
    for a moment
he is ennobled, a prince.

She gives the signal
    for their embrace;
over too soon. O, nevermore.

Bruised, she drags herself from
    his dead body,
finds her way back exhausted.

She is bathed, curtains are drawn.
    Ten thousand lives
settle inside her belly.

Now to the only labor she knows.
    She remembers
nothing of him, or their fall.

3. The Recluse

They make it plain
her term is over.
No one comes;
they let her starve.

The masses, her children,
whip up sweets
for a young beauty
who is getting fat.

Nothing to do.
Her ovaries paper,
her sperm sac dust,
she shrivels away.

A crew disassembles
her royal cell.
Outside, a nation
crowns its queen.

A Voice from Out of the Night

Remember me, I was a celebrity,
the famous beauty. All mirrors confirmed me,
the panel of judges ogled me
and cast a unanimous vote.
I was asked my opinion
on marriage, men, abortion,
the use of liquor and drugs;
that was a long time ago.

When my voice deepened
and a bristle
appeared under my chin,
when my blond hair
developed gray roots
and my waist thickened,
the rumors started.
When my legs became sticks
and small brown toads
spotted the backs of my hands,
everyone believed them.
I was accused of devouring children
and mutilating men;
they said I smelled of old age
and strong home remedies.
They cast me into the forest
but come to me secretly, in the dark,
in their times of trouble.
What could I have done to convince them
I was not guilty?
Loss of beauty was all
the proof they needed.

Young wives in love with your men,
kissing your babies: this
could be a warning, but what is the use?
Husbands will flee you,
sons will turn on you,
daughters will throw up their hands
and cry, "Not me! Not me!"

Small Poem About the Hounds and the Hares

After the kill, there is the feast.
And toward the end, when the dancing subsides
and the young have sneaked off somewhere,
the hounds, drunk on the blood of the hares,
begin to talk of how soft
were their pelts, how graceful their leaps,
how lovely their scared, gentle eyes.

Untitled

Yes, we were happy that Sunday, walking
through mild blue patches of phlox
and dark red wake-robin stands
along the creek. Don't ask me what
switch in my mind flashed on,
unbidden, the Algerian girl
who had a bottle jammed into her
to make her talk:

              I did not know
she was still there, my antilife,
with her dark red wound.

HOWARD NEMEROV

Ginkgoes in Fall

They are the oldest living captive race,
Primitive gymnosperms that in the wild
Are rarely found or never, temple trees
Brought down in line unbroken from the deep
Past where the Yellow Emperor lies tombed.

Their fallen yellow fruit mimics the scent
Of human vomit, the definite statement of
An attitude, and their translucency of leaf,
Filtering a urinary yellow light,
Remarks a delicate wasting of the world,

An innuendo to be clarified
In winter when they defecate their leaves
And bear the burden of their branches up
Alone and bare, dynastic diagrams
Of their distinguished genealogies.

BINK NOLL

Shutting the Curtains

The same sequence as the night before,
window by window the same two sounds:
the cords pulleying inside the rods,
the clicking of knobs against plaster
till the black glass glare is out of sight.
Now the first floor takes its nighttime shape
quiet in proportion and tidy
as if what could happen today has
and we are here, together at last,
the selves stretched as we wish and faces
involved in visible harmony.
If someone passing could imagine
our hidden needs, the lamplight at rest
on surfaces, their finish, their age
he would grow homesick with jealousy.
This our waking is not finished but floats
on into supreme intimacies
of our household closed upon itself.

Wedlock

When I wake and stir, he thumps his tail,
rolls over like a puppy and shares
his bright feelings about every day.
We rise and appear like twin planets
in the firmament, Joe and myself,
while the bonds between us equalize
like the huge forces of gravity
that tug our earth through happy daytimes.

The first week he moved he made me
feel like an ion with a stray charge,
a soul in search of its better half,
which he proved, with good will that will
never have to grow up and brain that
works in unclouded simplicity.
Two adults, we consented and joined
and we stay joined. We are company.

Now after four years he's like a wife
the way he sleeps with one eye open,
reads my mind, learns how not to annoy,
and thinks in the first person plural,
creature of habit all set to please
but also be pleased, who always wears
me down to start out somewhat early
into the excitement of the known.

Our routine is a *pas de deux* named
"Taking the Usual for What It's Worth"
and we might as well live in a hut
for all Joe cares. As soon as we start,
our archaic hearts are lifted up:
hound and his hunter, hunter and hound.
We act as we're bound to, partners that
dance out the words *meat* and *fire* and *house*.

We are tried and true. Every waking
it's the same: in one another's eyes
we grow big, renew our self-respect,
an old pair so fixed in their orbit
year after year that we dream the same dreams.
After he's dead, my ear will expect
his sounds, my hand will want the exact
shape of his head, and my house will cry.

ED OCHESTER

The Gift

One day
as I was lying on the lawn
dreaming of the Beautiful
and my wife was justifiably bitching
        out the window
at my shiftlessness and
the baby was screaming
because I wouldn't let him
eat my cigarettes,
a tiger cat leaped over the fence,
smiled at my wife,
let the baby pull his tail,
hummed like a furry dynamo
as I stroked him.

My wife took the car to get him some food,
my son began to sing his wordless song,
and I wrote a poem in the sand.

Now God give every man who's hopeless
a beautiful wife,
an infant son who sings,
and the gift of a sweet-faced cat.

My Penis

Ordinarily I call it "my cock," but
often there is a strange formality about it,
this rocket with wattles.
"Penis" and "Vagina," a dignified couple
immobile on a Grecian urn
or at times engaged in elegant ballet and
desiring frequent medical checkups.
"Cock" and "Twat," two funloving kids
traveling from Pittsburgh to Tangiers
with a hundred bucks in their pockets,
laughing at Baptists but loving God.

279

Alone, it's
crazy and laughable, like the man
who stands up at every Quaker meeting,
testifying to his version of the Truth—
a drag to others but a private solace,
refusing to sit down when others whisper
"shush," "shame," "time and place for everything"—
a dotty old turkey continually rising in wonder,
even on lonely winter evenings refusing
not to point to the stars.

My Teeth

The up-front ones are marvelous,
tiny dancers braving the wind,
shapely and disciplined.
But behind them, corruption,
molars who have lived riotously,
roots eaten by secret lusts
as their bodies disintegrate.
Even the bicuspids and incisors
are infected,
blood swollen
around stiff afflictions of plaque.

The stains of drugs and nicotine
have reached behind the skirts of the dancers,
and it is only a matter of time
before the curtain comes down for good
and the closed mouth
fosters a strange revolution,
the muffled tongue rising
like a brutalized peasantry
to taste its own power
at last.

Snow White

Dopey sez to Doc:
"Finally got me a blow job
from them faggots
over in Uncle Remus."
"Oh," sez Doc, "how wuz it?"
"Waell, didn't taste too bad."

Meanwhile,
Snow White's
tired of slaving
in their fucking kitchen &
getting humped by seven dwarfs.

Their dicks are big as gherkins
and the shitheads play frisbee
in the mine.
Who wouldn't be fed up?

As they're slobbering over dinner
she slices them
a poison apple salad and later

remodels the little cottage in the woods
with gingerbread.

FRANK POLITE

Lantern

Next year, I'm forty years old.
I don't know what hump I'm over.
To have made it this far, what
does that mean? Where am I?

Where have I been? Like you,
I've been places, New York, Asia,
great fields uncut by wire
or river, mountains leaping up,

and O yes, oceans. I felt my way
deeply into each, into the mind
shafts permitted me, into
a flower (perfect on mescaline,

I laughed & wept for hours),
into the tenderness of people . . .
I've loved, worshipped stones,
written poems to moon and stars,

and depending on the deep and dark
of my downheartedness, I lit
a flame in my forehead like a toad,
imagining myself, at various

times, Lord of Earth, Light in
the Forest, even . . . God.
Down the road with my lantern, I
lifted up the broken, the poor,

the ignorant, the hopeless, only
to come down to this: to be all of
them myself, at once. So what's
it all about? I don't ask anymore;

I am one with the insect and cloud.
I beg my life to lay me down at last,
gently if possible, or fast, the way
a horse, plunging into darkness,

kicks a stone out of its path.

Carmen Miranda

Backstage, eating bananas
with Carmen Miranda, she offers me
her hat. I thank her and take
a bunch of purple grapes, 3 hardboiled
eggs, a muskmelon and four
ears of corn. She says, Frank,

it wasn't always this way.
There were lean years in Madrid, Marseilles,
Cuernavaca, when dancing didn't pay
and my dear hats went unrefrigerated.
Fruit can be expensive to a poor girl . . .
Anyway, I danced as best I could
with pears, beans, and tangerines shaped
from wax or wood, but it wasn't
the same. You know what they say about
the heart that wears a false face
and vice versa, but why go into it?
It's enough to say I suffered
to dance with no hat at all. Better that

than a cheap imitation! Darling,
try a quince. Persimmons? Have a cumquat!
But, the disgrace of those days
forced me to sing as an escape. And now
my hats and I sing and dance, and do well.
Oh, there are times I feel the fruit
salad is, well, ridiculous; but it's the thing
I do best, if you know what I mean . . .

Before I left, I kissed her
on the cheek, and said, I'm no spokesman
but I think we'll always love you for it . . .
And back on the streets that night
I split the sky with cherry pits.

CAROLYN M. RODGERS

And When the Revolution Came

(for Rayfield and Lillie
and the whole rest)

and when the revolution came
the militants said
niggers wake up
you got to comb yo hair
the natural way
   and the church folks say oh yeah? sho
    'nuff . . .
and they just kept on going to church
gittin on they knees and praying
and tithing and building and buying

and when the revolution came
the militants said
niggers you got to change
the way you dress
and the church folk say oh yeah?
    and they just kept on going to church

with they knit suits and flowery bonnets
and gittin on they knees and praying
and tithing and building and buying

and when the revolution came
the militants said
you got to give up
white folks and the
                    church folk say oh yeah? well?
never missed what we never had
and they jest kept on going to church
with they nice dresses and suits and
praying and building and buying

and when the revolution came
the militants say you got to give up
pork and eat only brown rice and
health food and the
                    church folks said uh hummmm
and they just kept on eating they chitterlings and
going to church and praying and tithing and
building and buying

and when the revolution came
the militants said
all you church going niggers
got to give up easter and christmas
and the bible
cause that's the white man's religion
and the church folks said well well well well well

and then the militants said we got to
build black institutions where our children
call each other sister and brother
and can grow beautiful, black and strong and grow in
    black grace
and the church folks said yes, lord Jesus we been calling
    each other
sister and brother a long time

and the militants looked around
after a while and said hey, look at all
these fine buildings we got scattered throughout
the black communities some of em built wid schools and
    nurseries
who do they belong to?

and the church folks said, yeah.
we been waiting fo you militants
to realize that the church is an eternal rock

now why don't you militants jest come on in
we been waiting for you
we can show you how to build
    anything that needs building
and while we're on our knees, at that.

Mama's God

mama's God never was no white man.
her My Jesus, Sweet Jesus never was neither.
    the color they had was the color of
her aches and trials, the tribulations of her heart
    mama never had no saviour that would turn
        his back on her because she was black
            when mama prayed, she knew who she
            was praying to and who she was praying to
                didn't and ain't got
                    no color.

HERBERT SCOTT

Letter from a Working Girl

Mother Dear, I am being careful.
My knees chafe as I walk.
I hear them saying: As long
as we are together . . . !
Do not worry. On Sunday
I eat the Lord's body.
Each night I wash my underclothes
and hang them in the dark.
Someone spoke to me in the park
but I did not listen.

You were right to warn me
of those animals. On the street
I feel their eyes follow me
like dogs. I will not feed them.
I have met one nice young man
who reads the Bible, who hopes
to instruct me in passages
I do not understand. He comes
this evening. I hear his knock.
I will finish this letter later.

Help Is on the Way

1   Frankenstein's Wife Writes to Ann Landers

Dear Ann, I think I am losing my husband.
He never straps me to the bed anymore
or fiddles with my parts.
I haven't had a charge in weeks.
Sometimes I think he wants to do me in.
There were intimations of this last week
when I found water in my oil can.
Am I going crazy?
I have faulty wiring and poor compression,
yet he won't fix anything around my body.
Lately, strange arms appeared beneath the couch,
and a leg under the table,
and teeth in my teacup.
I began to put things together.
And finally, last night, he robbed the grave
of that little tramp
who died down the street.
What shall I do?
Should I sever connections?
I would like to make this marriage work.
But where have I failed? I try to keep neat.
Heaven knows it's difficult with no help
in the kitchen, and nothing to wear,
and vapor lock to contend with.
I think I am pregnant, and he won't pay the bills.
What will I do when they turn off the lights?

2 Ann Landers Replies to Frankenstein's Wife

Listen Toots, I've had letters,
but this one takes the cookies.
You are one of a kind.
Did you ever stop to think
the fault may be yours?
You may not have much to work with
but there is no excuse for being run-down.
Shock him with a frilly new nightgown,
set a nice table. It's the little things that count.
Have you checked your breath lately?
Personal hygiene is the ticket, and he'll stop
playing footsie with that leg under the table.
Give the rooster a roost to crow about
and he'll send the other chickens home
is my motto. I don't really think
he is trying to do away with you.
If he does, see a lawyer. If he doesn't,
see a psychiatrist. You may need help.

Butcher's Wife

Butcher's wife
weighs 300 pounds
is crazy jealous.
Saturday nights
he gets drunk
and lays a whore.
Later, at home, his wife
pulls off his pants
and shines a flashlight
on his pecker,
sniffs it, grabs his balls
and won't let go
until he confesses,
slaps his face
to make him sober up
enough to fuck her.
Next morning
for breakfast

she fixes him
eggs and toast
and waffles
a big center slice
of fried ham.

LUCIEN STRYK

The Liberator

Approaching the laboratory gate
He heard familiar squeals and, again,
Myriad rat's feet along maze-planks,
Then crows, yelps, mews: he was
Climbing the gangway of the Ark,
The Deluge boiling round his knees.

Entering, he glanced back where
The smashed glass door reflected head
And wobbly shins: the rest of him he
Must have left out in the drunken
Dark. Plucked on by cries of those he'd
Come to save, he passed frothed rows

Of test tubes, pickled embryos.
A swipe of the arm, and down they crashed,
Slicking the concrete floor. Still
The living urged him on: Out! Out!
It was a cry he'd learned to
Understand. When he reached the

Guinea pigs, unsnapped the toolbox
Lid and sheared the cage-wire, they licked,
All gratitude, the palm that
Offered crumbs. The rats, when sprung,
Scurried dizzily across the
Table strewn with cheese he'd cached

For weeks. And now, no longer
Running wild, the cocks, mongrels, cats
Fed beak by jowl together.
High above them on a stool, he
Smiled the smile of God, first
Work done, betrayals yet to come.

Away

Here I go again,
want to be somewhere else—
feet tramping under the desk,

I study travel brochures,
imagine monastic Hiltons,
the caravansary of my past.

Apples, cheese, a hunk of bread,
the road: what'll it be today?
I ask myself: the Seine,

Isfahan bazaar, three claps
of the hand, and Yamaguchi,
Takayama-roshi shouting—

Down, down, and breathe!
My feet go faster faster,
suddenly fly off.

Calm, breathing slowly.
I bow to Master Takayama
who smiles all the way from Japan.

Fishing with My Daughter in Miller's Meadow

You follow, dress held high above
        the fresh manure,
missing your doll, scolding Miller's horses

for being no gentlemen where they graze
        in morning sun.
You want the river, quick, I promised you back there,

and all those fish. I point to trees where
    water rides low
banks, slopping over in the spring,

and pull you from barbed wire protecting corn
    the size of you
and gaining fast on me. To get you in the meadow

I hold the wire high, spanning a hand across
    your freckled back.
At last we make the river, skimmed with flies,

you help me scoop for bait. I give you time
    to run away,
then drop the hook. It's fish I think

I'm after, you I almost catch, in up to knees,
    sipping minnowy
water. Well, I hadn't hoped for more.

Going back, you heap the creel with phlox and marigolds.

The Face

Weekly at the start
of the documentary
on World War II

a boy's face, doomed,
sharply beautiful,
floats in the screen,

a dark balloon
above a field of barbs,
the stench of gas.

Whoever holds the
string
will not let go.

Friendship

He writes again. Since his divorce
a fist has never left his chest.

290

He needs my words, and so I fill
a sheet—what joy it gives

to utter words to eyes that plead
from paper. I place the softest

on his cheek, his brow, a special one
upon his mouth. Sigh across

the page that he still has a friend.
Now off to do its loving work,

my scroll of bandages and kisses,
my dried and flattened heart.

CONSTANCE URDANG

The Old Maid Factory

This is the factory
Where they manufacture old maids
At one end of the assembly line
The women are jostled into their places
They wonder where they are going
What will happen to them
One says, "Where is my sister?"
But the foreman is not permitted to answer

First she will be hollowed out
Her juices extracted
Her natural organs replaced
By parts she is not permitted to name
Her five senses
Are replaced by substitutes
Guaranteed non-inflammable
Non-toxic
Her sister is replaced by a substitute

At the end of the assembly line
The old maid minces out
Into what she calls America
She has forgotten she is a woman
She has no sister
In her shrivelled brain
Something murmurs that life is an accident
She wonders how it happened to her

Bread

It was the anniversary of bread
the bread-celebration
on that day everything was bread
mattresses pillows blankets chairs
windows
(wanting to look out, the child
chewed a hole in the bread pane)
the musicians played instruments of bread
the mayor unveiled
a bread monument
in honor of bread

People came from every corner of the republic
laughing and pushing, crowding in the streets
a busload of pickpockets emptied itself in the square
everyone wanted the bread
that thrust up on long stalks from the ground, or
hung down on strings from the sky

This bread was of three kinds
yellow, with raisins
like little black buttons
or pink as the sunset
or white as a girl's veil
at her first communion
—it made no difference
the people ate it all

Riding out into the dusk
the buses were filled with bread
the roads were lined with bread
the people waved

Goodbye, goodbye to the bread
they were chewing and laughing
in the deserted streets maybe one or two
were left lying asprawl
pillowed in a doorway, dead-drunk on bread
under stars clustered thick as raisins

Safe Places

The retreat to Vermont was orderly at first
Everybody expecting to find
At the end of the macadam, the old dirt road
Leading back into childhood
Expecting the luster of the farmhouse windows
As firelight burnished twilight
To make up for all they had lost
All they had left behind

So they marched like an army of refugees
Carrying lamps and birdcages, mattresses and clocks,
Flowing along the highways of Vermont
Calmly as a river

But something went wrong

The simple hills that, from a plane
Look smooth and domesticated
Turned rough and wild;
Bears lurched through the wood
Travellers who wandered from the road
Lost all direction, starving, or seeing ghosts

Even the road grew treacherous.
As night fell, and neighbors
Eyed one another with suspicion
The safe places retreated from Vermont
Northward to Canada and the frozen void,
Or lay behind them, maybe, in the ruined cities.

The Roots of Revolution
in the Vegetable Kingdom

The blond witch
with her wand of water
is out there
stirring up the teeming earth

A soft cap of cloud
is pulled low over her eyes
she steps delicately between the rows
on dirty feet
nothing escapes
the soft sprinkling of her attention

Not even the broccolis are safe
the cauliflowers
thinking themselves invisible
in their green tents
even the carrots
their soft blunt noses busy
with underground nuzzlings
cannot ignore her

Spinach with its leafy arms
asparagus all thumbs and feathers
lumpen-potatoes
onions and radishes
she rouses them all
her repeated provocations
have disturbed them
see how they spring up
from the spongy soil

And the weeds she prods into life
with her pokings and pryings
how they thrust and sprout
festering like disease

The vegetables are taking over
demolishing fences
obliterating property lines
let there be no more owners
and no more ownership
no more plats lots liens mortgages

let there be no property
even in the suburbs
let there be only the earth and the seeds
and the harvests thereof

MONA VAN DUYN

Relationships

The legal children of a literary man
remember his ugly words to their mother.
He made them keep quiet and kissed them later.
He made them stop fighting and finish their supper.
His stink in the bathroom sickened their noses.
He left them with sitters in lonesome houses.
He mounted their mother and made them wear braces.
He fattened on fame and raised them thin.

But the secret sons of the same man
spring up like weeds from the seed of his word.
They eat from his hand and it is not hard.
They unravel his sweater and swing from his beard.
They smell in their sleep his ferns and roses.
They hunt the fox on his giant horses.
They slap their mother, repeating his phrases,
and swell in his sight and suck him thin.

Open Letter from a Constant Reader

To all who carve their love on a picnic table
or scratch it on smoked glass panes of a public toilet,
I send my thanks for each plain and perfect fable
of how the three pains of the body, surfeit,

hunger, and chill (or loneliness), create
a furniture and art of their own easing.
And I bless two public sites and, like Yeats,
two private sites where the body receives its blessing.

Nothing is banal or lowly that tells us how well
the world, whose highways proffer table and toilet
as signs and occasions of comfort for belly and bowel,
can comfort the heart too, somewhere in secret.

Where so much constant news of good has been put,
both fleeting and lasting lines compel belief.
Not by talent or riches or beauty, but
by the world's grace, people have found relief

from the worst pain of the body, loneliness,
and say so with a simple heart as they sit
being relieved of one of the others. I bless
all knowledge of love, all ways of publishing it.

Billings and Cooings from "The Berkeley Barb"
(Want-Ad Section)

. . . Couples sought (enclose photographs please)
by couple who've expeditiously run through
(and are eager for permutations *à quatre, à seize*)
all known modes of the sweet conjunction for two.

Gay guy needs, for a few conventional
dances and such, fem Lez to pose as date,
in return for which she can really have a ball
with her butch friend at parties he'll give in private.

*How bright the scholars who use a previous schooling
to get the further enlightenment they want!*
Well-rounded girl will do it hung from the ceiling
by ropes in exchange for a used copy of Kant.

A youth who pines in his present incarnation
but remembers with pleasure being a parakeet
seeks a girl just as reluctantly human
and formerly budgerigar, for a mate.

At Blank's bar, woman who'd like the *frisson*
of sex with an ex-guru should ask for Gus.
An A.C.-D.C. will share pad with someone
similarly ambidextrous.

Boy seeks cute girlfriend to share his sack
How startling now the classic or pastoral!
and lists his qualifications to attract:
"tall, dark, sensitive, handsome, sterile."

Student who can't remember the phone number
or the face of student he met at Jack's last fall,
but can't forget the hard nipples, would like her
to dial xx (transvestites need not call).

Delights they probably never knew they could have
nineteen-year-old will guarantee to disclose
to women between fifty and sixty-five
with unusually big feet or long toes.

How dazzling love's infinite variety!
How fertile is nature in her forms of joy!
Male seeks, in the area around Berkeley,
another male whose fetish is corduroy . . .

The Twins

My sweet-faced, tattle-tale brother was born blind,
but the colors drip in his head. He paints with his fingers.
All day with his pots and paper he follows me around
wherever I set up my easel, till I pinch his bat ears,

then before he goes he swears he didn't feel anything.
But he knows my feelings, sneaks them out of my skin.
The things he knows! Leaving me squeezed and sulking,
he pretends he felt them himself and tells everyone.

Nobody ever blames him. He's terribly talented.
The world, glimpsing itself through him, will grow
sick with self-love, it seems, and under his eyelid
lie down, in burning shame, with its own shadow,

whereas, on my canvas, it wears its gray and brown
like a fat beaver, and even as I sweat on my brush,
all forms, at its simple-minded toothy grin,
branches, limbs, trunks, topple in a watery backwash.

When he goes to sleep, he says, the world stays in his head
like a big spiderweb strung between ear and ear,
buzzing like telephone wires, and what he has heard
all night, next morning has happened, is true, is there.

Though it always comes back for me, thick, bathed,
     grateful,
everything has to be re-imagined each sunrise
when I crawl from my black comfort. But I can't make a
     phone call.
I have to talk to something in front of my eyes.

You'd never know we were close. When we meet strangers
they poke my round stomach and pat his long bare legs,
I gush, and he, or that's what it looks like, glares,
then he stomps on my oils and we fight like cats and dogs.

But when it rains sometimes, and he feels it and I hear it,
and he closes my eyes with his fingers to stop my raining,
and one tear falls before everything is quiet,
and his tear is the color of cinnamon on my tongue,

oh then we leave together and nobody can find us.
Not even our mother, if she came, could tell us apart.
Only the stars can see, who cluster around us,
my painted person crouched in his painted heart.

DIANE WAKOSKI

Ode to a Lebanese Crock of Olives

for Walter's Aunt Libby's diligence
in making olives

As some women love jewels
and drape themselves with ropes of pearls, stud their ears
with diamonds, band themselves with heavy gold,
have emeralds on their fingers or
opals on white bosoms,
I live with the still life
of grapes whose skins frost over with the sugar forming
     inside,
hard apples, and delicate pears;
cheeses,

from the sharp fontina, to icy bleu,
the aromatic chevres, boursault, boursin, a litany of
thick bread, dark wines,
pasta with garlic,
soups full of potato and onion;
and butter and cream,
like the skins of beautiful women, are on my sideboard.

These words are to say thank you
to
Walter's Aunt Libby
for her wonderful olives;
oily green knobs in lemon
that I add to the feast when they get here from Lebanon
(where men are fighting, as her sisters have been fighting
for years, over whose house the company stays in)
and whose recipes for kibbee or dolmas or houmas
are passed along.

I often wonder,
had I been born beautiful,
a Venus on the California seashore,
if I'd have learned to eat and drink so well?
For, with humming birds outside my kitchen window to
    remind of small elegance,
and mourning doves in the pines & cedar, speaking with
    grace,
and the beautiful bodies
of lean blond surfers,
dancing on terraces,
surely had I a beautiful face or elegant body,
surely I would not have found such pleasure
in food?
I often wonder why a poem to me
is so much more like a piece of bread and butter
than like a sapphire?
But with mockers flying in and out of orange groves,
and brown pelicans dipping into the Pacific,
looking at camelias and fuchsia,
an abundance of rose, and the brilliant purple ice plant
which lined the cliffs to the beach,
life was a "Still Life" for me.
And a feast.
I wish I'd known then

the paintings of Rubens or David,
where beauty was not only
thin, tan, California girls,
but included all abundance.

As some women love jewels,
I love the jewels of life.
And were you,
the man I love,
to cover me (naked) with diamonds,
I would accept them too.

Beauty is everywhere,
in contrasts and unities.
But to you, I could not offer the thin tan fashionable body
of a California beach girl.
Instead, I could give the richness of burgundy,
dark brown gravies,
gleaming onions,
the gold of lemons,
and some of Walter's Aunt Libby's wonderful olives from
    Lebanon.

Thank you, Aunt Libby,
from a failed beach girl,
out of the West.

JOHN WOODS

Outburst from a Little Face

He is crying there near the toilet.
Mother not enough.
Father gone into the roof altitudes.
Tired of seeing his little face
warped in shoe leather.
Afraid of the menstrual towels,
the bicker and shouting
of the storming ceiling.

Let me out of this dwarf.
I want my full voice.
I don't want to be the submarine
riding the pillow behind the sofa.
I want this thing between my legs
to hang heavy and gnarled as
the steaming grain of the table leg.

I'm tired of sitting on my lap
to reach the cereal.

Guns

Surely the day will come
when they will bring in the guns to the armory
and be given an acre and seeds
by the old sergeant with frank tears.
In Quincy, they will burn them in the vacant lot,
where the feed store failed, you remember,
and the bulldozers coming in the morning.
Children in arms, and the drunks let out
among the parishioners.
And out near the ore fills, where the freshets ran brown,
Billy Joe Smith, the harelip cousin,
will tamp down the sour dirt over his squirrel rifle.
What will grow there? A cordite daisy,
a squirrel arching his leg over it.
All the animals back, like cats,
to be shooed out of the privies.

Remember, then, in your canines, in your
trigger fingers, in the blood of your temples,
the belts of blue cartridges, Bofors pocking
the Stuka sky, John Wayne searching for something
in his chaps, sorry, it's gone. His grandchildren
will have to look it up in Webster's.
It starts with G, like God.

The Girl Who Had Borne Too Much

That girl has borne too much,
there, in her locked bed.
We need to see the caul flaming,

the drooled lip, ancestral greed
stamping its old medallion
on the childish brow, something
dragging a swollen foot
at the edge of our shadows.

But whatever walks her night corridors,
its hair burning, does not lie
in her arms. Now her face is smoothed
back to childhood.
               Child, and whoever
wears your young body in the bad nights,
we know that the whore
may breathe sweet milk,
and a lean christ lie back at ease
in the fat-rinded murderer.

Woods Gets Religion

(for Paul Zimmer)

Our church had no theology,
no saints but plenty of sinners,
no confessional but a cold baptistery.
Communion once a year, but cold
chicken and potato salad every
Bible meeting. The Book was ironbound
to be struck on, and sparks flew
from Hell revealed. Some wag
put a chicken leg in the offering,
the plate was passed so many times.
O Helen of the Organ, I chose
the Baptist Church for your
deep eyes, and your sweet tongue
was the only wafer I could not wash down.

Lying Down with Men and Women

When we came up from water, our eyes
drew to the front of our heads,
and we had faces. When we came up
on our knuckles, we held fruit to our mouths,

and wanted to know the chemistry
of sweetness.
              Then as we walked down
the earth's curve, trees and hills
got in our way, so we moved them
for roads and newsprint and wreckage.

Part of every day, the water mood and the tree mood
rise in our bodies, and we must
lie down a bit to honor our lost
tails and gills.
              When we lie on our backs,
we see so far away we try to give names to light,
like wild dogs we have taught
to lick our hands.
              And when we lie on our faces,
we see too close, the blank wall
at the end of the corridor.
              And so
we lie down with men and women
because we are terrified, and sometimes,
for that reason, we stand up and kill.

PAUL ZIMMER

Zimmer in Grade School

In grade school I wondered
Why I had been born
To wrestle in the ashy puddles,
With my square nose
Streaming mucus and blood,
My knuckles puffed from combat
And the old nun's ruler.
I feared everything: God,
Learning and my schoolmates.
I could not count, spell or read.
My report card proclaimed

These scarlet failures.
My parents wrang their loving hands.
My guardian angel wept constantly.

But I could never hide anything.
If I peed my pants in class
The puddle was always quickly evident.
My worst mistakes were at
The blackboard for Jesus and all
The saints to see.
                    Even now
When I hide behind elaborate mask
It is always known that I am Zimmer,
The one who does the messy papers
And fractures all his crayons,
Who spits upon the radiators
And sits all day in shame
Outside the office of the principal.

One for the Ladies at the Troy Laundry Who Cooled Themselves for Zimmer

The ladies at the Troy Laundry pressed
And pressed in the warm fog of their labor.
They cooled themselves at the windows,
The steam rising from their gibbous skins
As I dawdled home from school.
In warmer weather they wore no blouses
And if I fought the crumbling coke pile
To the top, they laughed and waved
At me, billowy from their irons.

Oh man, the ladies at the Troy Laundry
Smelled like cod fish out of water
And yet the very fur within their armpits
Made me rise wondering and small.

Zimmer Envying Elephants

I have a wide, friendly face
Like theirs, yet I can't hang
My nose like a fractured arm
Nor flap my dishpan ears.

304

I can't curl my canine teeth,
Swing my tail like a filthy tassel,
Nor make thunder without lightning.

But I'd like to thud amply around
For a hundred years or more,
Stuffing an occasional tree top
Into my mouth, screwing hugely for
Hours at a time, gaining weight,
And slowly growing a few hairs.

Once in a while I'd charge a power pole
Or smash a wall down just to keep
Everybody loose and at a distance.

Zimmer's Hard Dream

from Zimmer's Love Poem After a Hard Dream

In my most spectacular, technicolored dream
The great leaves slap my eyelids
As I smash through vegetation in pursuit
Of my rutting lady. My meat extends
And wavers like a palm log as I see
Her hard cheeks grinding through the bushes,
Her leg muscles bunching and breasts
Sliding like volcanoes. Oh sun!
My lady could crush me if she got advantage,
But I stun her with a great stone
And she goes down on her back,
Roaring like a hairy brontosaurus.
Oh then it is I spread her,
And crushed between her incredible thighs,
As pterosaurs clack and duckbills belch,
I raise the human race within my loins
And fire it off to home!

The
South

JOHN BEECHER

from **To Live and Die in Dixie**

II

Old Maggie's sweat would drip and sizzle
on that cast iron range she stoked
but she was grinding at the handle
of our great big ice cream freezer
that day she had her stroke
It put a damper on my mother's luncheon
All the ladies in their picture hats and organdies
hushed up until the ambulance took Maggie off
but soon I heard
their shrieks of laughter
like the bird-house at the zoo
while they spooned in
their fresh peach cream

III

Asparagus fresh from the garden
my dad insisted
went best on breakfast toast with melted butter
so Rob was on the job by six
He used to wake me whistling blues
and whistled them all day till plumb
black dark when he got off
Times Mother was away
he'd play piano for me
real barrelhouse
(I liked it better than our pianola classics)
and clog on the hardwood floor
Rob quit us once to paper houses on his own
but white men came at night and sloshed
paint all over his fresh-papered walls
took the spark plugs out of his Model T truck
poured sand into the cylinders

then screwed the plugs back in
so when Rob cranked it up next day
he wrecked the motor
He came back to work for us
but I can't seem to remember
him whistling much again

VI

Confederate veterans came to town
for their convention
and tottered in parade
while Dixie played and everybody gave the rebel yell
but the Confederate burying ground near school
where the battle had been
nobody seemed to care about
It was a wilderness of weeds and brambles
with headstones broken and turned over
The big boys had a den in there
where they would drag the colored girls
that passed by on the path
and make them do
what they said all colored girls
liked doing
no matter how much
they fought back and screamed

VII

The Fourth of July
was a holiday for everybody but people's cooks
Corinne was fixing us hot biscuit
when I marched into the kitchen
waving the Stars and Stripes
and ordered her to
"Salute this flag! It made you free!"
I just couldn't understand why Corinne
plumb wouldn't

IX

Spurgeon would daub designs on flowerpots
wheelbarrows
garbage cans
just anything he could get his hands on

though all he had was house-paint
and the kind of big flat brush
you slap it on with
My mother said
Spurgeon was what you call
a primitive
One Saturday evening
he was downtown window-shopping the pawnshops
gawking at all the jewelry
the pretty knives and pistols
when a mob came tearing round the corner
after another black man
but they made Spurgeon do

Aztec Figurine

"Ray-*hee*-nah!"
                    "*Ya voy, señora!*"
                                        All day on
the double with her mop and pail, huaraches
tattooing tile, small Aztec figurine
with no more bust or hip-span than a *chica*
at first communion. Three Caesareans
to pry her babies out. Her man is down
with ulcers. Even when he works he drinks
his little money up and lives with some
puta. Regina's shanty's built from cans
and crates high up the *Montuoso*. That's
the *barrio* without a water tap
for fifteen thousand people. Trucks come in
and sell it by the litre. There's a queue
at every out-house. Most just use a pot
and throw it in the street. Planes bomb the place
with DDT. At six Regina locks
her children in and goes to work. It's dark
when she gets home. She lights a candle then
beneath two pictures on the wall, Our Lady
of Guadalupe and by her side Fidel.

WENDELL BERRY

The Stones

I owned a slope full of stones.
Like buried pianos they lay in the ground,
shards of old sea-ledges, stumbling blocks
where the earth caught and kept them
dark, an old music mute in them
that my head keeps now I have dug them out.
I broke them where they slugged in their dark
cells, and lifted them up in pieces.
As I piled them in the light
I began their music. I heard their old lime
rouse in breath of song that has not left me.
I gave pain and weariness to their bearing out.
What bond have I made with the earth,
having worn myself against it? It is a fatal singing
I have carried with me out of that day.
The stones have given me music
that figures for me their holes in the earth
and their long lying in them dark.
They have taught me the weariness that loves the ground,
and I must prepare a fitting silence.

Earth and Fire

In this woman the earth speaks.
Her words open in me, cells of light
flashing in my body, and make a song
that I follow toward her out of my need.
The pain I have given her I wear
like another skin, tender, the air
around me flashing with thorns.
And yet such joy as I have given her
sings in me and is part of her song.
The winds of her knees shake me
like a flame. I have risen up from her,
time and again, a new man.

The Springs

In a country without saints or shrines
I knew one who made his pilgrimage
to springs, where in his life's dry years
his mind held on. Everlasting,
people called them, and gave them names.
The water broke into sounds and shinings
at the vein mouth, bearing the taste
of the place, the deep rock, sweetness
out of the dark. He bent and drank
in bondage to the ground.

The Grandmother

Better born than married, misled,
in the heavy summers of the river bottom
and the long winters cut off by snow
she would crave gentle dainty things,
"a pretty little cookie or a cup of tea,"
but spent her days over a wood stove
cooking cornbread, kettles of jowl and beans
for the heavy, hungry, hard-handed
men she had married and mothered, bent
past unbending by her days of labor
that love had led her to. They had to break her
before she would lie down in her coffin.

To Know the Dark

To go in the dark with a light is to know the light.
To know the dark, go dark. Go without sight,
and find that the dark, too, blooms and sings,
and is traveled by dark feet and dark wings.

from Inland Passages

I. The Long Hunter

Passed through the dark wall,
set foot in the unknown track,
paths locked in the minds of beasts

and in strange tongues. Footfall
led him where he did not know.
There was a country in the dark where
only blind trust could go.
Some joyous animal paced the woods
ahead of him and filled the air
with steepling song to make a way.
Step by step the darkness bore
the light. The shadow opened
like a pod, and from the height
he saw a place green as welcome
on whose still water the sky lay white.

DAVID BOTTOMS

Stumptown Attends the Picture Show

*on the first attempt at desegregation
in Canton, Georgia*

Word has come and Martha the ticket girl
stands behind the candy counter
eating popcorn and smoking Salems.
Beside her the projectionist,
having canned Vivien Leigh
and come downstairs to watch the real show,
leans folding chairs against the theater doors,
guards his glass counter
like saloon keepers in his Westerns
guard the mirrors hung above their bars.
Outside, good old boys line the sidewalk,
string chain between parking meters
in front of the Canton Theater,
dig in like Rebs in a Kennesaw trench.
From the street policemen and sheriff's deputies
address their threats to proper names,
try to maintain any stability.
Someone has already radioed the State Boys.

Through a glass door Martha watches
the moon slide over Jones Mercantile.
In front of Landers' Drugstore
a streetlight flickers like a magic lantern,
but Martha cannot follow the plot,
neither can the projectionist.
Only one thing is certain:
elements from different worlds are converging,
spinning toward confrontation,
and the State Boys are winding some county road,
moving in a cloud of dust toward the theater marquee.

TURNER CASSITY

L'Aigle a Deux Jambes

(on a photograph of Sarah Bernhardt in *L'Aiglon*)

Eagle into swayback Ganymede,
The predator and prey become one breed;

Crippling Time the only Metternich,
Ego the only cup. As pallid duke,

For all the jack boots and the ducal sash,
You still are the devouring mother—ash

The taste, compulsive the desire. If Jove
Had finally his nectar, what you have

Is this: bankruptcy, fright wig, and a limp.
But while you've alexandrine for your pimp

You ravish; cruel in the knowledge that,
Olympian at last, you serve your fate;

Intransigence your courage, myth your art.
A rarer bird, a truer Bonaparte,

Across the steppes of your decay—in drag—
You stump toward Moscow on a wooden leg.

Pacelli and the Ethiop

> The Italian government's representations to the Vatican's secretary of state, Cardinal Eugenio Pacelli, had their effect. The Holy See did not further condemn the potential aggressor.
>
> George W. Baer,
> *The Coming of the Italian-Ethiopian War*

Unlikely angels, although by and large well met,
The pontiff and the emperor embattle yet—
Their paradise Geneva's giant Follies set.

One is a stately, beady-eyed old barracuda,
One some crypto-Coptic, bearded living Buddha.
The League of Nations hears again the Lion of Judah:

"True, I am a slaver. Now, as true confessor,
I demand the Church inculpate the aggressor."
Whereat the Earthly Vicar, ever the recessor,

Recedes into his role as papal secretary:
"That queen whom you succeeded . . . Matabele Hari . . .
The fat one . . . Did you give her poison, Ras Tafari?"

"What is truth?" inquires the League, and then dissolves.
The exiled emperor is forced to sell his slaves;
The pontiff washes in the silver bowl that saves.

LUCILLE CLIFTON

At Last We Killed the Roaches

at last we killed the roaches.
mama and me. she sprayed,
i swept the ceiling and they fell
dying onto our shoulders, in our hair
covering us with red. the tribe was broken,
the cooking pots were ours again
and we were glad, such cleanliness was grace
when i was twelve. only for a few nights,

and then not much, my dreams were blood
my hands were blades and it was murder murder
all over the place.

Her Love Poem

Demon, Demon, you have dumped me
in the middle of my imagination
and i am dizzy with spinning from
nothing to nothing. It is all your fault
poet, fat man, lover of weak women
and i intend to blame you for it.
I will have you in my head
anyway i can, and it may be love you
or hate you but i will have you
have you have you.

Let There Be New Flowering

let there be new flowering
in the fields   let the fields
turn mellow for the men
let the men keep tender
through the time   let the time
be wrested from the war
let the war be won
let love be
at the end

Salt

For SJ and JJ

he is as salt
to her,
a strange sweet
a peculiar money
precious and valuable
only to her tribe,
and she is salt
to him,
something that rubs raw

317

that leaves a tearful taste
but what he will
strain the ocean for and
what he needs.

The Poet

i beg my bones to be good but
they keep clicking music and
i spin in the center of myself
a foolish frightful woman
moving my skin against the wind and
tap dancing for my life.

ANN DARR

For Great Grandmother and Her Settlement House

Over the mantel in the settlement house in Gary,
there is a picture of my children's father. He
is nine months old, sitting on his grandmother's
lap. She is seventy-nine with bristles
on her chin, and a champion heart under that
great round pincushion breast, disguised
as a watermelon.

Grandma said, no no no, but the Sunday class
gave the picture anyway, and I'm glad they did.
Now when we go by Gary we'll stop to see Grandmother,
though she died thirty years ago.
The children will say, looking at the madonna and child,
is that the time you peed in Great Grandmother's lap?
They will admire the Mona Lisa smile on Grandma's
    mouth;
they know the story well: how she kept on smiling
while the wide-eyed boy on her lap
soaked her right down to her corset. For them she is alive,
    and warm, and wet.

The Pot-Bellied Anachronism

I have this bulging belly because:

> of a deep desire for pregnancy
> long past the possibility.
> I wanted a baseball team, at least.

> it is my anchor to this role. If
> I had been trim and sleek and presentable,
> I would have disappeared with every
> young man who winked at me twice. This
> is known as insurance. Double-bellied indemnity.

> to keep my daughters from having
> to compete with me, after they learn
> I am more to the world than their mother.

> it is the "cross-I-bear," the burden for
> all those things I am guilty of. It will
> remind me every time I fold it into my lap
> that innocence has fled.

> it is my feminist posture. Way out front.
> Men's bellies are never regarded with derision,
> snickered about, offered a girdle.

> I am making a statement. That I can be any
> shape I want, even pudding-shaped and
> nobody can stop me.

Oblique Birth Poem

Labor Room: three handed
cribbage, interrupted by jack-pot
coming on. Back to the game. I win
three dollars and twenty cents . . .
Now!
I have never seen a birth before,
hold the mirror over here
and now in her garland of
cheese and while we are still
connected, I am towing you, my little
skiff, my boat, come into my arms,
onto my deck, sunlight has just

shone through, and the crazy doctor
bursts into song. Happy Birthday
he sings in his cracked voice and we
are all laughter.

GUY DAVENPORT

The Medusa

is Juno of the Ribbons in gelatin,
little more, as Lyman said to Agassiz,
than organized water, Hegel's brain
in a lace shawl, knit moonlight,
its dome of liquid glass
sealed by invisible sutures,
its spore sacs disguised as eyes
alternate with eyes, testicle eye,
testicle eye, petalwise radiant,
six sexes flowering in six eyes
fringed with pleats thin as wine
down the side of a glass
stitched to the dome with cobweb.
Its confetti of forty legs
hang below, mylar orchid roots,
a silverpoint page of da Vinci
on the purl and meander of rivers
that eddy, curl in countercurl,
like Isabella d'Este's hair.
This anatomy of water
with its crystal bowl of a hat
hung with sexual eyes and optical sexes
is named Medusa by the masters
of naming, Arethusa and Ariadne,
ladies whose fate was in mazes.
It is the Portuguese Man of War,
the sea nettle, the stinging jellyfish.

Builders with baskets of atoms
in the seven days, sticking the protozoa
together, called these humps of slime
bearded with transparent fern
The Electric Lady, Quintessential Venus,
Jezebel in Panoply, Hera of the Tassels.
This graceful sphere ringed
and dressed in Isolde hair,
crawfish-shy, improbably intricate,
and by any virtuoso craftsman's word
impossible, is fifty pounds of water
and four ounces of flesh,
is an electricity of convolute frills,
and is transparent. You may see
through it what's behind, a fish
rippled as in a mirror with a warp,
or coral squeezed and stretched
by this lens of fat water. To
copulate it rolls cogwheel fashion
around another which in turn
is rolling around another, eye
looking into eye, seeder into socket.
It is an hermaphrodite and can
if the press is great mate with six
at once and has been known,
what with the sea unsteady and itself so slick,
to shoot from among its lovers
two feet into the air.
It hatches not baby Circes but
anemones, carnivorous flowers,
pomegranates of the ocean which
like their Titan parents are
Venus and Mercury blended.
Headless, they are not beings
but the seeds of beings,
parent, egg, and infant in one,
bones of water, flesh of film.
Their progeny is the ghost octopus
with legs of smoke, the dozen-crotched-
and-eyed Medusa Cyanea,
fire in azure, quick to sting,
a ferociousness of light
in the cold dark of the seas.

JAMES DICKEY

The Cancer Match

Lord, you've sent both
And may have come yourself. I will sit down, bearing up
under
The death of light very well, and we will all
Have a drink. Two or three, maybe.
I see now the delights

Of being let "come home"
From the hospital.
Night!
I don't have all the time
In the world, but I have all night.
I have space for me and my house,
And I have cancer and whiskey

In a lovely relation.
They are squared off, here on my ground. They are fighting,
Or are they dancing? I have been told   and told
That medicine has no hope, or anything
More to give,

But they have no idea
What hope is, or how it comes. You take these two things:
This bourbon and this thing growing. Why,
They are like boys! They bow
To each other

Like judo masters,
One of them jumping for joy, and I watch them struggle
All around the room, inside and out
Of the house, as they battle
Near the mailbox

And superbly
For the street-lights! Internally, I rise like my old self
To watch: and remember, ladies and gentlemen,
We are looking at this match
From the standpoint

Of tonight
Alone. Swarm over him, my joy, my laughter, my Basic Life
Force! Let your bright sword-arm stream
Into that turgid hulk, the worst
Of me, growing:

Get 'im, O Self
Like a beloved son! One more time! Tonight we are going
Good   better and better   we are going
To win, and not only win but win
Big, win big.

The Sheep Child

Farm boys wild to couple
With anything   with soft-wooded trees
With mounds of earth   mounds
Of pinestraw   will keep themselves off
Animals by legends of their own:
In the hay-tunnel dark
And dung of barns, they will
Say   I have heard tell

That in a museum in Atlanta
Way back in a corner somewhere
There's this thing that's only half
Sheep   like a woolly baby
Pickled in alcohol   because
Those things can't live   his eyes
Are open   but you can't stand to look
I heard from somebody who . . .

But this is now almost all
Gone. The boys have taken
Their own true wives in the city,
The sheep are safe in the west hill
Pasture   but we who were born there
Still are not sure. Are we,
Because we remember, remembered
In the terrible dust of museums?

Merely with his eyes, the sheep-child may

Be saying   saying

I am here, in my father's house.
I who am half of your world, came deeply
To my mother in the long grass
Of the west pasture, where she stood like moonlight
Listening for foxes. It was something like love
From another world that seized her
From behind, and she gave, not lifting her head
Out of dew, without ever looking, her best
Self to that great need. Turned loose, she dipped her
*   face*
Farther into the chill of the earth, and in a sound
Of sobbing   of something stumbling
Away, began, as she must do,
To carry me. I woke, dying,

In the summer sun of the hillside, with my eyes
Far more than human. I saw for a blazing moment
The great grassy world from both sides,
Man and beast in the round of their need,
And the hill wind stirred in my wool,
My hoof and my hand clasped each other,
I ate my one meal
Of milk, and died
Staring. From dark grass I came straight

To my father's house, whose dust
Whirls up in the halls for no reason
When no one comes   piling deep in a hellish
*   mild corner.*
And, through my immortal waters,
I meet the sun's grains eye
To eye, and they fail at my closet of glass.
Dead, I am most surely living
In the minds of farm boys: I am he who drives
Them like wolves from the hound bitch and calf
And from the chaste ewe in the wind.
They go into woods   into bean fields   they go
Deep into their known right hands. Dreaming of me,
They groan   they wait   they suffer
Themselves, they marry, they raise their kind.

R. H. W. DILLARD

Hats

Annie appears, arrayed
In an amazing assortment
Of hats.

They stagger above her
Like a happy drunk
Looking for the familiar lamppost.

What a strange creature,
The Martian must think,
Taking a quick snap
From the step of his lander,
I hope this shot comes out.

All of my friends
Are astounded. They
Applaud, not really knowing
What is expected of them.
As always, they have done
The right thing.

Her walk is a dance
Taller than telephone poles.
Birds light lightly
On the brims.

The grass is alert
Underfoot for droppings.
Three small hats do fall:
The Sudanese felt tarboosh
And the two York Harbor
Paper fireman's hats.
They bounce like dervishes,
Like water drops on a hot roof.

What a strange creature,
You must think. So do I.
Odd that she should prove
So lovely. Odder still

How her eyes are friendly
Like the tracks of birds,
How her hands are safe
As the eyelids of birds.

JOSEPHINE JACOBSEN

The Class

The small black blobs on the beach are the heads
of children. Defectives:
the imbeciles could not come, and the morons
have graduated to lives.
Five sit under the sun at the tide's edge.

Everything moves: like a motion of silence a sailboat
goes on the sea's brilliant shiver;
the glittery palms make the sound of raining,
clouds change shape, waves curl over.
The five stay still as five struck in one pose.

They are out for an outing in the free great air:
they face the Caribbean;
the air will not bear them up, nor the sea,
nor the sand grow an herb to heal,
nor the thick white clouds transport them elsewhere.

This is no lesson the voice gives.
They listen, listen in a secret school,
their faces lifted: conscienceless, on their skin
the tongue of the tide says, *Cool* . . .
and in glazed brightness the sun says, *Live* . . .

The Planet

For Erlend

From the center of the Sea of Tranquility—
a dry sea and a grainy—
see shining on the air
of that stretched night, a planet.

See it as serene and bright, very bright,
a far fair neighbor;
conceive what might be there
after the furious spaces.

Green fields, green fields,
oceans of grasses, breakers of daisies;
shadows on those fields,
vast and traveling,

the clouds' shadows.
And something smaller:
in the green grass, lovers in each other's
arms, still, in the grass.

The clouds will water the fields
the stream run shining
to the sea's motion; the sea shining
as the clouds travel and shine,

so shine the daisies, as
the light in the seas
of the lovers' eyes. The innocent planet
far and simple, simple because far:

with lovers, and fields for flowers,
and a blue sky carrying clouds;
and water, water: the innocent planet,
shining and shining.

Yellow

Yellow became alive.
Materialization took place.
First logically with lemons,
then fresh butter.

Also a chairleg.
After that it appeared
to carve the curve of clouds
and, as sun, shatter them.
The stars grew yellower
yellow whirls on wheels on whirls
leaves flew yellow
the corn sprang
yellow and the crows
winged with a yellow nimbus.
Finally his face
had brilliant yellow
in its grain.
Outside the madhouse hung the yellow sun.

The Interrupted

Of the goddess there is only the marble shoulder and one
keen breast, lifted in a shout or love.
The axle is all that remains of the race.

On the smashed frieze, the forelegs, jubilant,
spring from no stallion: spring in the glass case
under the shadow of outside almond bloom.

On a stump, leafless, the slender headless youth
leans on his elbow, tenderly in stone,
to watch something in absence.

Acanthus cannot shake, though wind from the sea comes in:
the acanthus is a scrap from a scrap of column.
It is stopped short and waits for us.

The noble plunge of the stallion, the race, the shout,
the eyes' view, the acanthus moved by the wind
achieve themselves in this stone room—

of the company of their unbroken peers, the lords.
These escape from their maker's limit to rejoice us
with hope. These are the interrupted.

ETHERIDGE KNIGHT

Dark Prophesy: I Sing of Shine

And, yeah, brothers,
while white/america sings about the unsink
able molly brown
(who was hustling the titanic
when it went down)
I sing to thee of Shine
the stoker who was hip
enough to flee the fucking ship
and let the white folks drown
with screams on their lips
(jumped his black ass into the dark sea, Shine did,
broke free from the straining steel).
Yeah, I sing of Shine
and how the millionaire banker stood on the deck
and pulled from his pocket a million dollar check
saying Shine Shine save poor me
and I'll give you all the money a black boy needs—
how Shine looked at the money and then at the sea
and said jump in muthafucka and swim like me—
And Shine swam on—Shine swam on—
how the banker's daughter ran naked on the deck
with her pink tits trembling and her pants roun her neck
screaming Shine Shine save poor me
and I'll give you all the cunt a black boy needs—
how Shine said now cunt is good and that's no jive
but you got to swim not fuck to stay alive—
And Shine swam on—Shine swam on—
how Shine swam past a preacher afloat on a board
crying save me nigger Shine in the name of the Lord—
how the preacher grabbed Shine's arm and broke his
    stroke—
how Shine pulled his shank and cut the preacher's throat—
And Shine swam on—Shine swam on—
And when the news hit shore that the titanic had sunk
Shine was up in Harlem damn near drunk—
and dancing in the streets.
Yeah, damn near drunk and dancing in the streets.

Feeling Fucked/Up

Lord she's gone done left me done packed/up and split
and i with no way to make her
come back and everywhere the world is bare
bright bone white   crystal sand glistens
dope death dead dying and jiving drove
her away made her take her laughter and her smiles
and her softness and her midnight sighs—

Fuck Coltrane and music and clouds drifting in the sky
fuck the sea and trees and the sky and birds
and alligators and all the animals that roam the earth
fuck marx and mao fuck fidel and nkrumah and
democracy and communism fuck smack and pot
and red ripe tomatoes fuck joseph fuck mary fuck
god jesus and all the disciples fuck fanon nixon
and malcolm fuck the revolution fuck freedom fuck
the whole muthafucking thing
all i want now is my woman back
so my soul can sing

PAUL LAWSON

Survey

We're up in a balloon
with so many beliefs to be
shattered our voices quaver

below, the people
seem to be shouting we're gods

the dogs believe in us—they
bark—they're all we hear
except an occasional ooga
at a crossroads
translation is impossible

but the visibility is good
you can see everything here
look
somebody's pulling a slingshot
back (that lousy son of a bitch)
they say one puncture and we'd
go poof (don't think of it)
happily we're out of range
we can relax
in our basket
and skim along above the treetops
awed by the scenery of our
beautiful bodies, sharing the
last of the bread
and our imaginary hotdogs

watch it! Fasten your belt
the bag's beginning to lurch
wipe the mustard out of your eye
look around for an open field
we must descend, not that we've
had enough sky or lost faith in
it but for the sake of our images
and stomachs. Straighten your
tie, people are bound to take us
in, though we are fallen
or because we have fallen so far

The Ambassadors

When we heard it announced
that our country had been abolished
we looked around from the top of the
embassy, loving the station
no way to tell the sky from the water
and, sickened, went inside
to start packing

back of the funny tick-tick
we sensed lions dreaming our bones

in the infirmary was a man who'd
had his bowels removed
thankful that his stomach was left in

when the embarkation tickets were
distributed (without names, to underline
our identity) and we realized
we wouldn't have a home again
we knew we had to be
something other than a nation
and went back to packing
and unpacking
discarding, reclaiming
questioning
hurting one another
waiting for a destination
listening to everyone cry
and occasionally thinking of the
stomach man

someone mentioned Pocahontas
who left England for Virginia
in sixteen seventeen
and died off Gravesend

CYNTHIA MACDONALD

Accomplishments

I painted a picture—green sky—and showed it to my
   mother.
She said that's nice, I guess.
So I painted another holding the paintbrush in my teeth,
Look, Ma, no hands. And she said
I guess someone would admire that if they knew
How you did it and they were interested in painting which
   I am not.

I played clarinet solo in Gounod's Clarinet Concerto
With the Buffalo Philharmonic. Mother came to listen and
   said
That's nice, I guess.
So I played it with the Boston Symphony,

Lying on my back and using my toes,
Look, Ma, no hands. And she said
I guess someone would admire that if they knew
How you did it and they were interested in music which I
    am not.

I made an almond soufflé and served it to my mother.
She said, that's nice, I guess.
So I made another, beating it with my breath,
Serving it with my elbows,
Look, Ma, no hands. And she said
I guess someone would admire that if they knew
How you did it and they were interested in eating which I
    am not.

So I sterilized my wrists, performed the amputation, threw
    away
My hands and went to my mother, but before I could say
Look, Ma, no hands, she said
I have a present for you and insisted I try on
The blue kid gloves to make sure they were the right size.

RICHARD MATHEWS

dear patty dear tania

you are so beautifully thin and naive
i wince as they peel your brain
its grey fibers are so twisted by now
you are a sweet precious thing
gone jive gone by gone sour
wash brain by dada hurts and mama kill
patty cake sweet good you done gone

where could you

your startling innocence hits
even the wisest of us below the belt
they've had you reeling before
the tapes and cameras have
always been rolling around you

i am in london as i write this
patty sitting in the hot spot cafe
this is really true it's on
earls court road and cheap
filling but hardly hot like the hunger
you began your martyrdom to feed

your startling innocence has us
turning in all our graves
there's no chance to cut up out
of this one all the irreparable da-da-
damage has been done

i'm writing this more plainly
than i've written anything
for years i'm reading it to
as many people as i can because
i see beneath that fragile
skin of yours all the precarious
real sense of all of us
ripped out of our minds
by sudden violence
america
i've got myself
at gunpoint don't worry
i'm blowing my brains out if they don't
release you i'm giving them an ultimatum
holding myself hostage and there's no way out

PETER MEINKE

This Is a Poem to My Son Peter

this is a poem to my son Peter
whom I have hurt a thousand times
whose large and vulnerable eyes
have glazed in pain at my ragings
thin wrists and fingers hung

boneless in despair, pale freckled back
bent in defeat, pillow soaked
by my failure to understand.
I have scarred through weakness
and impatience your frail confidence forever
because when I needed to strike
you were there to be hurt and because
I thought you knew
you were beautiful and fair
your bright eyes and hair
but now I see that no one knows that
about himself, but must be told
and retold until it takes hold
because I think anything can be killed
after a while, especially beauty
so I write this for life, for love, for
you, my oldest son Peter, age 10,
going on 11.

Cheerios

you are what you eat & I
I am a sexmad wheatgerm
floating in holes of cheerios
stamped out of Kansas farmland
where in late August
the All-American sun
drives ripe farmgirls into barns
and shadows as pitchforks
are abandoned like Neptune's
trident while he rolled in the springs
with Ceres, seeds exploding
everywhere, pine cones and
pomegranates, ears of corn
popeyed with heat
bunches of grapes swollen
in the wagon while we
danced & sang & drank
& ate and the god laughed
& chanted, crying
gobble it all in excess of

the minimum daily adult requirements
screw hunger
look longer
live younger

Happy at 40

STOP: if you're racing at night
over cobblestones winking like turtles
to meet an important party in 15 minutes
when an ancient winedark man reels out
of a one-eyed bar with parachutes
sagging from the ceiling and croaks
A tugboat captain
is a tough captain
skip the bus, forget about the party
follow him into the bar if
you want to be happy at 40

LOOK: if you're in Paris or Munich
or Barcelona drinking beer with a whore
who weighs over 200 pounds
and is not pretty
when you see a friend of the family's
from your home town approaching
be certain you stand up and say Mr. Barnes
I'd like you to meet
my friend Marie who is showing me
this marvelous city,
if you want to be happy at 40

LISTEN: lies are all around us
it's only sporting, life is tricky
like poetry, lies, lies abound,
testing you, setting you up
for an occasional truth
like this:
if you see a woman leap over a hedge
marry her on the spot
take her forcibly on the greensward for
your life depends on it
if you want to be happy
at 40.

336

JIM WAYNE MILLER

A House of Readers

At 9:42 on this May morning
the children's rooms are concentrating too.
Like a tendril growing toward the sun, Ruth
moves her book into a wedge of light
that settled on the floor like a butterfly.
She turns a page.
Fred is immersed in magic, cool
as a Black Angus belly-deep in a farm pond.

The only sounds: pages turning softly.
This is the quietness
of bottomland where you can hear only the young corn
growing, where a little breeze stirs the blades
and then breathes in again.

I mark my place.
I listen like a farmer in the rows.

Growing Wild

Writing you this, I can feel a dewclaw
pushing through the skin an inch above my thumb.
I'll sign this letter with a muddy paw.

Since you've been gone
I've grown a little wilder every day,
like a dog on one of those abandoned farms
out in the scrub-pine country between the rivers.

I'm living in just one room of the house,
I've turned it into a lair.
I wake there by the bones of my last meal.
I'm eating rare steaks, loving the taste of blood.
Yesterday, grabbling in the creek,
I caught six red horse with my hands
and ate them for supper.

Late in the afternoon I sit out back
and watch the woods creep closer to the house.
Rabbits come up into the grass and nibble.

Sometimes they sit for minutes at a time
watching me warily. They know I can't be trusted.
Tomorrow or the next day I may pounce
and bolt one squealing, beating heart and all,
snapping his bones between my teeth.

I walk in the woods at night and strange scents
curling from folds of wind
stir whines and whimperings in my throat.

If you don't come home soon
I know I'll range farther and farther off
into my woodsy dreams.
When you do return, you'll find the grass
knee-high around the house, the doors all open,
chewed bits of fur and feathers in the bedroom,
bones buried in your bedroom slippers.
I will have taken up
with some skinny, yellow-eyed bitch from the woods.

By late summer, lovers parked by cattle bars
will swear they saw me running with wild dogs
that drag down sheep and cattle between the rivers.

VASSAR MILLER

Homecoming Blues

The ashes have waited for me in the ash tray,
but say nothing.
The towel hanging on the rack that I have longed to see
somehow says nothing.
My dogs who have already forgotten how much they
    missed me
say nothing either.
        And O O O O
I wish I could call my mother
or eat death like candy.

Encounter

I was content with the pseudonym
of my own name, with the disguise
provided by my body,

snapped to when anybody called me,
answered to the image captured in
eyesight's polaroid

posted for all the curious who passed,
lived, a stranger in my own skin,
because my friends defined me,

till at your word, I, somnambulist,
awakened astonished in the streets
of my identity,

and there you left me, but not before
your flesh, breathed in a muted sentence,
instructed me in mine.

Eden Revisited

"We'll talk all night until we swoon away," you promised,
friend of my innocence and of no more than that,
the only rule allowing us to talk.

*

Words were my lawyers once before Judge Life.
Now when he passes sentence,
silence and I stand side by side.

No longer are words the currency in my country.
I have been thrown into jail
more times than one for passing counterfeit.

*

My mother's best friend gave a leaf to her.
She recorded it in words, saying,
"Given to me in 1912 by Helen."

Though Freud was lurking those days in Vienna,
bidding us unravel our lives in words,
people still spoke.

And those two girls, my mother and Helen,
not knowing Victoria was dead,
still moved inside their skins as though not touching them.

So, now I view their leaf, more durable than breath,
but bruised and breaking under each minute more,
frayed reconciliation between truth and lie.

LARRY RUBIN

The Manual

I found it in the bottom drawer
Under her wedding linen
And reading it was like eating the wild apples
That grew in my grandfather's orchard
Till I was sick with ferment and love
And ran for relief, racing the rain in my bowels
But now my canals were thick with the freight of their
    fourteen years
And the dreams came thick and heavy
At the point where dew descends
At the moment of belief in those printed words
When the diagrams exploded in my dreams

And I was putting the book back in the drawer
Under her wedding linen
When she came in and saw me
And asked if I understood
Smoothing the folds in something she'd bought as a bride
I saw the bewilderment in my mother's eyes
And quietly closed the drawer, and lied

The Brother-in-Law

Haunt him, Mona! Haunt him, demon sister!
He who filled your bed for twenty years,
Inflating placentas, till you withered in
His bursting gifts, and burrowed into safer

Ground, he will betray those nights; he's found
A woman newer in the flesh, and has pushed
Your grave below his bed.
                              They will wed,
But I who was your lover first, before
I knew what women hid—by the manhood
I had then, I conjure you to wall
Their nights, and lie between their straining parts.
Haunt him in his massive hour—
                                    child, I call.

The Son, Condemned

On this black night of rain
I damn the darkness of my father's eyes—
When I try to phone him, the static
In the storm shoots wild lights
From the receiver; my eardrum's scorched
And his voice does not get through.
I thought I saw his image on the screen
But all the dots got jumbled in the hectic air
And if I touch the rabbit ears I'll burn.
This night all rods are wired to his revenge:
He wanted grandsons forged in chains of light
And now he'll spot the withered link, and strike.

LEON STOKESBURY

Beef

When the fat woman's two brats
went with their noses running
toward the wrong Steak House rest-
room door, her husband laughed and laughed
and caught them just in time. He
stopped them, set them straight, then

came back grinning, saying "Well
they're safe for a few more years."
He steered them a proper course
toward a proper watered harbor,
safe from strange equipment
and stranger squalls and thighs. He grinned. He
slashed and tore broiled steak. He
wolfed down dark red catsup with his french fries.

Gifts

They say that blood is salt. I've
tasted yours, and they are right.
So let's get on with our big painting
exchange. In mine, I've placed you
in a black pasture, with black horses,
your red eyes clearly discerned. But,
and I observe you're having the same
problem, here in the middle distance
isn't really the right place for you
somehow. Over more to the left,
I think, yes, under that smeared vision
of crows, way out in those dark, waist-high
weeds, there, leaning against that
huge pile of horseshit, yes, and a little
nearer the vanishing point, thank you.

DABNEY STUART

The Refugee

While he talked the wireless man listened
For news of the fog lifting
The storm cutting down the mountains.

He'd thought it was midnight when he started
But who knew what time it was
The weather all over you like this.

He'd lost his clothes on the barbed wire
Piece by piece   *It was all right*
He said   *The fog fit all right.*

He thought he'd cut himself once
But couldn't see what it was
He wiped off his thigh   *Damn fog*

Felt like blood anyhow   Half the time
He had a hard on he said
The way that stuff seemed to love him.

The rest of us sat there thinking we saw him
A woman knitted a sweater with one arm
I looked for a window.

He'd kept the right direction
Eating everything in sight
When he ate his eyes he began to have visions.

He said he saw men armed with fences
Barbed wire fences bordering a road
His limbs flapped like clothing on the barbs.

He walked down the middle
He saw his penis standing ahead of him like a lighthouse
His eyes blinked from it like a beacon.

Steered clear of that he said
The worst was thinking I'd been walking
In the same place   *That was the worst.*

He said the fog kept him from being sure
He said he just kept going   Kept going
He said we didn't know how relieved he was to be here.

The fog caressed me   My groin ached
His voice burned my eyes   *We couldn't bear*
Your beating the door I said

We had to let you out.

A Lesson in Oblivion

One afternoon as I was wandering around
The grounds I happened on my keeper,
Goaltender, hardy watchdog of the lone
Prayree, immaculate conception,
And I posed him some hoary questions:

Would you paint the Taj Mahal
With a frayed matchstick? Would
You try to stuff a sea squid
Into a thimble? Would you
Keep trying? Would you cross

An eagle and a rattlesnake and kneel
before their issue, or print its likeness
on your currency? Would you buy
Consolidated Nerve Gas at 50 and seven/eighths
Or support basic research

Into the possibility of transplanting
A Teflon stomach? Would you run
It up the flagpole, give it a run
For its money, give it a whirl,
Accept the nomination, in short

If you had the chance
Would you do it the same way
All over again
Without changing a thing?
                                    And he said

Yes. Except I'd have your tongue cut out.

ROBERT WATSON

The Glass Door

Was I moving through the invisible glass
    Between life and death,

344

When I walked through the glass door
  I thought was open?
The glass fell on me like icicles or knives,
  My clothes turned red and then my eyes.

After the nurse sponged my face the surgeon
  With needle and thread
Mended me as if I were a tattered coat.
  "You will be the same as ever
After a month on crutches and two with a cane."
  But I am not the same.

I would have sworn our sliding glass door was open
  Nothing between in and out.
In daylight I walk as a man in darkness
  Hands out to feel
What the darkness holds, to test for walls
  That shatter,

For invisible curtains between what we see
  And what we think we see
On rainy nights staring beyond the windshield
  Or out the kitchen window
Washing glasses in the sink. Telescopes are useless.
  Everything we cannot see is here.

Is There Life Across the Street?

When I call to the dead to speak, the graves
At midnight are silent. In the moonlight
The tombs are white houses on dark green lawns,
A city of houses without windows
Or doors. Even the wind is speechless now.

The graveyard lies across the street from me,
My own house of red brick where my wife sleeps,
And I insomniac lean against the iron
Fence that keeps back the living from the dead
What should I anticipate? They won't tell.

My parents, other relatives live there,
And friends. Day follows day, year follows year
Until I know more people on that side
Than this. The living city shrinks, the silent
Grows. I have never gone anywhere,

Never travelled on a slow boat to China,
Skied the alps or dove from a coral reef.
I have climbed the nearest hill and there
Climbed a tree I climbed in childhood to see
The world I would explore in years to come:

It is my stamp collection buried in a drawer,
The atlas on its shelf, a telescope
I never use. Too young for one war
Too old for the next, I have lived in peace,
Some would say monotony. Not me.

My first lover lies under that little stone.
She married a brother of my wife and grew
Churchy near the end. He married again.
How I'd like to see her when my time comes
But I suppose the dead don't see . . . or touch.

No matter how much I ponder I can't
Figure out what the dead do. They're like
A gas, I guess, escaped from dust. One part there
In the grave, the rest expanding out, out
To form the atmosphere we breathe. I give up.

It is hard for me to believe the dead
Don't exist under the white stones under
The green lawns behind the iron fence,
Asleep as my wife is asleep upstairs.
Whether I'm right or wrong doesn't matter:

It's the comfort of belief, not the truth
That counts for me. At midnight at this division
Between life and death, holding to the fence—
Sleepy now—two worlds merge: the mood has clouded
Over, a ground fog rises. Are the dead

Rising to enfold me? I cross the street
Enter my darkened house, ascend to bed.
I have travelled more than round the world,
Further than Mars to the white houses across
The street and back to my brick house, my sleeping wife.

JOANIE WHITEBIRD

Star

out of Chaos
came a man walking,
unsteadily at first
but walking all the same

a woman
looked out
saw him walking
and loved him for it
          (because
   from where she was
                Inside
     he looked like
          a star
                    shining alone
                         at sun rise)

and she too
came out of Chaos,
            timid and unsure
but walking all the same

when the man
looked back at her,
he knew
but he kept walking

they walked a long way
in the clean and precise
                    New World
               gaining strength

                              and certitude
                                 in their new selves

before he spoke to her

"as children
we dreamed
lovers to be inseparable—
as stars, we learn
only the limitless
can support

our polarity"
he kissed her once
and began to move away
turning and spinning
                    into the distance

where he touched her
one tear fell

then
came a great rushing
of wind and lights;
the known universe fell away
                    completely
and time and space
became a frozen blue
in the distance
shone one star
that kept her immobile
                    hypnotized

and she began to sing
the song of his light,
and she sang
until it became
her light also

slowly,
after cycles
and more cycles
had passed,
a third light came
            then a fourth
                        a fifth
after eons
there appeared
        walking and holding hands,
                    two children,
                        bathed in stars

JAMES WHITEHEAD

He Records a Little Song for a Smoking Girl

Smoking all that much has got her eyes
Pinched and a little lined—so the misery
Of cigarettes deserves a song. Prize
For doing anything, catastrophe
In small doses, smoke cuts into a face
Almost as deep as Benzedrine and booze.

Still she's a lovely girl in every place
Because she is so young. O she will lose
Her surfaces of head in love and time
Though all the rest stay smooth and be close-pored.
Her legs would make a blind man smile, and rime—
Her belly and the thing in sweet accord
Years from now will cry, Forgive, forgive
My cigarettes, I swallowed smoke alive.

About a Year After He Got Married He Would Sit Alone in an Abandoned Shack in a Cotton Field Enjoying Himself

I'd sit inside the abandoned shack all morning
Being sensitive, a fair thing to do
At twenty-three, my first son born, and burning
To get my wife again. The world was new
And I was nervous and wonderfully depressed.

The light on the cotton flowers and the child
Asleep at home was marvelous and blessed,
And the dust in the abandoned air was mild
As sentimental poverty. I'd scan
Or draw the ragged wall the morning long.

Newspaper for wallpaper sang but didn't mean.
Hard thoughts of justice were beyond my ken.
Lord, forgive young men their gentle pain,
Then bring them stones. Bring their play to ruin.

A Local Man Remembers Betty Fuller

Betty Fuller cried and said, Hit me.
I did. Which made her good and passionate
But Betty Fuller never came. Fate
Decreed that Betty Fuller would not see
The generosity a lively house
And loyal husband bring. She lost her mind
In Mendenhall. She got herself defined
As absolutely mad. A single mouse
Caused her to run exactly down the line
Of a wide road, running both north and south
With execrations pouring from her mouth.

She's out at Whitfield doing crazy time
And she can't possibly remember me
Among the rest. I'm satisfied she can't.

REED WHITTEMORE

The Fall of the House of Usher

It was a big boxy wreck of a house
Owned by a classmate of mine named Rod Usher,
Who lived in the thing with his twin sister.
He was a louse and she was a souse.

While I was visiting them one wet summer, she died.
We buried her,
Or rather we stuck her in a back room for a bit, meaning
    to bury her
When the graveyard dried.

But the weather got wetter.
One night we were both waked by a twister,
Plus a screeching and howling outside that turned out to be
    sister
Up and dying again, making it hard for Rod to forget her.

He didn't. He and she died in a heap, and I left quick,
Which was lucky since the house fell in right after,

                                            Like a ton of brick.

from **The Seven Days**

III. On First Knowing God

At breakfast I had french toast
(I nomenclate thee french toast)
And drank several cups of coffee
(This will soon be arithmetic)
And came back to my bathroom
And emptied my new bowels
And said to the pines, Who is God?

The wind was up, the pines
Noisy but recondite.
An ant crawled up my shirt.
I took off my shirt and baked,
And looked at Mount Crotched and dozed.
Who was to tell me, tell me?
Not the leaves, not the pines,
Not the sun, not the ant.
Had I made nothing would speak to me?
I went to the finch in the leaves
And said, Someone must say.
But he flew away.

How about you, robin,
You on the stump?
But the robin zipped to the underbrush
And a hush fell on the brush
And I understood as I stood
Bare to the waist on a stone
That the robin had known.
The stone upheld me.

To my porch then did I walk
And did to the mountain cry,
God, God am I.

Science Fiction

From my city bed in the dawn I see a raccoon
On my neighbor's roof.
He walks along in his wisdom in the gutter
And passes from view

On his way to his striped spaceship to take his disguise off
And return to Mars as himself, a Martian
Raccoon.

JONATHAN WILLIAMS

from Strung Out with Elgar on a Hill

March 2:

all you ask is
one person, one person only
to look at you
for real
scratch your back
suck your cock
put his arms
around you
one person
one person only

for that
you
may
cry
your
heart
out

March 2:

stop all the literary shit,
look up from the floor of the valley
at my glands and ducts
(as much *out there* as in here)

I see the Emotions
in their ranks,
moving east

three solar-plexus clouds from Utah loom
above the massive wall
of the Maroon Bells:

here comes Rage
seething
over the lost lover

now Despair,
blue and black

and now Hunger,
no color,
for the next lover

*　　*　　*

March 4:

awake
3 a.m.,
from a dream:

a pillar of silver smoke,
a tornado of light
in Aspen's sky
over Washington's landscape

I begin to feel like Sappho,
on fire to sleep against
the breasts of her latest school girl discovery

O Geriatrical Poet—Paedophile & Ogre!!!

how many steps from
Oscar and the grooms;
Douglas and his farm
boys, whom he dug
"because they are warm and human"?

when Renate wrote
"I had wanted simply a hand in my hair"
she wrote it like it was

light
on Red Butte

I could see
my hand in your blond hair—
if you wanted it there

* * *

March 6:

IN TE, ORPHEUS, SPERAVI: NON CONFUNDAR IN AETERNUM!

thinking of Anton Bruckner,
the Master of Sentences,
an old man in Wien,
absolutely alone,
alone his whole bleeding life,
beloved of not one man
or not one woman
in the entire Austro-Hungarian Empire

his thing about
fires, looking at the charred
bodies, pinching servant-girls' bottoms,
counting all the leaves
on trees—

they bring
tears
to the eyes

heaven in his heavy heart,
loins locked apart by heavenly art . . .

later
he became Hitler's
favorite composer

* * *

March 8:

ON ARRIVING AT THE SAME AGE AS JACK BENNY

my Ol' Kentucky Pal,
Professor Davenport, donning his Dear-Abby drag,
advises:

354

DON'T CHASE!

he suggests Socrates sat on a bench in the gym,
the lovers came flocking
for the simple reason he was the best talker in town

(but, could be, they just figured
all that potato nose and all,
he was strictly gangbusters downstairs?)

((vide:
Ovid))

these kids, they listen to talk:
tell 'em, Soc, baby!

Chorus:

SOCKITTOMESOCKITTOME—
SOCKITTOMESOCKITTOME!!!

* * *

March 9:

clean sheets, *again*,
just in case

MILLER WILLIAMS

Getting Experience

The first real job I had was delivering drugs
for Jarman's Pharmacy in Bascum, Arkansas.

If everyone was busy or in the back I sold things.
A cloudy woman with pentecostal hair

softly asked for sanitary napkins.
She brought the Kleenex back unwrapped in twenty
   minutes.

Shame said Mr. Jordan, we shouldn't make a joke
of that and made me say I'm sorry and fired me.

When I found out what the woman wanted
I had to say I did what everyone said I did.

That or let them know I hadn't heard of Kotex.
Better be thought bad than known for stupid.

The first hard fight I had was after school
with Taylor Wardlow West in Bascum, Arkansas.

Ward West chased me home from school when I was lucky.
My father said Ward West was insecure.

Go smile at him he said and let him know
you mean to be his friend. My father believed in love.

All day I smiled and twisted in my seat to see him
all hate and slump by himself in the back of the room.

After school he sat on my chest and hit me
and then his little brother sat on my chest and hit me.

And then his little sister sat on my chest and hit me.
She made me so ashamed I tried to kick her

and kicked Ward West in the face. When he could see
I was rounding the corner for home. Jesus, Jesus, Jesus.

Next day everybody told me over and over
how I had balls to make those stupid faces,

him the son of a bitch of the whole school
and how I surely did kick the piss out of him.

Ward had to go to the dentist. Also his father beat him.
He didn't come to school for two days.

Then he left me alone. He said I was crazy.
Everybody thought I was a little crazy.

Although with balls. I just let them say I was.
Better be thought mad than known for stupid.

Sneeze, belch or fart. Choose if you have a choice.
Nobody's going to think you're good and sane and smart.

The Neighbor

". . . thou, and thy sons, and thy wife,
and thy sons' wives with thee."

No one knows what the banging is all about
or the drilling that buzzes like a swarm of gnats
above the clover between his woods and the wash

or why it is he never came into the store
to pick up his almanac
or goes to Grange anymore

or why his sons have all come back from the city
and their fair wives with them

or why he walks the long fences of his farm
picking up sometimes a twig
turning it in his fingers
and letting it fall.

The main fact is which does make us uneasy
he's set about building something in his barn

and it's big.

The Northeast

A. R. AMMONS

Imperialist

Everybody knows by now
that the weeds are mine
& knows I don't feel
altogether sorry for them:
but they I think
resent being owned or
written into roses.

Ballad

I want to know the unity in all things and the difference
between one thing and another
    I said to the willow
and asked what it wanted to know: the willow said it
wanted to know how to get rid of the wateroak
that was throwing it into shade every afternoon at 4 o'clock:
    that is a real problem I said I suppose
and the willow, once started, went right on saying
I can't take you for a friend because while you must
be interested in willowness, which you could find nowhere
    better than right here,
        I'll bet you're just as interested in wateroakness
which you can find in a pure form right over there,
a pure form of evil and death to me:
I know I said I want to be friends with you both but the
willow sloughed into a deep grief
and said
if you could just tie back some of those oak branches
until I can get a little closer to mastering that domain
of space up there—see it? how empty it is
and how full of light:
        why I said don't I ask the wateroak if he would mind
withholding himself until you're more nearly even: after

all I said you are both trees and you both need water and
light and space to unfold into, surely the wateroak will
understand that commonness:
   not so you could tell it, said the willow:
      that I said is cynical and uncooperative: what could
you give the wateroak in return for his withholding:
what could I give him, said the willow, nothing
that he hasn't already taken:
   well, I said, but does he know about the unity in
all things, does he understand that all things have a
common source and end: if he could be made
to see that rather deeply, don't you think he might
      give you a little way:
   no said the willow he'd be afraid I would take all:
would you I said:
or would you, should the need come, give him a little way
back:
      I would said the willow but my need is greater than
his
and the trade would not be fair:
maybe not I said but let's approach him with our powerful
concept that all things are in all
   and see if he will be moved

Rocking

The cock sparrow with a sweet
tweetering
did it on-and-off
fluttering four times quick
on the porch caves:
the hen sparrow seemed
moved no further than
injunction's
"propagate the species":
well, the sun's breaking
out, maybe she'll like that,
or maybe she means her
propriety to send
that earnest little
rooster off again.

Satisfaction

Still I'm for upper
buzzardry: the high
easy fix
of the actual meal:
hunger lofts:
descent's a nasty dinner.

ALVIN AUBERT

Blood to Blood

it may be a little different
nowadays but when i was a boy
everyblackoneofus had his own
private lynching. carried it
'round with him in his front
pocket, close to his private
parts. blood to blood.

There Were Fierce Animals in Africa

there were fierce animals in Africa.
their king a noble white savage who swung
across a continent on a plaited vine.
that was before hemingway gave me
my first lesson in the mysteries of
kilimanjaro. even before i heard water
dance to the syncopated beat of
the congo. not to mention that lake
dutifully and ceremoniously dubbed
victoria. from whose enthronement
in colonized black minds all bounty
was taught to flow. there were all
these things and more in Africa.
but no people, no people.

even the man man was nothing
but a mean abstraction. a sundown
dance viewed from a cool veranda.

One More Time

> *Within this black hive to-night*
> *There swarm a million bees*
> Jean Toomer, *Cane*

you should have, jean, stopped them.
those strange bees you saw going
in and out the moon. you lying flat
on your back, spine sucked by old bitch earth.
you should have plucked their looney wings
from space. fell them from that fantastic
height. nipped that mysterious drill.
still, i wonder, whatever harsh master
they danced to—what might he have done
taking me through them by surprise
a raw handed strappling twelve in the raspish
milk-sticky shade leaves of a neighbor's
fig tree. in heat for the cool interior
of the fig. soft seed succulent and
sacramental on the young tongue. jean.
you should have iced them jazzy bees.

Levitation

or telling time

The old man raises his bones
among the lithe skaters. glides
through their insouciant frolick.
weaves his intricate warp into
the weft of their rush and roar.
The old man spread his
rheumatic wings, floats his
ancient craft above the ponderous
strokes of the laborious skaters.
Featherless wrinkled bird.
lighter than air. parched
goosepimply skin—my heart
soars with that intrepid flyer.

AMIRI BARAKA

Horatio Alger Uses Scag

Kissinger has made it, yall. He's the secretary
of state, U.S.A. The anglo-snakes have called him
mooing to their side, his bag-time with rocky helped
a lot. His ol lady, was once, they say, rocky's main
squeeze . . . intellectually. But Henry, the k, pushes through
his dangerous glasses. His wine smile sloshes back and forth
he's thinking, as he speaks. A fast man on his feet. The
        subject,
a cold threat to the a-rabs (it makes him feel vaguely
        nationalistic,
but not in an irresponsible way, him bein a jew and all
ya know) . . . but they hired him not for his jewishness
        "grrr . . . he sd
what is that," but for his absolute mastery of the art of
bullshitting
And so, he lays it all out
across the U.N. decks for all
to hear, and be afraid. His freckles, even,
show, so synonymous with america is this
fat priapic mackman
A-rabs, he says, you betta
be cool with that oil & shit
& beyond us all, you cdda laught
is the realization that the shadowy figure
in the arab getup, is yo man, rocky, makin
                                    the whole thing
                                    perfect

At the National Black Assembly

        "EEK

        a nigger
communist," the lady democrat
nigrita squeeked, eek
an "avowed"
nigger
communist, & almost swooned

except you cd hear static chattering
from her gold necklace chairman
Strauss dialing trying to get through
her papers spilled
& the autographed picture
of Teddy K. & Georgie W.
hugging each other in
the steam bath
fell out.

You see she
say I cant not be
you see
with you niggers
with no nappy head commie
America's been good
to me. The democrats, God
bless' em, have alllllllways

done good
by us
by colored folks
you see she say I studied
commies, them chinese maoists
specially (She scooped her papers
up & thought deliciously
about the time her man
Scoop J & she licked on the same ice
cream
cone
right down to the hairs!
Specially them
Maoists, I studied

      They tacktix
She say, They tacktix
is to take over
the microphone &
be against the
democrats)
           sweeping out
           wrist radio tittering
           Strauss waltzes &
           Proposed ripoffs
           Straight from Watergate

Going to the airport
interviewed by WLIE

She smiled powdering her

conversation

    & caught a plane

      to

        petit bourgeois

          negro

            heaven

ELIZABETH BISHOP

12 o'Clock News

gooseneck lamp

As you all know, tonight is the night of the full moon, half the world over. But here the moon seems to hang motionless in the sky. It gives very little light; it could be dead. Visibility is poor. Nevertheless, we shall try to give you some idea of the lay of the land and the present situation.

typewriter

The escarpment that rises abruptly from the central plain is in heavy shadow, but the elaborate terracing of its southern glacis gleams faintly in the dim light, like fish scales. What endless labor those small, peculiarly shaped terraces represent! And yet, on them the welfare of this tiny principality depends.

pile of mss.

A slight landslide occurred in the northwest about an hour ago. The exposed soil appears to be of poor quality: almost white, calcareous, and shaly. There are believed to have been no casualties.

typed sheet

Almost due north, our aerial reconnaissance reports the discovery of a large rectangular "field," hitherto unknown to us, obviously man-made. It is dark-speckled. An airstrip? A cemetery?

envelopes

In this small, backward country, one of the most backward left in the world today, communications are crude and "industrialization" and its products almost nonexistent. Strange to say, however, signboards are on a truly gigantic scale.

ink-bottle

We have also received reports of a mysterious, oddly shaped, black structure, at an undisclosed distance to the east. Its presence was revealed only because its highly polished surface catches such feeble moonlight as prevails. The natural resources of the country being far from completely known to us, there is the possibility that this may be, or may contain, some powerful and terrifying "secret weapon." On the other hand, given what we *do* know, or have learned from our anthropologists and sociologists about this people, it may well be nothing more than a *numen*, or a great altar recently erected to one of their gods, to which, in their present historical state of superstition and helplessness, they attribute magical powers, and may even regard as a "savior," one last hope of rescue from their grave difficulties.

typewriter eraser

At last! One of the elusive natives has been spotted! He appears to be—rather, to have been—a unicyclist-courier, who may have met his end by falling from the height of the escarpment because of the deceptive illumination. Alive, he would have been small, but undoubtedly proud and erect, with the thick, bristling black hair typical of the indigenes.

From our superior vantage point, we can
clearly see into a sort of dugout, possibly a
shell crater, a "nest" of soldiers. They lie
heaped together, wearing the camouflage
"battle dress" intended for "winter warfare."
They are in hideously contorted positions, all
dead. We can make out at least eight bodies.

ashtray

These uniforms were designed to be used in
guerrilla warfare on the country's one snow-
covered mountain peak. The fact that these
poor soldiers are wearing them *here*, on the
plain, gives further proof, if proof were
necessary, either of the childishness and
hopeless impracticality of this inscrutable
people, our opponents, or of the sad
corruption of their leaders.

PHILIP BOOTH

Lines from an Orchard
Once Surveyed by Thoreau

I've lived by the world's rules
long enough. That season is over.
There's no ladder, no word that the bees
haven't already given. My feet
press cider back to the roots.
The orchard quiets; I sip
at its silence, letting the nectar
change me. What else
need I know, when there's
nothing to know, save
for the wisdom of trees?
I conduct myself like a naked monk.
Were I to open
to any more fullness, I think I'd
turn into a woman.

The Incredible Yachts

The incredible yachts: stays
and halyards geared to tension,
banks of winches on deck;
they blew into harbor
this evening: richly cruised men
wed to aluminum hulls
and fleet women: they raced
to get here. Once at anchor
in this stormed harbor,
in this indelible weather,
they bobbled the tide with
their empties: none of them
cared to know in truth
what harbor they were in.

JOHN MALCOLM BRINNIN

Dachau

Such a merry suburb!
Flats of ice cream colored building blocks,
acres of laundry, strenuous underwear!
In no-man's-land,
even the dump trucks & bulldozers waltz.

At the site itself,
clouds bulge the hub caps
of my Hertz
Mercedes-Benz, go shivering across
the muddy saucers of a parking lot.
Vast engines, far off, chomp.
The wind,
stage-managing Bavaria,
hurries another thousand extras
down a street far right.
Everything wants to be historical.

370

A neat red arrow
bids me take a cinder path.
Already half way toward the brute
meters of a poem scanting nothing,
I sketch out words:
here poison seeped from Christ's jackboot;
here, on a dog pack, huge rose-windows flicked
hyssops of warm blood. Walpurgisnacht!
All-powerful,
the leathery archangel raised his wing;
the long freights squealed to their dead stop;
the choirs rose.

Inside the compound gate:
thin leaks of rust,
tar paper clawed by rain,
barbed wire piled like tumbleweed,
a small sweet stench of mice,
the grassy alleys of the shanty dead. . . .

Unutterably surprised,
I cannot see. Somehow, I find a wall.
My toes clenched in my shoes,
I choke on air.

Families out from Munich—slouch hats,
plus fours, pigtails & reptile shoes—
come crunching the loud path.
Their voices—gentle, almost lyrical—
reach through my dark. *"Er ist ein Jude,"*
a woman whispers, perhaps to a child,
"er weint für alle Juden."

My wall weeps with me, pocks
my forehead with its miniature decay.

A locomotive in a tantrum
brings me to. I hear
its huff-huff-huff & idiotic shriek,
& then
the chuckle of a bird
quite new to me.
Drained, refreshed,
my credit cards intact,

I blow my nose,
I pull myself together.
There is much to see:
bunkers, barracks, crematoria. . . .

WILLIAM BRONK

After the Spanish Chroniclers

Crossing the Western Ocean to the edge of the world
or beyond it, and coming at last to the landed rim,
what it astounded them to find so far
from home, was men. They couldn't believe it at first.
Some never acknowledged; one was said to have kept
haunches of Indians hanging for his meat. Fair game.

Suppose that we, like them, should find somewhere
in a farther distance, others. It has to be us.
This is the curious thing: we have to be
whom we find there. Different customs; not our skins,
but nevertheless. Well, it doesn't matter, I guess.
But we're extensible; we don't leave room.

The Continuance

The time they misdirected themselves to a wake
and, coming to the coffin, found a corpse of the wrong sex
who was no one they knew, they knelt and nuzzled their
    fists.

It was get out, of course, without guffaw
and around the corner to where they should have been
but helpless with hidden laughter the whole time.
They cherished the joke; in the back of their minds, even
    more,
was the look of the roomfull of faces they didn't know.
The separate cruelty.

How almost all
of life is unspeakable. Disjunctiveness.
They thought of that. Incongruence.

                    It seems
as though, on a journey, we wake in the night. We must
have stopped somewhere—no telling where. In the light,
we look at the others, look at ourselves, invent
procedures to pass time, are as intent
at this as if we came for the purpose. The rules
change. It is uncertain what they are. We go on.

The Mask the Wearer of the Mask Wears

Yes, look at me; I am the mask it wears,
as much am that which is within the mask.
Nothing not mask but that. That every mask.

The mask will fall away and nothing lost.
There is only the mask-wearer, the self-aware,
the only aware, aware of only the self.

Awake, it dreams: is every character;
is always more; is never only that.
It contemplates; tries any mask of shape.

Any is nothing. Any is not what is.
But that it should be. That it should seem to be.
That it be no more than that, and yet should be.

And that it turn to look, look favorably,
look lovingly, look long, on what there is.

Go Ahead; Goodbye; Good Luck; and Watch Out

You get to Gilead, let me know. That balm,
supposed to be so good for human hurts
—all wounds, holes, hollows, hungriness—
you tell me if it's there, and how it works.

Till the time comes, I'll look for further ways
with the old lack, the void, push it along
ahead of me in the only way we have
to carry this luggage of ours of hungriness
like an empty bag. What else is there to do?
No kind of balm. You look, though. Let me know.

373

HAYDEN CARRUTH

Speaking for Them

August. Hear
the cicadas
splitting their skins.

The bleeding cow
has rubbed her neck on barbed
wire against the flies,

which return, crawling
in her eyes. She looks up,
a sorrow, raising her great
head in slowness, brown eyes rising
like pools in the earth.

Then the elms. There marching
down the knoll by the fence slowly,
a dead march. Shall we have

Memorial Day for the elms,
those veterans? Here are the oldest,
stricken and proud, lifting

poor broken arms in sleeves
of ragged bark.

Blackeyed susans bow their heads,
crazy swallows
turn somersaults in the air.

ALAN DUGAN

On a Professional Couple in a Side-Show

She is the knife-thrower's lady:
around her outline

374

there is a rage of knives.
Unharmed, he hopes, inside,
she is love's engine
of dark business
and the target of design.

What does she think of this?
The same, reversed: money is money
and spangled tights.
Those whistling knives of his
are kitchened at night.

Untitled Poem

I never saw any point
to life because I suffered
all the time, but now
that I am happy or bored
for whole days out of pain
I regret my past inactions.
Oh I could do nothing else.

I am almost too old
to learn about human life
but I try to, I
watch it curiously and try
to imitate its better processes.
So: First pleasures after hard times,
Hello in time for goodbye.

Untitled Poem

Two shots down and I'm exalted,
so I have the choice: do I give out
the passion of the day to whiskey, arts and crafts,
and lose tomorrow's to the shakes and nausea,
or do I be a joiner with the bourgeoisie
and cool it, feed, do labor, and make sleep?
Ah how I envy my iron-gut youth
when I could drink and talk all night
and get to work next morning, work the day,
and come home to a woman saying honey.

On When McCarthy Was a Wolf Among a Nation of Queer-Queers

At thirty, when the faiths give out,
and all the pleasures of light and air
go grey along with love, oh I began
to play the game: "Assumption of Faiths,"
and took up spiritual hobbies. God,
sports, and country were not enough
for one American, so I became
a joiner lapsing from the faiths.
May whiskey, money, and analysis
survive me through committee days
and may the night yield sex,
in which release whole moments pass.

As for the rest, left-left politics
was out of law, so I read books and bit
my thumbnails to the quick
in false despair: I am still here.

STEPHEN DUNN

California, This Is Minnesota Speaking

I tell my friend in California
I am so in control
my dream is
to be slightly out of control.
He understands, he's from California
and tells me
he has beaten up his wife at a party
and runs a nude group
and when he taught at medical school
dispensed drugs to hopheads.
(As kids in New York we played
stickball, drank Mission Orange,
ate Devil Dogs.)
I tell him I've been to the edge

of myself a few times,
and the atmosphere there is rarefied
and terrifying.
I ask him what it's like
to live there, on the edge,
and he says "Listen, I'm becoming a sad
old man, save your romantic bullshit
for some midwesterner,"
and, standing here on the flat land,
I sense what he means,
solid ground beneath me, never a chance
that the wild gesture you begin on Tuesday
will be more than thin air
on Wednesday, the perpetual safety
of unfinished business.
And I say "Listen, my shoulders
sometimes want to leave for the moon,
this peace in my gut is expensive,"
and he starts to talk about the price
of ecstasy,
the fact that there's no middle
where he is, no place to return to
except either up or down,
and I can hear seagulls on his end
of the phone, the surf, the daily redefinition
of the state he's in,
and I want to let myself drift
out of control, toward him,
toward the dumb, childish universe
where you open a door and walk in
and no one's there except yourself
and you say hello and see if you can survive.

Building in Nova Scotia

Before the grass could be planted
stones had to be picked
every day for a week
and then my wife took her urine somewhere
and in the evening she was pregnant
        it was a miracle
when the rocks were gone how the seed
took hold, changed,

if they had investigated her belly for prints
I would have been guilty, especially my lips
on the evening the news came—
the next day a tern, hunting for fish,
stopped in midair before it dove
     I tell you it was beautiful
how the sky gave way
to our house when it was finished
and the small imperialist in my body
gathered in the stars

RICHARD EBERHART

Long Term Suffering

There will be no examination in Long Term Suffering,
The course will come to an end as planned.
I have found that examinations are useless,
We have altogether too short a time to spend.

Time, ladies and gentlemen, is the great examiner.
I have discovered that this is true.
It is what you write as you go through the course
Is the only determinant and determinator of you.

Long Term Suffering is for those of all ages
In our tussling University, our bulging classroom.
It may be that I will profess near madness,
It may be that you will write out your doom.

All that you will have at the end of the course
Is writings you indite, or poems you make,
If you make them. Words, words in a sea flow;
At any rate, a lot of heartbreak.

Save your papers. It may be that years later,
Forty, maybe, you would like to look back
At your course in Long Term Suffering,
And note how strangely you had to act.

Reading Room,
The New York Public Library

In the reading room in the New York Public Library
All sorts of souls were bent over silence reading the past,
Or the present, or maybe it was the future, persons
Devoted to silence and the flowering of the imagination,
When all of a sudden I saw my love,
She was a faun with light steps and brilliant eye
And she came walking among the tables and rows of
  persons,

Straight from the forest to the center of New York,
And nobody noticed, or raised an eyelash.
These were fixed on imaginary splendours of the past,
Or of the present, or maybe of the future, maybe
Something as seductive as the aquiline nose
Of Eleanor of Aquitaine, or Cleopatra's wrist-locket in
  Egypt,
Or maybe they were thinking of Juliana of Norwich.

The people of this world pay no attention to the fauns
Whether of this world or of another, but there she was,
All gaudy pelt, and sleek, gracefully moving,
Her amber eye was bright among the porticoes,
Her delicate ears were raised to hear of love,
Her lips had the appearance of green grass
About to be trodden, and her shanks were smooth and
  sleek.

Everybody was in the splendor of his imagination,
Nobody paid any attention to this splendour
Appearing in the New York Public Library,
Their eyes were on China, India, Arabia, or the Balearics,
While my faun was walking among the tables and eyes
Inventing their world of life, invisible and light,
In silence and sweet temper, loving the world.

RUSSELL EDSON

When the God Returns

When the God returns he gives the world to mannequins
and toys. Dummies in store windows receive the world
as though the world had always been theirs. Dolls that
children played with are suddenly the masters; families
are consigned to shelves and playrooms.
The world crawls with motherless toys that murmur, mama.
Naked female mannequins, without vaginas, walk the
roads at night like human ghosts . . .
A Raggedy Ann confronts a family at dinner. The painted
smile is suddenly full of small animal teeth. She orders
them out of the dining room into a closet.
They must obey.
She wants to cut mother's head off. She wants to cut father's
penis off. She wants to open junior to see what's inside of
junior.
They must obey . . .

The Little Lady

A female hand puppet refuses to let the puppet master put
his hand up under her dress.
No no, it is too embarrassing, she weeps.
Oh please, little lady, my hand is your life, says the puppet
master.
Oh no, that cannot be, she weeps, have I no other life
except indignity?
I assure you, little lady, there's nothing *there*.
Nothing there . . . ? she weeps. Surely I'm not without
woman's treasure?
Only a tunnel of pretty cloth; the passage where I put my
hand to make you dance.
. . . But you haven't said you love me.
Please, little lady . . .
No no, we'll have to be married first, that's only fair, she
weeps.

And so the puppet master makes up another of the puppets
　　into a little justice of the peace, and has him perform the
　　marriage.
Now, little lady . . . ?
Now, and *forever*, my love, she says with the puppet master
　　making her voice with his falsetto . . .

The Prophylactic

He had hitched a chicken to a cart.
Go chicken, go, he screamed.

Not that the chicken doesn't try, for the man pleased is
　　prophylactic to chicken-murder.

A woman cries from a window, what is it that the chicken
　　is so put to do?

It's the harness or the pot —Do you think I give space on
　　earth to this feathered beast other than I milk its purpose
　　into mine! screamed the man.

Then beat it with a whip, fool; best that it run from pain
　　than consider the weight of the load, cried the woman.

No, the threat of death wins it to my will, screamed the
　　man, for the man pleased, as well the chicken knows, is
　　prophylactic to chicken-murder.

But the cart proves too heavy for the chicken. It turns to the
　　man and says, as you see I have tried, but the cart proves
　　too heavy; and I curse my ancestors for being chickens
　　rather than horses.

IRVING FELDMAN

So It Happens

So it happens
when Messiah stands
among us, this lost relation,

a small, forgotten cousin
from the other side who looks
with eager puzzlement into
our faces he half-recognizes,
half-guesses from the photo
he carries. Touchingly, with
wonder and disappointment,
he says, "It isn't you, Marsha,
Judy, Sam! Why am I always
lost and lose my way to
the appointed heart?" and goes off
while we cry out, "Mistake!
we are the very ones, look again,
seek us still in ourselves!"
—and yearn indeed to become
those pure incalculable names.

ROBERT FRANCIS

A Fear

Against a falling snow
I heard him long ago

A young man who could prove
Old Goethe could not love

Old love he both denied
And equally decried.

If I were young and cold
I'd be afraid to scold

The old in love for fear
The god of love might hear

And hearing me might freeze
My five extremities.

Spell

To be near
Yet not to wake
The sleeper, to hear
The poised antiphony
Of breath taken,
Breath released, to see
The petal lips parted,
The fluid hair
Poured on the pillow
Like some rare metal
Curiously spun,
To be there,
Oh, to be there.

Though a Fool

The wayfaring man though a fool
Will often fare as well
As one who has been to school
And knows how to scan and spell.

The scholar is melancholy
Too often on his way
While the fool may well be jolly
Though why he cannot say.

Bouquets

One flower at a time, please
however small the face.

Two flowers are one flower
too many, a distraction.

Three flowers in a vase begin
to be a little noisy

Like cocktail conversation,
everybody talking.

A crowd of flowers is a crowd
of flatterers (forgive me).

One flower at a time. I want
to hear what it is saying.

Cromwell

After the celebrated carved misericords
And various tombs, the amiable sexton
Shows you by St. Mary's door the stone
Where Cromwell's men sharpened their swords.

Was it not a just, a righteous, war
When indiscriminate Irish blood
Flowed for the greater glory of God
Outside St. Mary's door?

If righteousness be often tipped with steel,
Be rightly tipped, psalm-singing men
Will help themselves to holy stone
To whet their zeal.

So you have both: the mellow misericords
Gracing the choir
And just outside the door
The swords.

LOUISE GLÜCK

The Gift

Lord, You may not recognize me
speaking for someone else.
I have a son. He is
so little, so ignorant.
He likes to stand
at the screen door calling
oggie, oggie, entering
language, and sometimes
a dog will stop and come up
the walk, perhaps
accidentally. May he believe
this is not an accident?
At the screen
welcoming each beast in
love's name, Your emissary.

384

The Mirror

Watching you in the mirror I wonder
what it is like to be so beautiful
and why you do not love
but cut yourself, shaving
like a blind man. I think you let me stare
so you can turn against yourself
with greater violence,
needing to show me how you scrape the flesh away
scornfully and without hesitation
until I see you correctly,
as a man bleeding, not
the reflection I desire.

Gretel in Darkness

This is the world we wanted.
All who would have seen us dead
are dead. I hear the witch's cry
break in the moonlight through a sheet
of sugar: God rewards.
Her tongue shrivels into gas. . . .

        Now, far from women's arms
and memory of women, in our father's hut
we sleep, are never hungry.
Why do I not forget?
My father bars the door, bars harm
from this house, and it is years.

No one remembers. Even you, my brother,
summer afternoons you look at me as though
you meant to leave,
as though it never happened.
But I killed for you. I see armed firs,
the spires of that gleaming kiln—

Nights I turn to you to hold me
but you are not there.
Am I alone? Spies
hiss in the stillness, Hansel,
we are there still and it is real, real,
that black forest and the fire in earnest.

WILLIAM HEYEN

Riddle

From Belsen a crate of gold teeth,
from Dachau a mountain of shoes,
from Auschwitz a skin lampshade.
Who killed the Jews?

Not I, cries the typist,
not I, cries the engineer,
not I, cries Adolf Eichmann,
not I, cries Albert Speer.

My friend Fritz Nova lost his father—
a petty official had to choose.
My friend Lou Abrahms lost his brother.
Who killed the Jews?

David Nova swallowed gas,
Hyman Abrahms was beaten and starved.
Some men signed their papers,
and some stood guard,

and some herded them in,
and some dropped the pellets,
and some spread the ashes,
and some hosed the walls,

and some planted the wheat,
and some poured the steel,
and some cleared the rails,
and some raised the cattle.

Some smelled the smoke,
some just heard the news.
Were they Germans? Were they Nazis?
Were they human? Who killed the Jews?

The stars will remember the gold,
the sun will remember the shoes,
the moon will remember the skin.
But who killed the Jews?

The Children

I do not think we can save them.
I remember, within my dream, repeating
I do not think we can save them.
But our cars follow one another
over the cobblestones. Our dim
headlamps, yellow in fog, brush past,
at the center of a market square,
its cathedral's great arched doors.
I know, now, this is a city
in Germany, two years
after the Crystal Night. I think ahead
to the hospital, the children.
I do not think we can save them.

Inside this dream,
in a crystal dashboard vase,
one long-stemmed rose unfolds
rows of soft red light.
Its petals fall, tears, small
flames. I cup my palm to hold them,
and my palm fills to its brim,
will overflow.
Is this the secret, then?
Now I must spill the petal light, and drive.

We are here, in front of the hospital,
our engines murmuring. Inside,
I carry a child under each arm,
down stairs, out to my car.
One's right eyeball hangs on its cheek
on threads of nerve and tendon,
but he still smiles, and I love him.
The other has lost her chin—
I can see straight down her throat
to where her heart beats
black-red, black-red.
I do not think we can save them.

I am the last driver in this procession.
Many children huddle in my car.
We have left the city. Our lights
tunnel the fog beneath arches of linden,

toward Bremerhaven toward
the western shore.
I do not think we can save them.
At the thought, lights
whirl in my mirror, intense
fear, and the screams of sirens.
I begin to cry, for myself, for the children.
A voice in my dream says
this was the midnight you were born.

Later, something brutal happened, of course,
but as to this life I had to, I woke,
and cannot, or will not, remember.
But the children, of course, were murdered,
their graves lost, their names lost,
even those two faces lost to me. Still,
this morning, inside the engine of my body,
for once, as I wept and breathed deep,

relief, waves of relief, as though the dreamed
rose would spill its petals forever.
I prayed thanks. For one night, at least,
I tried to save the children,
to keep them safe in my own body,
and knew I would again. Amen.

DANIEL HOFFMAN

The Sonnet

(Remembering Louise Bogan)

The Sonnet, she told the crowd of bearded
        youths, their hands exploring
            rumpled girls,
            is a sacred

vessel: it takes a civilization
        to conceive its shape or know
            its uses. The kids
            stared as though

          a Sphinx now spake the riddle of
                    a blasted day. And few,
                              she said, who would
                                   be *avant-garde*

consider that the term is drawn
          from tactics in the Prussian
                    war, nor think
                              when once they've breached

the fortress of a form, then send
          their shock troops yet again
                    to breach the form,
                              there's no form—

. . . they asked for her opinion of
          "the poetry of Rock."
                    After a drink
                              with the professors

she said, This is a bad time,
          bad, for poetry.
                    Then with maenad
                              gaze upon

the imaged ghost of a comelier day:
          I've enjoyed this visit,
                    your wife's sheets
                              are Irish linen.

JOHN HOLLANDER

The Lady of the Castle

Venus Pudica stands, bent. Where her hand is
Cupping her marble mound a mystery has
Come into being as the sculptor hides what
          Stone could not show yet,

Nor bronze expound. The goddess may be guarding
Herself, or in a special mode of pointing
Out (should we call it "curving in"?) her temple,
          Teaching her children

The central and precious, where they may be found.
Or indeed, as the girls say, she is hiding
Nothing, nor instructing—she is caressing
       That which she barely

Touches, warming those feelings which for her are
Wisdom blossoming even within marble.
What her maker buried she loves, and thereby
       We are revealed it.

Far in the minimal North, some contracted
Hand or eye has carved into senseless clunch an
Impudent and schematic presence, done in
       Primal intaglio,

A circle head perched on a larger circle
Of lady body, spidery legs drawn up
And outward showing off on the church tower
       Under the clock, and

Cut in a sort of Linear C, her slit.
Her hands touch nothing but her knees held open.
It is not she who joys in it, nor teaches;
       But from beneath her

A very well-hung personage indeed is
Climbing up toward her, as if far from having
Merely no words for things, their sculptor had no
       Method of using

Images for them: no things, only actions.
And thus translated into language her wedge
Would be a "Let's-get-up-on-her-and-in-there."
       Hieroglyphic

Of nature's own cuneiform, she sits high
But almost hiding in the irrelevance
Of a religious building now to the young
       Mums of the village.

Ignored, then, or misread by mythographers
—Myopically concluding that a corpus
Christi lies beneath a bungled cross—as a
       Crude Deposition,

She with her terrible thin cut is not to
Be any the less feared by those who read signs
And remember instances of their wide truths
        Narrowed in darkness:

Hers is the closed door into the stone again.
The soft traps having long since sprung, the marble
Self-adoring dolls long crumbled, hers is the
        Linear kingdom.

from **Something About It**

Its Lunch

On the shining china, white and gold,
    A cold toad
Graced with pieces of lettuces, and
Unless eaten at once, somewhere past
Chambers of mauve and peacock, behind
The strings of candied stanzas, in a
    White tiled room,
A child will go on being tortured.

BARBARA HOWES

Jim

Sat there
In a folding chair
Awaiting his father:

Sixteen
Is young, if it means
Only more beatings,

Or older
When the boy was ordered
Monthlong to his room last year—

That June crept
By in exploding slow-motion; he erupted
July 1st, like a puppy

Ran each four corners
Of the yard, while his mother's
Eyes were grey with tears . . .

Then last week his father loomed
In the doorway:—so framed,
He was shot four times;

Sound
Catapulted against the background
Hill, the slag-dark ground,

To ricochet
From that squat tannery
Which was the future.

This much older
Boy, is he in second child-
Hood now? Can he recall

More than that he sat there
In a folding chair
Waiting for his father?

Monkey Difference

The monkey difference
  From Catholic and
    Protestant comes down to
      Most peoples' fix on guilt . . .

A maxi-skirted papacy
  Fears female more
    Than monkey; its guillotine,
      Childbed, falls on woman

Each year . . . No monkey'd be named
  Calvin: hatred of bodily
    Love is not simian, nor the
      Puritan icehouse his,

Where a dressmaker's
   Dummy can hang
      In that abattoir
         Till the 20th child . . .

Monkey: his simon-pure,
   Active body may be
      A hieroglyph
         For life, pinpointing

It . . . In his leaf
   Cathedral he's on his own,
      Is monkey, as long as, leaping,
         Flying, he lands—and holds on.

ERICA JONG

Divorce

Eggs boiling in a pot.
They click
like castanets.
I put one in a cup
& slice its head off.

Under the wobbly egg white
is my first husband.
Look how small he's grown
since last we met!

"Eat me," he says agreeably.
I hesitate, then bite.

The thick yolk runs down
my thighs.

I take another egg
& slice its head.
Inside is my second husband.
This one's better done.

"You liked the white," I say,
"I liked the yolk."

He doesn't speak
but scowls as if to say:
"Everyone always eats me
in the end."

I chew him up
but I spit out
his jet-black hair,
the porcelain jackets from his teeth,
his cufflinks, fillings,
eyeglass frames. . . .

I drink my coffee
& I read the *Times*.

Another egg is boiling in the pot.

Sexual Soup

A man so sick that the sexual soup
cannot save him—

the chicken soup of sex
which cures everything:
tossed mane of noodles,
bits of pale white meat.
the globules of yellow fat
like love . . .

But he is a man so sick
no soup can save him.

His throat has healed into a scar.
Rage fills his guts.
He wants to diet on dust.

I offered to feed him
(spoon by spoon)
myself.

I offered my belly as a bowl.
I offered my hands as spoons,
my knees as tongs,
my breasts as the chafing dish
to keep us warm.

I offered my navel
as a brandy snifter.

"My tongue is gone," he said,
"I have no teeth.
My mouth is with my mother in the grave.
I've offered up my hunger to the air,
my nostrils to the wind,
my sex to death,
my eyes to nothingness & dust."

"What do you lust for then?"
I asked.

"I lust for nothing."

GALWAY KINNELL

from **The Dead Shall Be Raised Incorruptible**

In the Twentieth Century of my trespass on earth,
having exterminated one billion heathens,
heretics, Jews, Moslems, witches, mystical seekers,
black men, Asians, and Christian brothers,
every one of them for his own good,

a whole continent of red men for living in unnatural
    community
and at the same time having relations with the land,
one billion species of animals for being sub-human,
and ready to take on the bloodthirsty creatures from the
    other planets,
I, Christian man, groan out this testament of my last will.

I give my blood fifty parts polystyrene,
twenty-five parts benzene, twenty-five parts good old
   gasoline,
to the last bomber pilot aloft, that there shall be one acre
in the dull world where the kissing flower may bloom,
which kisses you so long your bones explode under its lips.

My tongue goes to the Secretary of the Dead
to tell the corpses, "I'm sorry, fellows,
the killing was just one of those things
difficult to pre-visualize—like a cow,
say, getting hit by lightning."

My stomach, which has digested
four hundred treaties giving the Indians
eternal right to their land, I give to the Indians,
I throw in my lungs which have spent four hundred years
sucking in good faith on peace pipes.

My soul I leave to the bee
that he may sting it and die, my brain
to the fly, his back the hysterical green color of slime,
that he may suck on it and die, my flesh to the advertising
   man,
the anti-prostitute, who loathes human flesh for money.

I assign my crooked backbone
to the dice maker, to chop up into dice,
for casting lots as to who shall see his own blood
on his shirt front and who his brother's,
for the race isn't to the swift but to the crooked.

To the last man surviving on earth
I give my eyelids worn out by fear, to wear
in his long nights of radiation and silence,
so that his eyes can't close, for regret
is like tears seeping through closed eyelids.

I give the emptiness my hand: the pinkie picks no more
   noses,
slag clings to the black stick of the ring finger,
a bit of flame jets from the tip of the fuck-you finger,
the first finger accuses the heart, which has vanished,
on the thumb stump wisps of smoke ask a ride into the
   emptiness.

In the Twentieth Century of my nightmare
on earth, I swear on my chromium testicles
to this testament
and last will
of my iron will, my fear of love, my itch for money, and
    my madness.

from Lastness

A black bear sits alone
in the twilight, nodding from side
to side, turning slowly around and around
on himself, scuffing the four-footed
circle into the earth. He sniffs the sweat
in the breeze, he understands
a creature, a death-creature
watches from the fringe of the trees,
finally he understands
I am no longer here, he himself
from the fringe of the trees watches
a black bear
get up, eat a few flowers, trudge away,
all his fur glistening
in the rain.

And what glistening! Sancho Fergus,
my boychild, had such great shoulders,
when he was born his head
came out, the rest of him stuck. And he opened
his eyes: his head out there all alone
in the room, he squinted with pained,
barely unglued eyes at the ninth-month's
blood splashing beneath him
on the floor. And almost
smiled, I thought, almost forgave it all in advance.

When he came wholly forth
I took him up in my hands and bent
over and smelled
the black, glistening fur
of his head, as empty space
must have bent
over the newborn planet
and smelled the grasslands and the ferns.

from **The Call Across the Valley of Not Knowing**

Of that time in a Southern jail,
when the sheriff, as he cursed me
and spat, took my hand in his hand, rocked
from the pulps the whorls
and tented archways into the tabooed realm, that underlife
where the canaries of the blood are singing, pressed
the flesh-flowers
into the dirty book of the
police-blotter, afterwards what I remembered most
was the care, the almost loving,
animal gentleness of his hand on my hand.

Better than the rest of us, he knows
the harshness of that cubicle
in hell where they put you
with all your desires undiminished, and with no body to
    appease them.

And when he himself floats out
on a sea he almost begins to remember,
floats out into a darkness he has known already;
when the moan of wind
and the gasp of lungs call to each other among the waves
and the wish to float
comes to matter not at all as he sinks under,

is it so impossible to think
he will dream back to all the hands black and white
he took in his hands
as the creation
touches him a last time all over his body?

MAXINE KUMIN

Life's Work

Mother my good girl
I remember this old story:

you fresh out of the Conservatory
at eighteen a Bach specialist
in a starched shirtwaist
begging permission to go on tour
with the nimble violinist you were
never to accompany and he
flinging his music down
the rosin from his bow
flaking line by line
like grace notes on the treble clef
and my grandfather
that estimable man I never met
scrubbing your mouth with a handkerchief
saying no daughter of mine
tearing loose the gold locket
you wore with no one's picture in it
and the whole German house on 15th Street
at righteous whiteheat. . . .

At eighteen I chose to be a swimmer.
My long hair dripped through dinner
onto the china plate.
My fingers wrinkled like Sunsweet
yellow raisins from the afternoon workout.
My mouth chewed but I was doing laps.
I entered the water like a knife.
I was all muscle and seven doors.
A frog on the turning board.
King of the Eels and the Eel's wife.
I swallowed and prayed
to be allowed to join the Aquacade
and my perfect daddy
who carried you off to elope
after the fingerboard snapped
and the violinist lost his case
my daddy wearing gravy on his face
swore on the carrots and the boiled beef
that I would come to nothing
that I would come to grief. . . .

Well, the firm old fathers are dead
and I didn't come to grief.
I came to words instead
to tell the little tale that's left:
the midnights of my childhood still go on

the stairs speak again under your foot
the heavy parlor door folds shut
and "Au Clair de la Lune"
puckers from the obedient keys
plain as a schoolroom clock ticking
and what I hear more clearly than Debussy's
lovesong is the dry aftersound
of your long nails clicking.

Amanda Dreams She Has Died and Gone to the Elysian Fields

This morning Amanda
lies down during breakfast.
The hay is hip high.
The sun sleeps on her back
as it did on the spine
of the dinosaur
the fossil bat
the first fish with feet
she was once.
A breeze fans
the deerflies from lighting.
Only a gaggle of gnats
housekeeps in her ears.
A hay plume sticks out of her mouth.

I come calling with a carrot
from which I have taken
the first bite.
She startles
she considers rising
but retracts the pistons
of her legs and accepts
as loose-lipped as a camel.

We sit together.
In this time and place
we are heart and bone.
For an hour
we are incorruptible.

DENISE LEVERTOV

Libation

Raising our glasses, smilingly
we wish one another not luck
but happiness. After half a lifetime
with and without luck,
we know we need more than luck.
It makes no difference that we're drinking
tomato juice, not wine or whiskey—
we know what we mean,
and the red juice of those virtuous
vegetable-fruits is something we both enjoy.
I remember your wonder, as at a miracle,
finding them growing on sturdy vines
in my old aunt and uncle's sun-room
ripe to pluck at the breakfast table!
We were twenty-three, and unappeasably hungry ...

We agree on tomatoes, then—and happiness?
yes, that too: we mean growth, branching,
leafing, yielding blossoms and fruit and the sharp odor
          of dreams.
We mean knowing someone as deeply,
no, deeper, than we've known each other,
we mean being known. We are wishing each other
the luck not to need luck. I mill
some pepper into my juice, though,
and salt in the ancient gesture; and what would be wrong
with tipping out half a glass
for the gods?
      We smile.
After these months of pain we begin
to admit our new lives have begun.

February 1975

The Poem Rising by Its Own Weight

The poet is at the disposal of his own night.
                                        Jean Cocteau

The singing robes fly onto your body and cling there silkily,
you step out on the rope and move unfalteringly across it,

and seize the fiery knives unscathed and
keep them spinning above you, a fountain
of rhythmic rising, falling, rising
flames,

and proudly let the chains
be wound about you, ready
to shed them, link by steel link,
padlock by padlock—

                    but when your graceful
confident shrug and twist drives the metal
into your flesh and the python grip of it tightens
and you see rust on the chains and blood in your pores
and you roll
over and down a steepness into a dark hole
and there is not even the sound of mockery in the distant air
somewhere above you where the sky was,
no sound but your own breath panting:
then it is that the miracle
walks in, on his swift feet,
down the precipice straight into the cave,
opens the locks,
knots of chain fall open,
twists of chain unwind themselves,
links fall asunder,
in seconds there is a heap of scrap-
metal at your ankles, you step free and at once
he turns to go—

but as you catch at him with a cry,
clasping his knees, sobbing your gratitude,
with what radiant joy he turns to you,
and raises you to your feet,
and strokes your disheveled hair,
and holds you,

                holds you,
                        holds you
close and tenderly before he vanishes.

JAMES MERRILL

Voices from the Other World

Presently at our touch the teacup stirred,
Then circled lazily about
From A to Z. The first voice heard
(If they are voices, these mute spellers-out)
Was that of an engineer

Originally from Cologne.
Dead in his 22nd year
Of cholera in Cairo, he had "known
No happiness." He once met Goethe, though.
Goethe had told him: *Persevere*.

Our blind hound whined. With that, a horde
Of voices gathered above the Ouija board,
Some childish and, you might say, blurred
By sleep; one little boy
Named Will, reluctant possibly in a ruff

Like a large-lidded page out of El Greco, pulled
Back the arras for that next voice,
Cold and portentous: "All is lost.
Flee this house. Otto von Thurn und Taxis.
Obey. You have no choice."

Frightened, we stopped; but tossed
Till sunrise striped the rumpled sheets with gold.
Each night since then, the moon waxes,
Small insects flit round a cold torch
We light, that sends them pattering to the porch . . .

But no real Sign. New voices come,
Dictate addresses, begging us to write;
Some warn of lives misspent, and all of doom
In ways that so exhilarate
We are sleeping sound of late.

Last night the teacup shattered in a rage.
Indeed, we have grown nonchalant
Towards the other world. In the gloom here,
Our elbows on the cleared
Table, we talk and smoke, pleased to be stirred

Rather by buzzings in the jasmine, by the drone
Of our own voices and poor blind Rover's wheeze,
Than by those clamoring overhead,
Obsessed or piteous, for a commitment
We still have wit to postpone

Because, once looked at lit
By the cold reflections of the dead
Risen extinct but irresistible,
Our lives have never seemed more full, more real,
Nor the full moon more quick to chill.

The Octopus

There are many monsters that a glassen surface
Restrains. And none more sinister
Than vision asleep in the eye's tight translucence.
Rarely it seeks now to unloose
Its diamonds. Having divined how drab a prison
The purest mortal tissue is,
Rarely it wakes. Unless, coaxed out by lusters
Extraordinary, like the octopus
From the gloom of its tank half-swimming half-drifting
Toward anything fair, a handkerchief
Or child's face dreaming near the glass, the writher
Advances in a godlike wreath
Of its own wrath. Chilled by such fragile reeling
A hundred blows of a boot-heel
Shall not quell, the dreamer wakes and hungers.
Percussive pulses, drum or gong,
Build in his skull their loud entrancement,
Volutions of a Hindu dance.
His hands move clumsily in the first conventional
Gestures of assent.
He is willing to undergo the volition and fervor
Of many fleshlike arms, observe
These in their holiness of indirection
Destroy, adore, evolve, reject—
Till on glass rigid with his own seizure
At length the sucking jewels freeze.

ROBERT MORGAN

Mountain Bride

They say Revis found a flatrock
on the ridge just
    perfect for a natural hearth,
and built his cabin with a stick

and clay chimney right over it.
On their wedding night he lit
    a fire to dry away the mountain
chill of late spring, and flung on

applewood to dye
the room with molten color while
    he and Martha that was a Parrish
warmed the sheets between the tick

stuffed with leaves and its feather
cover. Under that wide hearth
    a nest of rattlers,
they'll knot a hundred together,

had wintered and were coming awake.
The warming rock
    flushed them out early.
It was she

who wakened to their singing near
the embers and roused him to go look.
    Before he reached the fire
more than a dozen struck

and he died yelling her to stay
on the big four-poster.
    Her uncle coming up the hollow
with a gift bearham two days

later found her shivering there
marooned above a pool
    of hungry snakes,
and the body beginning to swell.

ROBERT PACK

The Mugger

He will know me when we meet, his blade
clicking open, telling him. I offer
my cape, embroidered in Persia. It is not
what he wants. I show him the secret pocket
in my attaché case and hand him the key.
He rejects it. My Diner's card, Mobil Oil,
a hundred dollars cash—he throws them
over his shoulder. I show him my mother's picture.
She has always loved me, I tell him
more gruffly than I mean to. He pauses,
lights fire to it, letting it burn back
to his fingertips, glinting on the knife blade.
He says nothing and moves back a step.
A heart is tattooed on his hand. His slick hair
is sweetly perfumed. I take off my tie.
I take off my shoes, my argyle socks.
His lips open, he has one golden tooth.
I stand naked before him. He eyes me
like a doctor. I tell him I was a happy child.
I tell him I am good to my wife,
that my children trust me. He slides my clothes
into the gutter with his foot. Down the street,
where I cannot see, I hear a cry—or a cheer!
I recall the night of my election,
the crowd, and my prepared remarks.
I tell him my plans. I describe my house,
how my fruit trees have grown, how one can smell
the blossoms in the wind at twenty yards—
like his hair. The blade is still. Its glint
reminds me of the pond where I hunted turtles
as a boy at dawn when the mist came up.
I tell him how I made my sister haul the pail
to put them in, her hair golden as his tooth.
He tells me to get dressed, but I have more
to say: change is possible, reason
never rests until it leads men to the truth
where justice dwells. I take more plans
from the attaché case, insisting that he read.

He shuts his knife. I demand that he study them.
They are for him. I have done everything for him.
He tries to move away, but I have him now.
I put the key into his ear and turn it
until he promises to let me keep
his gold tooth as a pledge. He tells me
he has always loved his wife, that his children
are happy. Soon his garden will be ripe.
My plans are coming true. Nothing can stop me now.

MARGE PIERCY

To the Pay Toilet

You strop my anger, especially
when I find you in restaurant or bar
and pay for the same liquid, coming and going.
In bus depots and airports and turnpike plazas
some woman is dragging in with three kids hung off her
shrieking their simple urgency like gulls.
She's supposed to pay for each of them
and the privilege of not dirtying the corporate floor.
Sometimes a woman in a uniform's on duty
black or whatever the prevailing bottom is
getting thirty cents an hour to make sure
no woman sneaks her full bladder under a door.
Most blatantly you shout that waste of resources
for the greatest good of the smallest number
where twenty pay toilets line up glinty clean
and at the end of the row one free toilet
oozes from under its crooked door,
while a row of weary women carrying packages and
    babies
wait and wait and wait to do
what only the dead find unnecessary.

A Proposal for Recycling Wastes

Victim not of an accident
but of a life that was accidental
she sprawls on the nursing
home bed: has a photo
of herself at seventeen with long
brown hair, face paprikaed
with freckles, like a granddaughter
who may live
in San Diego. In Decatur
love picked her up
by the scruff and after
out of work wandering dumped
her in Back of the Yards Chicago.
A broken nose, the scar of love;
stretch marks and a tooth lost
each child, love like
tuberculosis, it happens.
And generation used
her like a rutted highway
the heavy trucks trundling
their burdens all day and all
night. Her body was a thing
stuffed, swollen, convulsed
empty, producing for the state
and Jesus three soldiers and one
sailor, two more breeding wombs
and a (defunct) prostitute.
The surviving corporal drives
hack, one mother waits tables;
the other typed, married into
the suburbs and is den
mother to cubscouts.
The husband, cocksman, luckless
horse and numbersplayer, security
guard and petty thief, died
at fifty-two of cancer
of the colon.
Now like an abandoned car
she has been towed here
to fall apart.
She wastes, drugged,

in a spreading pool
of urine.
Surely she could be used,
her eyes, her heart
still strangely sturdy,
her one good kidney
could be salvaged for the rich
who are too valuable at seventy-four
to throw away.

SONIA SANCHEZ

So This Is Our Revolution

nigguhs with naturrrals
still smoken pot drinken
shooten needles into they arms
for some yestuhday dreams.
sistuhs fucken other sistuhs'
husbands
        cuz the rev o lu shun dun
freed them to fight the
enemy (they sistuhs)
                yeh.
                    the
revo lushun is here
               and we still
where our fathas /
                muthas were
twenty yrs ago
              cept we all look
prettier.
        cmon brothas.   sistuhs.
how bout a fo /
              real /   revolu/shun
with a fo / real
              battle to be fought
outside of bed /
              room / minds.

like. there are children
to be taught to love they blk / selves
a blk / culture
                    to be raised on this
wite / assed / universe.
                            how bout a
fo / real
        sun inspired life
                            while
these modern / day / missionary /
    moon / people
go to the moon
            where they belong.

MAY SARTON

Bears and Waterfalls

Kind kinderpark
For bear buffoons
And fluid graces—
Who dreamed this lark
Of spouts, lagoons,
And huge fur faces?

For bears designed
Small nooks, great crags,
And Gothic mountains?
For bears refined
Delightful snags,
Waterfalls, fountains?

Who had the wit to root
A forked tree where a sack
Of honey plumps on end,
A rich-bottomed fruit
To rouse a hearty whack
From passing friend?

410

Who ever did imagine
A waterspout as stool,
Or was black bear the wiser
Who sat down on this engine
To keep a vast rump cool,
Then, cooled, set free a geyser?

Who dreamed a great brown queen
Sleeked down in her rough silk
Flirting with her huge lord,
Breast-high in her tureen?—
"Splash me, delightful hulk!"
So happy and absurd.

Bear upside-down, white splendor,
All creamy, foaming fur,
And childhood's rug come true,
All nonchalance and candor,
Black pads your signature—
Who, above all, dreamed you?

When natural and formal
Are seen to mate so well,
Where bears and fountains play,
Who would return to normal?
Go back to human Hell?
Not I. I mean to stay,

To hold this happy chance
Forever in the mind,
To be where waters fall
And archetypes still dance,
As they were once designed
In Eden for us all.

Burial

The old man who had dug the small pit
Opened the two boxes with a penknife
And let the ashes fall down into it,
The ashes of this husband and his wife,
My father and my mother gently laid
Into the earth and mingled there for good.

We watched the wind breathe up an ashen breath
And blow thin smoke along the grass—
And that was all: the bitterness of death
Lifted to air, laid in the earth. All was
Terribly silent where four people stood
Tall in the air, believing what they could.

CHARLES SIMIC

Solitude

There now, where the first crumb
Falls from the table
You think no one hears it
As it hits the floor

But somewhere already
The ants are putting on
Their Quakers' hats
And setting out to visit you.

Ax

Whoever swings an ax
Knows the body of man
Will again be covered with fur.
The stench of blood and swamp water
Will return to its old resting place.
They'll spend their winters
Sleeping like the bears.
The skin on the breasts of their women
Will grow coarse. He who cannot
Grow teeth, will not survive.
He who cannot howl
Will not find his pack . . .

These dark prophecies were gathered,
Unknown to myself, by my body
Which understands historical probabilities,
Lacking itself, in its essence, a future.

412

Poem Without a Title

I say to the lead
Why did you let yourself
Be cast into a bullet?
Have you forgotten the alchemists?
Have you given up hope
Of turning into gold?

Nobody answers.
Lead. Bullet. With names
Such as these
The sleep is deep and long.

Fork

This strange thing must have crept
Right out of hell.
It resembles a bird's foot
Worn around the cannibal's neck.

As you hold it in your hand,
As you stab with it into a piece of meat,
It is possible to imagine the rest of the bird:
Its head which like your fist
Is large, bald, beakless and blind.

LOUIS SIMPSON

Isidor

Isidor was always plotting
to overthrow the government.
The family lived in one room. . . .
A window rattles,
a woman coughs,
snow drifts over the rooftops . . .
despair. An intelligent household.

One day, there's a knock at the door. . . .
The police! A confusion. . . .
Isidor's wife throws herself
on the mattress . . . she groans
as though she is in labor.
The police search everywhere,
and leave. Then a leg comes out . . .
an arm . . . then a head with spectacles.
Isidor was under the mattress!

When I think about my family
I have a feeling of suffocation.
Next time . . . how about the oven?

The mourners are sitting around
weeping and tearing their clothes.
The inspector comes. He looks in the oven . . .
there's Isidor, with his eyes
shut fast . . . his hands are folded.
The inspector nods, and goes.
Then a leg comes out, and the other.
Isidor leaps, he dances . . .

"Praise God, may His Name be exalted!"

Sensibility

Her face turned sour.
It broke into tears.
She wept, she wept.
The streams were wide and deep.
Wide and deep were the streams
of time that were flowing toward me.
Neither she nor I could control
the flow of her tears,
and so, in the middle of summer,
this tender girl and I
were married in rain-water.

American Dreams

In dreams my life came toward me,
my loves that were slender as gazelles.
But America also dreams. . . .
Dream, you are flying over Russia,
dream, you are falling in Asia.

As I look down the street
on a typical sunny day in California
it is my house that is burning
and my dear ones that lie in the gutter
as the American army enters.

Everyday I wake far away
from my life, in a foreign country.
These people are speaking a strange language.
It is strange to me
and strange, I think, even to themselves.

The Wall Test

When they say "To the wall!"
and the squad does a right turn,

where do you stand? With the squad
or the man against the wall?

In every case
you find yourself standing against the wall.

W. D. SNODGRASS

The Men's Room in the College Chapel

Here, in the most Unchristian basement
of this "fortress for the Christian mind,"
they close these four gray walls, shut out shame,
and scribble of sex and excrement,
draw bestial pictures and sign their name—
the old, lewd defiance of mankind.

The subversive human in his cell—
burn his vile books, stamp out his credo,
lock him away where no light falls,
and no live word can go back to tell
where he's entombed like Monte Cristo—
still, he'll carve his platform in the walls.

In need, men have painted the deep caves
to summon their animal, dark gods;
even the reviled, early Christians
prayed in catacombs to outlawed Good,
laid their honored dead and carved out graves
with pious mottos of resistance.

This is the last cave, where the soul
turns in its corner like a beast
nursing its wounds, where it contemplates
vengeance, how it shall gather to full
strength, what lost cause shall it vindicate,
returning, masterless and twisted.

What We Said

Stunned in that first estrangement,
We went through the turning woods
Where inflamed leaves sick as words
Spun, wondering what the change meant.

Half gone, our road led onwards
By barbed wire, past the ravine
Where a lost couch, snarled in vines,
Spilled its soiled, gray innards

Into a garbage mound.
We came, then, to a yard
Where tarpaper, bottles and charred
Boards lay on the trampled ground.

This had been someone's lawn.
And, closing up like a wound,
The cluttered hole in the ground
A life had been built upon.

In the high grass, cars had been.
On the leafless branches, rags
And condoms fluttered like the flags
Of new orders moving in.

We talked of the last war, when
Houses, cathedral towns, shacks—
Whole continents went into wreckage.
What fools could do that again?

Ruin on every side—
We would set our loves in order,
Surely, we told each other.
Surely. That's what we said.

BARRY SPACKS

My Mother's Childhood

When she still used words, my mother told
of her childhood: they were poor, her father
peddled insurance door-to-door
in Portland, where the firehouse bell
would ring *no school* come heavy snow
and she'd stand—her little shrug, her sheepish
grin—in the candy factory yard,
waiting, patient child in the cold,
for sometimes an upper window would open,
someone would throw down gum, lumps
as large as little pumpernickels;
grey, but tasty. How she chewed!
She never wondered then, was it pure?
rejected?—chewed till her jawbones ached
and the tears welled in her eyes—they only
threw to her, to her, because
she waited,
and was good.

"Who Then Is Crazy?"

At evening I pause, neglected pen
in hand like a miniature fasces, eyes
revealing a hurt no calm nor healthy
children nor even guiltless sleep
can heal, for look, the crazies run
in the streets, they gnaw
their nails for blood . . .

I think it is their pain for which
I yearn—who then is crazy?—feeling
nothing, the horror
of feeling nothing,
they fuck for their lives
in heatless rooms.

Teaching the Penguins to Fly

The penguins must have had it once,
some drive and wingspan, back before
they joined up in committees to waddle
on slow-moving ice floes, flapping rhetorical
vans. My daughter's first ambition
was teaching them to fly, and she hasn't
forgotten: a poster of Emperor penguins
hangs on her bedroom wall where Beatles
still remain, and Aquarius,
her sign—the fuzzy young and vaguely
gazing adults, all of them look
like kids who've lost their expedition
leader. Emperors. Most of them show
color enough at the neck for the mythseeking
eye to propose, from vestigial yellows,
ancestor roc-macaws. Fifteen,
already the culture-heroine knows
it's nothing like easy to start them moving;
she'll leap and flap her arms to teach
the huge idea: up on the toes,
higher, higher, lift those wings!—
trials down ice-slicked runways, lengthy

political sessions, building the Movement,
until the strongest risk the winter
sky, shedding their dickies, becoming
through generations enormous budgies
who sing in the jungle, in general bird,
the epic tale of the odd liberator
in shirt and jeans who beat the air
with her arms, who sang them
Woody Guthrie, who
brought the revolution
uncramping their lives.

RUTH STONE

Periphery

You are not wanted
I said to the older body
Who was listening near the cupboards.
But outside on the porch
They were all eating.
The body dared not
Put its fingers in its mouth.
Behave, I whispered,
You have a wart on your cheek
And everyone knows you drink.
But that's all right, I relented,
It isn't generally known
How clever you are.
I know you aren't appreciated.
The body hunted for something good to eat,
But the food had all been eaten by the others.
They laughed together carelessly outside the kitchen.
The body hid in the pantry near the refrigerator.
After a while it laughed, too.
It listened to all the jokes and it laughed.

Bargain

I was not ready for this world
Nor will I ever be.
But came an infant periled
By my mother sea,
And crying piteously.

Before my father's sword,
His heavy voice of thunder,
His cloud hung fiery eyes,
I ran, a living blunder.

After the hawker's cries,
Desiring to be shared
I hid among the flies.

Myself became the fruit and vender.
I began to sing.
Mocking the caged birds
I made my offering.

"Sweet cream and curds . . .
Who will have me,
Who will have me?"
And close upon my words,
"I will," said poverty.

Beginning to Live

I'm beginning to understand that man in old boots
Who sits on his front porch looking at the wood pile;
A bottle of booze behind his wash basin.
He is waiting for snow.
In the wet air crows and bluejays set up a rollick
And try for the sun. But the heifers, grazing through
    November,
Slog in the sticky clay, their cloven marks filling up
With rain among the moonstone mushrooms.
Those women who gathered squaw-wood, their eyes
Were not clear. They were red rimmed, smoke irritated;
But stoic from looking at the brown quiet of fallen pine
    needles.
Sitting here saying things to myself, the long staccato drill

Of leg-rubbing insects stops for a moment when the rain
   begins.
A leaf imitating a dying butterfly falls in reluctant spirals.
I will sit here drinking until it snows and then
I'll go in and build a fire.

JOHN TAGLIABUE

December 1970

You never frightened me
and you were never oppressive
I do not feel you looming   you did not plant guilt
      you never put moral meanings
         around our necks like Ideals or tomb stones
you are never a weight
I do not think your body can decay
and your mind is not like a Library or School of
   Philosophy or an Engineering Building
You were fully here
You were largely present
You do not hang around like a Puritan or Stoical Corpse
   saying do this or finish that
You didn't even mind my preaching (this sort of stuff)
      You could accept it
the way the holy universe accepts Christmas
You were not wilful and you made no slaves

You

Deck out
         the Decalogue
said the tipsy Captain to the Scrubbing Sailors;
the waves insisted on knocking them down;
the air insisted on caressing them and singing
   to them,
the fish insisted on nibbling at them like dreams,

421

the Magna Carta and the Carta Geographica and the
    Magnet Wheel
insisted on following them, so everytime they came up
    spouting
they were all nationalistic, humanistic and above all
Transcendental Misfits. Their fitful dancing late
    at night
on the Waters of the World like the Belly of Creation
aroused Gossip. Theologians predicted. But when they
    Returned Home
with Mermaids or Pearls or Treasures in their High Hands
    they became the Rulers
that are now seen sitting on any Cliff like the
    Title above a Poem.

JAMES TATE

Teaching the Ape to Write Poems

They didn't have much trouble
teaching the ape to write poems:
first they strapped him into the chair,
then tied the pencil around his hand
(the paper had already been nailed down).
Then Dr. Bluespire leaned over his shoulder
and whispered into his ear:
"You look like a god sitting there.
Why don't you try writing something?"

My Great Great etc. Uncle Patrick Henry

There's a fortune to be made in just about everything
in this country, somebody's father had to invent
everything—baby food, tractors, rat poisoning.
My family's obviously done nothing since the beginning
of time. They invented poverty and bad taste
and getting by and taking it from the boss.

O my mother goes around chewing her nails and
spitting them in a jar: You should be ashamed
of yourself she says, think of your family.
My family I say what have they ever done but
paint by numbers the most absurd disgusting scenes
of plastic squalor and human degradation.
Well then think of your great great etc. Uncle
Patrick Henry.

ROBERT PENN WARREN

from Homage to Theodore Dreiser on the Centennial of His Birth (August 27, 1871)

1. Psychological Profile

Who is the ugly one slump-slopping down the street?
Who is the chinless wonder with the potato-nose?
Can't you hear the soft *plop* of the pancake-shaped feet?

He floats, like Anchises' son, in the cloud of his fine new
    clothes,
Safe, safe at last, from the street's sneer, toward a queen
    who will fulfill
The fate devised him by Venus—but where, oh when!
    That is what he never knows

Born with one hand in his pants and one in the till,
He knows that the filth of self, to be loved, must be clad
    in glory,
So once stole twenty-five dollars to buy a new coat, and
    that is why still

The left eye keeps squinting backward—yes, history
Is gum-shoeing closer behind, with the constable-hand
    that clutches.
Watch his mouth, how it moves without sound, he is
    telling himself his own old story.

Full of screaming his soul is, and a stench like live flesh
    that scorches.
It's the screaming, and stench, of a horse-barn aflame,
And the great beasts rear and utter, their manes flare up
    like torches.

From lies, masturbation, vainglory, and shame,
He moves in his dream of ladies swan-necked, with asses
    ample and sweet,
But knows that no kiss heals his soul, it is always the
    same.

The same—but a brass band plays in the distance, and the
    midnight cricket,
Though thinly, asseverates his name. He seeks amid the
    day's traffic a sign—
Some horseshoe or hunchback or pin—that now, at last,
    at the end of this street

He will enter upon his reality: but enters only in-
To your gut, or your head, or your heart, to enhouse
    there and stay,
And in that hot darkness lie lolling and swell—like a
    tumor, perhaps benign.

May I present Mr. Dreiser? He will write a great novel,
    someday.

2. Vital Statistics

On the wrong side of the tracks—that was where
He was born, and he never let you forget it, and his
    sisters
Had hot crotches and round heels.
He knew the gnaw of hunger, and how the first wind of
    winter feels.
He was born into the age of conspicuous consumption,
    and knew
How the heart, in longing, numbly congeals

Nothing could help nothing, not reading Veblen or even
    Freud, for
The world is a great ass propped high on pillows, the cunt
Winks.

Dreiser,
However, could not feel himself worthy. Not,
At least, of love. His nails, . .
Most horribly, were bitten. At night,
Sometimes, he wept. The bed springs
Creaked with the shift of his body, which,
In the Age of Faith and of Contempt of the World,
Would have been called a sack
Of stercorry: i.e., that matter the body ejects.
Sometimes he wept for the general human condition,
But he was hell on women.

He had never loved any woman, he confessed,
Except his mother, whose broken shoes, he,
In childhood, had once caressed,
In the discovery of pity.

               Have you ever
Seen midnight moonlight on the Wabash,
While the diesel rigs boom by?
Have you ever thought how the moonlit continent
Would look from the tearless and unblinking distance of
   God's wide eye?

3. Moral Assessment

You need call no psychiatrist
To anatomize his pain.
He suffers but the pain all men
Suffer in their human kind.
No—suffers, too,
His nobility of mind.

He denies it, he sneers at it,
In his icy nightmare of
The superlative of self;
Tries to, but cannot theorize past
The knowledge that
Others suffer, too, at last.

He is no philosopher.
His only gift is to enact
All that his deepest self abhors,
And learn, in his self-contemptive distress,
The secret worth
Of all our human worthlessness.

THEODORE WEISS

Ways of Loving

First there is the student
who so adores his teacher
he must satisfy that feeling: he runs
off with the teacher's wife.

And then there is another,
of a gratitude akin to worship,
who much later, out of very gratitude
and worship grown resentful,

feels obliged—if he's to know
some freedom and a sense of selfhood—
to attack his teacher, to excoriate
the hand that's led him this far.

And likewise a young painter
out of admiration for an older rubs
out a lovely sketch. How else possess
this man who means so much to him?

Or earlier no other cared enough
to need to draw a magic circle
of rude rallies and vituperations
hemmed a portrait of the man who vexed

the drawer since the former
had anticipated, so subdued, many
of the feelings, inspirations, of him
offended: Blake, Will Blake,

beat in magnificent fury
against *The Works of Sir Joshua
Reynolds, Knt.,* who understood enough—
in this the more insufferable—

to realize ". . . when me
they fly I am the wings." And so,
those wings ripped off and trampled on,
the teacher knows success.

RICHARD WILBUR

A Shallot

The full cloves
Of your buttocks, the convex
Curve of your belly, the curved
Cleft of your sex—

Out of this corm
That's planted in strong thighs
The slender stem and radiant
Flower rise.

April 5, 1974

The air was soft, the ground still cold.
In the dull pasture where I strolled
Was something I could not believe.
Dead grass appeared to slide and heave,
Though still too frozen-flat to stir,
And rocks to twitch, and all to blur.
What was this rippling of the land?
Was matter getting out of hand
And making free with natural law?
I stopped and blinked, and then I saw
A fact as eerie as a dream.
There was a subtle flood of steam
Moving upon the face of things.
It came from standing pools and springs
And what of snow was still around;
So that the freeze was coming out,
As when a set mind, blessed by doubt,
Relaxes into mother-wit.
Flowers, I said, will come of it.

Piccola Commedia

He is no one I really know,
The sun-charred, gaunt young man
By the highway's edge in Kansas
Thirty-odd years ago.

On a tourist-cabin veranda
Two middle-aged women sat;
One, in a white dress, fat,
With a rattling glass in her hand,

Called "Son, don't you feel the heat?
Get up here into the shade."
Like a good boy, I obeyed,
And was given a crate for a seat

And an Orange Crush and gin.
"This state," she said, "is hell."
Her thin friend cackled, "Well, dear,
You've gotta fight sin with sin."

"No harm in a drink; my stars!"
Said the fat one, jerking her head.
"And I'll take no lip from Ed,
Him with his damn cigars."

Laughter. A combine whined
On past, and dry grass bent
In the backwash; liquor went
Like an ice-pick into my mind.

Beneath her skirt I spied
Two sea-cows on a floe.
"Go talk to Mary Jo, son,
She's reading a book inside."

As I gangled in at the door
A pink girl, curled in a chair,
Looked up with an ingénue stare.
Screenland lay on the floor.

Amazed by her starlet's pout
And the way her eyebrows arched,
I felt both drowned and parched.
Desire leapt up like a trout.

"Hello," she said, and her gum
Gave a calculating crack.
At once, from the lightless back
Of the room there came the grumble

Of someone heaving from bed,
A Zippo's click and flare,
Then, more and more apparent,
The shuffling form of Ed,

Who neither looked nor spoke
But moved in profile by,
Blinking one gelid eye
In his elected smoke.

This is something I've never told,
And some of it I forget.
But the heat! I can feel it yet,
And that conniving cold.

MARYA ZATURENSKA

Once in an Ancient Book

Once, in an ancient book,
Remembering what I read,
Lines scattered to the wind
Or buried in the sand,
Words quoted, widely spread,
Now lost to humankind
In a dry, dead land,

Still, still, some glory thrives,
Blooms and has many lives,
Through deepest memory
Retains strange influence—glows
In clear serenity
Through longing or repose.

It tells how beauty flows
In some obscure delight
Through pain, through failing sight,
Through subterranean streams
Of love, through the very soul
Longing to be made whole,
Or sees the dark made bright—
Sees also from a height
Some secret goal.

New York City

JACK ANDERSON

Going to Norway

I asked my parents,
"Have you ever thought
of going to Norway?
You are Andersons
and deserve to know
Norway, where we all began.
Do you not wonder
how things are in Norway?
I know that I wonder."
And my parents said,
                    "Yes,
we shall go to Norway,
we are Andersons
and want to see where
our people began.
We are growing old:
we must go now."
                  Yet they stayed
on the dock, staring
at the water
as ship after ship
sailed toward the north,
toward Norway.
              So I said
to my parents, "Now,
you must leave now.
These are the boats
that are leaving for Norway.
It is not long
or far."
          Then my parents said,
"Yes, we want to see
Norway: we are Andersons.
But it is so far."

                    They stayed
where they were, watching
the boats leave for Norway
and trying to picture it,
even testing a few words
of that dear language
on their tongues

                    —but standing
still, never moving,
never climbing aboard,
though I kept pleading,
"Please, now, you must leave now
if you want to see Norway."
"Norway?" they murmured,
"Norway? Ah, where is that?"
They stood very still,
grayness crept through their hair;
it frightened me to see them
growing so old,
for I had not thought
such a thing possible.
At last I said,
                    "I must go
to Norway. I am
an Anderson
and want to know
where all of us began.
I must go now."
                    They stood
on the dock, waving
out at the water, and I
waved back over the water
which darkened between us
with distance and tears.

JOHN ASHBERY

Mixed Feelings

A pleasant smell of frying sausages
Attacks the sense, along with an old, mostly invisible
Photograph of what seems to be girls lounging around
An old fighter bomber, circa 1942 vintage.
How to explain to these girls, if indeed that's what they
    are,
These Ruths, Lindas, Pats and Sheilas
About the vast change that's taken place
In the fabric of our society, altering the texture
Of all things in it? And yet
They somehow look as if they knew, except
That it's so hard to see them, it's hard to figure out
Exactly what kind of expressions they're wearing.
What are your hobbies, girls? Aw nerts,
One of them might say, this guy's too much for me.
Let's go on and out, somewhere
Through the canyons of the garment center
To a small café and have a cup of coffee.
I am not offended that these creatures (that's the word)
Of my imagination seem to hold me in such light esteem,
Pay so little heed to me. It's part of a complicated
Flirtation routine, anyhow, no doubt. But this talk of
The garment center? Surely that's California sunlight
Belaboring them and the old crate on which they
Have draped themselves, fading its Donald Duck insignia
To the extreme point of legibility.
Maybe they were lying but more likely their
Tiny intelligences cannot retain much information.
Not even one fact, perhaps. That's why
They think they're in New York. I like the way
They look and act and feel. I wonder
How they got that way, but am not going to
Waste any more time thinking about them.
I have already forgotten them
Until some day in the not too distant future
When we meet possibly in the lounge of a modern airport,
They looking as astonishingly young and fresh as when
    this picture was made

But full of contradictory ideas, stupid ones as well as
Worthwhile ones, but all flooding the surface of our minds
As we babble about the sky and the weather and the
    forests of change.

Farm Implements and Rutabagas in a Landscape

The first of the undecoded messages read: "Popeye sits
    in thunder,
Unthought of. From that shoebox of an apartment,
From livid curtain's hue, a tangram emerges: a country."
Meanwhile the Sea Hag was relaxing on a green couch:
    "How pleasant
To spend one's vacation *en la casa de Popeye*," she
    scratched
Her cleft chin's solitary hair. She remembered spinach

And was going to ask Wimpy if he had bought any
    spinach.
"M'love," he intercepted, "the plains are decked out in
    thunder
Today, and it shall be as you wish." He scratched
The part of his head under his hat. The apartment
Seemed to grow smaller. "But what if no pleasant
Inspiration plunge us now to the stars? *For this is my
    country*."

Suddenly they remembered how it was cheaper in the
    country.
Wimpy was thoughtfully cutting open a number 2 can
    of spinach
When the door opened and Swee'pea crept in. "How
    pleasant!"
But Swee'pea looked morose. A note was pinned to his
    bib. "Thunder
And tears are unavailing," it read. "Henceforth shall
    Popeye's apartment
Be but remembered space, toxic or salubrious, whole or
    scratched."

Olive came hurtling through the window; its geraniums
    scratched

436

Her long thigh. "I have news!" she gasped. "Popeye,
   forced as you know to flee the country
One musty gusty evening, by the schemes of his wizened,
   duplicate father, jealous of the apartment
And all that it contains, myself and spinach
In particular, heaves bolts of loving thunder
At his own astonished becoming, rupturing the pleasant

Arpeggio of our years. No more shall pleasant
Rays of the sun refresh your sense of growing old, nor
   the scratched
Tree-trunks and mossy foliage, only immaculate darkness
   and thunder."
She grabbed Swee'pea. "I'm taking the brat to the
   country."
"But you can't do that—he hasn't even finished his
   spinach,"
Urged the Sea Hag, looking fearfully around at the
   apartment.

But Olive was already out of earshot. Now the apartment
Succumbed to a strange new hush. "Actually it's quite
   pleasant
Here," thought the Sea Hag. "If this is all we need fear
   from spinach
Then I don't mind so much. Perhaps we could invite
   Alice the Goon over"—she scratched
One dug pensively—"but Wimpy is such a country
Bumpkin, always burping like that." Minute at first, the
   thunder

Soon filled the apartment. It was domestic thunder,
The color of spinach. Popeye chuckled and scratched
His balls: it sure was pleasant to spend a day in the
   country.

Clausa Germanis Gallia

Five years after Pastorius had written about "the
    threatening movements of war"
and had taken his ship to America,
a certain person
        lifted heavy robes proudly
        up over his left arm to display
an aging but handsome thigh. *Le Roi Soleil.*
That drooping regal lip and eye initiated
        many
        less than necessary acts.

In September, sixteen eighty-eight, after secret conferences
    at Versailles,
Louis XIV authorized—for certain "limited French
    aims"—
an invasion of the Rhineland.
He meant it as a quick war (and a cheap one),
but nothing ever goes quite as planned.
The Dauphin rapidly captured
Heidelberg, Mayence, Philippsburg, Mannheim,
    Frankenthal, Speyer, some twenty cities
in a muddy, cold campaign.
but this easy success
depended on "the enemy," a Grand Alliance of northern
    troops,
being away fighting Turks in the east.
When the Turks were unexpectedly defeated
and that great sickle of Grand Alliance troops turned
    west,
Louvois, the general, consulted with Louis on strategy,
asking him
to let him "devastate" the Palatinate, to put a barrier
    between the enemy and France.
All food, all fodder, all houses, all towns, cities, all
    that could keep up troops—all was ordered
burned and destroyed.
It was an expensive operation
which Voltaire described later:
Directions were given (it was midwinter)

438

"to the citizens of all those flourishing and well-ordered
    towns, to the inhabitants of the villages"
that they leave.
Men, women, old people and children filled the roads and
    fields. Few were killed,
but all were made homeless.
The destruction was methodical. Mannheim was torn
    stone from stone, and then Louvois suggested
shipping the stones away,
that nothing be left with which to rebuild. Louis:
    "I do not doubt you will execute this
with all diligence." He saved some chapels,
but no houses anywhere. All went down in the laborious
    flood of fire and demolition.
Voltaire said,
if Louis personally had seen the suffering,
he would "himself have extinguished the flames," but
    "in the midst of pleasures,
he signed the destruction of an entire country."
To celebrate it,
he had a medal struck that said
CLAUSA GERMANIS GALLIA, Gaul is closed to
    Germany.
This was the logic, and of course what is logical must be
    done.
Europe was "horror-struck." The Germans called the
    French "Huns." Napoleon said of it, later:
"Only Wellington and I
are up to these things."

As the burning went on, some officers had difficulty
being ruthless enough.
Tesse let the people of Heidelberg
put out fires he had started. D'Uxelles "failed" to
    demolish castles and went slow with the torch.
Louis was angry. Louvois wrote, "The King
will remember those who don't obey . . . Everything must
    be burned."
The details of how farm women wept,
reddened with flame, and their men waited
and killed the French in their hearts
go unrecorded. Palatinate children afterward
grew up malnourished and stunted and, grown,
grasped at any hope. Some explored Boehme,

some the cabala, the Rosy Cross,
some looked for a "new Christianity,"
and some read the letters now coming back from
   "Amerika."

All One

She held his head of close hard hair
that knotted in the wet,
and his lips against hers
were large but soft yet.
After she kissed him,
she could not keep her eyes
from casually or not casually
questioning his eyes.
She saw there dark. Past dark, light:
both in his gaze,
and she wondered which the white
and which the darkness was.
So the old tangle
of longing limb and limb
found her forgetting
which was her or which was him.

The Last Families in the Cabins

At a bend in the Bally-Dale road,
in a low growth of woods
an unused log cabin still stands,
its adze-squared timbers weathered
into black bars between the mortar,
and some of the bottom logs thrust out.
"There are few cabins left in these hills,
none lived in at the present time,"
the Reverend Elmer Johnson says. "In my young days,
when I began the flour route
for my uncle, Joseph Schultz, the miller,
in the late eighteen eighties,
there were still four families
lived in cabins. Only the poorest
by that time would live so.
My uncle gave me orders

my first day with the wagon,
when I would come to such and such a cabin,
a woman would come out,
and would have with her a receptacle.
She would say how much flour she needed.
I should give her what she asked.
As I was told, so it happened.
I came to a cabin, the woman came out.
She reckoned, so many loaves of bread,
and the children should have a small cake,
so she explained how much she needed.
I tried to give her more, but she refused.
'Only so much,' she said.
Then she said, 'I don't have money.'
'It's no matter,' I said as I was ordered,
and closed the wagon up and drove away.
Because people could not pay
was no reason why they should not eat."

OLGA CABRAL

The Factory

They said the furnaces were cold
the rusted doors unhinged
the vats were empty
and the soap
no longer cried.

They said the chimneys
had not smoked
in almost thirty years
they said the factory was dead
in that country of the graves.

Some gray men came
a delegation
dressed in business suits
showed me how clean
they kept the bones
how neat the warehouses

and showed me shelves
mile after mile
of ashes teeth and hair
all neatly ticketed—
the factory's byproducts
of soapmaking.

They showed me inventories
businesslike receipts
and endless requisitions
written on doors
by clerks who marked an "X"
with yellow chalk.

I left.   They were polite.
Had no way to detain me.
They shook my hand
said: Come back soon.
Then showed me to the border.

I looked back.
Were the chimneys red?
Was the factory on fire?
I said: It happened long ago.
It will not be again.

Safe across sinister borders
in my own country
I came to my own house
to my own door:
there was the yellow chalk sign
the factory's "X."

Lillian's Chair

Lillian had just arisen from her chair.
She has gone into her garden to commune with snails
to answer the birds' questions.
She has left her shawl and her cane
and that iron leg brace.
Won't she need her shawl in the garden?
Won't she be feeling the cold?

And she has forgotten her sling
thrown it carelessly aside—
the crumpled black satin
in which she cradled her dead arm
for seventeen years.
In one hand she took her straw basket
in the other her pruning shears:
"That bush needs seeing to," she muttered
and went looking for red clover, queen anne's lace.

What is she doing so long in the garden?
Where has she gone with her red hair?
She just grew tired of sitting and watching.
A vivid light pulled her into the leaves.
Woolen shawl, satin sling, iron brace—
she just walked out on them all.

Left us this empty chair.

GREGORY CORSO

Eastside Incidents

Aside from ashcans & halljohns & pigeoncoops
there were the sad backyards
the hot July stoops
There were those mad Valenti kids who killed my cat
with an umbrella
There was Dirty Myra who screwed the Rabbi's son
in the cellar
And there was Vito & Tony & Robby & Rocco
I see them now
eating poisoned mushrooms and vomiting air
killing Mr. Bloom the storekeeper
and getting the chair
I see them now
but they aren't there

Body Fished from the Seine

He floats down the Seine
The last victim of the FLN
He's Arab, he's soft, he's green
"He's a long time in the water been"
They're dragging him up now
Rope around his waist against the prow
Like a wet sponge he bounces and squirts
Somehow you feel though dead it hurts

I turned to Allen & Peter—what amazed them
Was not so much the sad victim
But how a big glass-top tourist boat
Stopped and had the tourists take note
They fresh from Eiffel and Notre-Dame
—A break of camera calm

God Is a Masturbator

Folks, sex has never been
more than a blend
of bodies doing for one
another
that which pleases
them and evolution
to do
either in desire
or in desperation
or in necessity
It serves no purpose
other than love
and life's purpose
Sexualists
are a product of sex
We are made by sex
Sex made the Salvation Army
We are sex
There is nothing dark
about this magic
And those pangs of lust
which make you sick
Those unthinkable dreams

444

which fill you with doubt
—as long as wild joys emit
from an enthusiastic spirit
eat the dust! *shout!*
Thank God one's thoughts
excite as much as flesh
Thank God there's a place
in all this he and she
and he and he
and she and she
for a me and me—

EDWARD FIELD

The Reservoir

The ancient reservoir,
an underground lake beneath the city,
has been closed to the public by the government
due to stringent budget cuts.

The news fills me with dismay.
It was the only thing I cared about
in that city of minarets, domes, and ruined palaces.
And to think I could have seen it
but passed it by, dismissing it
as a minor tourist attraction, not worth
spending fifteen minutes or fifty cents on.

I suppose there was nothing much to it:
You could go out on it in a boat,
though never all the way.
Imagine a city having a source of sweet water under it,
not needing aqueducts or to use the polluted river.

And maybe even it was a city underground,
now flooded, as the sewers of modern Jerusalem
once were Roman streets.

Too late I realize it was one of the important things.

It was closed for centuries
before being rediscovered and opened again.
And even if the population
never thought or even knew about it
still its presence must have affected them.
Like a desert is an energy accumulator,
a mountain a magnetic pole,
bodies of water give off an exciting influence.

Now it is shut again
and those carved pillars of limestone
that stretch away into the gloom
may collapse and the whole thing fill up with garbage,
become a sewer instead of a reservoir,
that underground lake, sacred to dervishes,
lost track of, and profaned.

And for how long, O my people,
I cry from the bottom of my wretched heart,
will it still be possible to reopen it, and explore?

The Lost, Dancing

after Cavafy

When the drums come to your door
do not try to shut them out,
do not turn away and resist them,
for they have come to tell you what you need to hear,
they are your fate.
When Antony heard them
he knew then that he had lost Egypt forever.
He did not shriek or tear his clothes
for he always knew they would come someday.
What the drums speak to you
is so inevitable you have to agree with them—
nothing else could be right.
So when the drummers and dancers come to your door
your life changes,
and with no bitterness
but with a sad smile
—after all what you had you had,
you loved the way few men love—

and as someone who was worthy of such a kingdom,
join the army of the lost, dancing,
follow the drums
and turn and wave goodbye
to the Alexandria you are losing.

Rio de Janeiro
Carnival, 1974

ISABELLA GARDNER

That Was Then

Union Pier Michigan. We called it Shapiro
Shangri La. People said I needed a passport.
I was the only Shicksa there. Kolya Shura
Manya Tanya and Sonya, Sulya Myra and
Vera they were there. And Riva a young girl then.
Soda pop and ice cream parlors, no bars,
Delicatessens but no liquor stores.
They spoke fractured English fractured Yiddish
and fractured Russian when they did not want
their children to understand. Most husbands
drove down from Chicago fridays but mine
came to me thursdays bringing the squat green
bottles of Chilean white wine I drank
(he was angry if I forgot to buy
cucumbers). My daughter then five, now in
Bedlam, chased butterflies and thirty years
ago my infant son, now for some years
lost, was happy too. I washed his diapers
in a tub and hung them up in the sun.
Instead of a play-pen, my husband, Seymour,
called Simcha which means joy, made a paddock
for him. Dan did not like to be cooped up
(nor did Rose, my daughter Rosy; nor did she)
not then, not later, never. Dan was last
seen in Columbia South America.
Simcha little Rosy   littler Daniel

and the Shicksa we were all of us joy—
full then in Shapiro Shangri La when
we were young and laughing. On the lake beach
the women waded and grossiped. The men,
supine on the hot sand sucked in the sun
through every work and city tired pore
and on the blithe beach played chess needling each
other, "singing" they called it. The Shicksa
swam and her daughter, round pink Rosy made
castles out of sand and when the big rough
boys' unseeing feet crushed her battlements
she cried. (as she would later, as she did
later, as she does now and must again
in inexorable time) Ah but then
it was different. The first summer at our
Michigan Shangri La we shared one half
a cottage with Seymour's sister Molly
Molly the matriarch and my mother
too Molly ample Yiddishe mama
bountiful heart bountiful flesh married
to tender Ben Blevitsky book-binder
and Bolshevik, not Communist though he
thought he was and paid his Party dues.
He pressed on me, a bemused fellow traveller
The Daily Worker which I occasionally
scanned. Aside from Ben's misguided fealty
to a party that betrayed his each, his
every dream, he taught the Shicksa wisdom,
ancient, Hebraic, of the heart and pulse.
This Shicksa loved him all his life. He died
attacking Zionists. In the debate
the heckling struck his heart and aged eighty two
gentle Ben Blevitsky fell down and died.
That first summer the Shicksa shared the stove
with Molly who wouldn't let her cook
a meal but did teach her to cook kugel
and fix gefilte fish. (It was only
the Shicksa's second marriage and so she
had not yet lost her appetite for cooking,
that came after the fourth marriage when
she recklessly played house with a fifth man)
Political not pious there was not
kept, a kosher kitchen. Molly and Ben
once took the bus to Chicago saying

they'd be back saturday night for supper
saying Be well Bellotchka but don't cook!
Later Molly cheeks streaming with laughter
crowed to cronies "The Shicksa cooked a haser
for the Shabbas!" Stuck with cloves it was,
the scored cuts thumbed full of dark brown sugar
hot powdered mustard and the fresh squeezed juice
of sweet oranges and the whole ham smeared
with that luscious mixture and therewith glazed
and all ate that haser with high delight
the Blevitskys, Molly, Ben, and their Bob and Riva
Rose, Simcha and his Bellotchka—the cook
ate and ate while the infant Daniel slept.
      That was then. That was then.

ALLEN GINSBERG

I Am a Victim of the Telephone

When I lay down to sleep dream the Wishing Well it rings
"Have you a new play for the brokendown theater?"
When I write in my notebook poem it rings
"Buster Keaton is under the brooklyn bridge on Frankfort
   and Pearl . . ."
When I unsheath my skin extend my cock toward
   someone's thighs fat or thin, boy or girl
Tingaling—"Please get him out of jail . . . the police are
   crashing down"
When I lift the soupspoon to my lips, the phone on the
   floor begins purring
"Hello it's me—I'm in the park two broads from Iowa . . .
   nowhere to sleep last night . . . hit 'em in the mouth"
When I muse at smoke crawling over the roof outside my
   street window
purifying Eternity with my eye observation of grey
   vaporous columns in the sky
ring ring "Hello this is Esquire be a dear and finish your
   political commitment manifesto"

When I listen to radio presidents roaring on the convention
    floor
the phone also chimes in "Rush up to Harlem with us
    and see the riots"
Always the telephone linked to all the hearts of the world
    beating at once
crying my husbands gone my boyfriend's busted forever
    my poetry was rejected
won't you come over for money and please won't you
    write me a piece of bullshit
How are you dear can you come to Easthampton we're
    all here bathing in the ocean we're all so lonely
and I lay back on my pallet contemplating $50 phone
    bill, broke, drowsy, anxious, my heart fearful of the
    fingers dialing, the deaths, the singing of telephone bells
ringing at dawn ringing all afternoon ringing up
    midnight ringing now forever.

Kral Majales

And the Communists have nothing to offer but fat cheeks
    and eyeglasses and lying policemen
and the Capitalists proffer Napalm and money in green
    suitcases to the Naked,
and the Communists create heavy industry but the heart
    is also heavy
and the beautiful engineers are all dead, the secret
    technicians conspire for their own glamor
in the Future, in the Future, but now drink vodka and
    lament the Security Forces,
and the Capitalists drink gin and whiskey on airplanes but
    let Indian brown millions starve
and when Communist and Capitalist assholes tangle the
    Just man is arrested or robbed or had his head cut off,
but not like Kabir, and the cigarette cough of the Just man
    above the clouds
in the bright sunshine is a salute to the health of the blue
    sky.
For I was arrested thrice in Prague, once for singing drunk
    on Narodni street,
once knocked down on the midnight pavement by a
    mustached agent who screamed out BOUZERANT,

once for losing my notebooks of unusual sex politics
   dream opinions,
and I was sent from Havana by plane by detectives in green
   uniform,
and I was sent from Prague by plane by detectives in
   Czechoslovakian business suits,
Cardplayers out of Cézanne, the two strange dolls that
   entered Joseph K's room at morn
also entered mine, and ate at my table, and examined by
   scribbled,
and followed me night and morn from the houses of lovers
   to the cafés of Centrum—
And I am the King of May, which is the power of sexual
   youth,
and I am the King of May, which is industry in eloquence
   and action in amour,
and I am the King of May, which is long hair of Adam
   and the Beard of my own body
and I am the King of May, which is Kral Majales in the
   Czechoslovakian tongue,
and I am the King of May, and in a few minutes I will
   land at London Airport,
and I am the King of May, naturally, for I am of Slavic
   parentage and a Buddhist Jew
who worships the Sacred Heart of Christ the blue body of
   Krishna the straight back of Ram
the beads of Chango the Nigerian singing Shiva Shiva in
   a manner which I have invented,
and the King of May is a middleeuropean honor, nine in
   the XX century
despite space and the Time Machine, because I heard the
   voice of Blake in a vision,
and repeat that voice. And I am King of May that sleeps
   with teenagers laughing.
And I am the King of May, that I may be expelled from
   my Kingdom with Honor, as of old,
To show the difference between Caesar's Kingdom and the
   Kingdom of the May of Man—
and I am the King of May, tho paranoid, for the Kingdom
   of May is too beautiful to last for more than a month—
and I am the King of May because I touched my finger to
   my forehead saluting
a luminous heavy girl trembling hands who said "one
   moment Mr. Ginsberg"

before a fat young Plainclothesman stepped between our
    bodies—I was going to England—
and I am the King of May, returning to see Bunhill Fields
    and walk on Hampstead Heath,
and I am the King of May, in a giant jetplane touching
    Albion's airfield trembling in fear
as the plane roars to a landing on the grey concrete, shakes
    & expels air,
and rolls slowly to a stop under the clouds with part of
    blue heaven still visible.
And *tho* I am the King of May, the Marxists have beat me
    upon the street, kept me up all night in Police Station,
    followed me thru Springtime Prague, detained me in
    secret and deported me from our kingdom by airplane.
Thus I have written this poem on a jet seat in mid Heaven.

NIKKI GIOVANNI

Revolutionary Dreams

i used to dream militant
dreams of taking
over america to show
these white folks how it should be
done
i used to dream radical dreams
of blowing everyone away with my perceptive powers
of correct analysis
i even used to think i'd be the one
to stop the riot and negotiate the peace
then i awoke and dug
that if i dreamed natural
dreams of being a natural
woman doing what a woman
does when she's natural
i would have a revolution

ARTHUR GREGOR

The Guide

If I could choose a role
for what of me continues
when the body goes
let me be guide to one
whose aim is
the full unfolding of the soul.

An incomparable mission this
which, encumbered with
the body's intricacies
none may declare openly.
Only when direct speech or touch
become subtle promptings
can such guiding be.

Or so it seems to me
for I know that I cannot alone
accomplish the next step,
cannot guess where the next crossing is
the landing where
what is needed for
the deepening I crave
is right and ready for me.
Can only plead

that it may be,
can break
the hold of security,
keep one foot raised in readiness
but must wait, wait
until the guide
I've come to trust
places it
on what I will accept
as the right track.

Who must surely shudder with
delight
which in this life
only the anticipated lover knows

as—cradling me as air does—
he—the bodiless—
takes me further, on to

where I yearn to get.
What mission of unearthly love!
To help an ignorant earthling on
to the radiance that he—the bodiless—
is now possessed of!

The Beacon

Your eyes I can see in the dark.
They have waited, wanted, are ready
pulsing like stars.
Your hands I can feel in the dark.
They are naked, bare to the touch
they protect themselves for
when they are not as now they are
naked and ready in the dark.

Here in this room with me
your eyes, your hands declare
what they've longed for
are received and receive in return.
It is all they have ever wanted
if only once to be full and
to fill. Everything of meaning
has promised them this—their due,

and I'm here in this room with you.

Gradually as we flow toward each other
a shape arises
what we cannot see
who we cannot say
but have the distinct impression
it is a shape that has always
resided in us but has waited for this
for us to be ready for this

and has now stepped out of us
here in this room in the dark:
a vaporlike shape white as the light
a boatman gathers from the stars

454

a shape that has the glow
and disembodiedness
characteristic of only the spirits
attributed only to gods.

A Nameless Recognition

On your way home you stopped to shop
looked around as you were going in
and recognized yourself in me
some steps away. Then you went in
and I went on. Of course the outcome
could have been otherwise, but not
what had already taken place.
That we had seen each other in
each other's face without disguise
had beheld what is not yours nor mine:
a nameless recognition we might not
have reached had our shyness and
each other's namelessness been breached.

MARILYN HACKER

Alba: March

Coming home to the white
morning light in my studio. Ten o'clock;
down the block construction workers stop
for coffee, beer, a drop of booze. It's cold;
they trample frozen mud. White
sunlight quivers in my head,
slivers in puddles breaking last night's freeze.
I finger keys in my woolly pocket, holding
a grocery bag striped golden with light.

All around the south windows
plants doze and shiver awake
as a new leaf breaks and uncurls. I unpack

a green enamel pot, black pepper, milk, eggs,
with the light melting my legs, like
that boy's long calves last night,
warm moons on my own
when we had grown drunk with kissing
stretched on slippery cool sheets.
I kissed his eyes, mouth, feet. I kissed his knees,
ate honey from the flower between his thighs
and felt it rise with sap against my tongue.
He was so young. His cheeks, as smooth as mine,
tasted of pears and wine, and that smile
was not for painters. While I held him
it swam above my drowned eyes.
Now I organize papers, inks, pens.
I'll draw the coleus again, its leaves
a curvilinear trap for light.

SANDRA HOCHMAN

I Want to Tell You

In Memory of Pablo Neruda

I want to tell you what it feels like not to touch.
It's terrible. Your head blows up
Until it feels like a balloon floating somewhere
And your feet are filled with helium and your light
In the sky—only nothing is there. No arm, no wrist,
No thigh. The thighs go first. Feeling gone.
Then the nipples. Then your arms.

Not to make love is unbearable.
Taking hold of the resting place you
Bob into sleep, but it isn't sleep. It isn't relief—it's
The sleep of the prisoner with the terrible bars
Of the body shining in the distance. And that's why the
  womb

Shines like linoleum
Under the stars, marvelous in its pursuit
Of a poor piece of flesh that will lovingly
Cover it up. Oh hear me, amazons, mistresses, wives,
Let air fly through the body, let all women dance
Into kingdoms of where loving is not getting even.

RICHARD HOWARD

Again for Hephaistos, the Last Time

> ... translate for me till I
> accomplish my corpse at last.
> W. H. Auden

What do we share with the past?
Assurance we are unique,
even in shipwreck. The dead
take away the world they made
certain was theirs—they die
knowing we never can have it.

As each of *us* knows, for even
a nap is enough to confirm
suspicions that when we are not
on the scene, nothing else is.
Call it the comfort of dying:
you *can* take it all with you.

"The ship is sinking": Cocteau managed to stage his
     whisper
while a camera was "well trained" (according to
     Stravinsky)
on the televised deathbed in Paris some dozen years ago;

his sparrow had fallen one day before this master forger
(who was hardly your *miglior fabbro*, although you had
     translated
his tangle of true and false. Ginifers into your own
     Tintagel)—

457

finding Piaf had "gone on," as she always did, ahead
of time and tonsillitis, how could *he* help finding, too,
the vessel on the rocks, the wreck within easy reach?

Predeceased, your gaudy predecessor in death gave up
the ship—high season for sinking: Harlequin Jean,
escorted
or just flanked by MacNeice and Roethke, alien
psychopomps.

Yours though were quite as unlikely, every bit as
outlandish.
This weekend, waves of applause (prerogative of popes!)
broke in the wake of a coffin leaving Santa Maria

sopra Minerva—Magnani, with Pablo Neruda your peer
on Sunday's appalling front page, though scarcely your
pal:
Verga you loved, but had you stayed up late enough to see

"Mamma Roma" in his *Lupa?* Even heard of her? Like
most
performers—like Piaf—she was, I suspect, as absent
from your now immortal reckonings as Rod McKuen et al.

You were not very fond of volcanoes—in verse or voice
either,
and to violent Anna preferred a predictable Donna Elvira
who could always repeat her crises on key, on cue,
encore!

Cocteau, you conceded, though stagy, had the *lacrimae
rerum* note,
but did *you?* The *Times,* this morning, declared you had
failed to make,
or even make your way inside, "a world of emotion."

I wonder. Given your case, or given at last your
encasement,
who knows? Only the poems, and to me at least they
speak volumes:
your death makes a leap-day this fall, this autumn you
would say.

But my *personal* knowledge is odd, my evidence suspect
even:

on a club-car up to Cambridge, two freshmen scribbled a
  note—
"Are you Carl Sandburg?" "You've ruined," you wrote
  back, "mother's day."

Was that emotion? Was this—the time backstage at the Y
when impatient to read to the rustling thousands out front,
  you asked
(possessing no small talk—and with you I possessed no
  large)

why it was I no longer endured a difficult mutual friend.
"Because he calls everyone *else* either a kike or a
  cocksucker,
and since, Wystan, both he and I are . . . well, both of
  them . . ."

"My *dear*," you broke in, and I think you were genuinely
  excited,
"I never knew you were Jewish!" No, not a world of
  emotion—
say, for the time being, as you said, the emotion of a
  world.

> Only those poets can leave us
> whom we have never possessed.
> What did you leave me? The unsaid,
> mourning, hangs around me,
> desperate, not catastrophic,
> like a dog having a bad time.
>
> The difference, then, between
> your death and all those others
> is this: you did not take
> a certain world away, after
> all. After you, because of you,
> all songs are possible.

October 1, 1973

DAVID IGNATOW

In a Dream

at fifty I approach myself,
eighteen years of age,
seated despondently on the concrete steps
of my father's house,
wishing to be gone from there
into my own life,
and I tell my young self,
Nothing will turn out right,
you'll want to revenge yourself,
on those close to you especially,
and they will want to die,
of shock and grief. You will fall
to pleading and tears of self-pity,
filled with yourself, a passionate stranger.
My eighteen-year-old self stands up
from the concrete steps and says,
Go to hell,
and I walk off.

I'm Here

The radio said, Go to your shelters,
in such a low whisper that we stood there
in front of the set, not wanting to understand
it was not part of a play. The color
of the blast came high over the horizon.
We stood watching it, still unable to realize
that we were being killed, for real.

We ran and are still running, it seems,
though our bodies have long since dropped
from us. We could be the wind rushing
through the trees or the stars moving out
to the perimeter. We know we felt ourselves
vanishing in flame and wind
and it seemed as though we were becoming
one or the other.

How then can we still speak to you
without body or voice? Do you know
there is another world, very silent,
which penetrates this one you're in?
Without your knowledge or your feeling it
you hear every word I speak but do not see
or feel me anywhere at all. I have no sight
or touch of you but I speak because I am
from nowhere in particular. And now
can you tell me what it is to live?

Are you lying in a cave at rest?
Or waiting crouched for the enemy,
or do you have your family with you still,
comforting them with food?
What is your situation?
Once having been human like you, if I may presume
nothing for you has changed in form, body
or mind. I hunger for a voice to fill
an emptiness in my speech,
which perhaps is what makes me invisible.
You can speak to me by standing perfectly still
where you are and breathing regularly.
Then I'll understand that all is well
again for the human and leave,
content with my condition.

Their Mouths Full

Let there be ripeness, said the Lord.
And men bowed down to see brown in the pod
and to its meat palpable and sweet.
And of this fruit you shall eat
for your wisdom, said the Lord.
And of none other, lest you die.
And the men ate of the ripened fruit
and rejoiced in its taste
and of the seed split between their teeth,
for these two were sweet of their kind;
and so it happened that unripened fruit
was looked on with scorn
and beaten down from its branches

in the Lord's name as sinful
and the work of death.
And men sat themselves down to grow
palpable and sweet to one another
in the sun and it was then time to die,
ripening, and they died,
blessing their maker,
their mouths full of one another.

KENNETH KOCH

from The Art of Love

Life Is Full of Horrors and Hormones . . .

Life is full of horrors and hormones and so few things
    are certain
So many unknown—but the pleasure of coupling with a
    creature one is crazy about
Is something undisputed. So don't be afraid to spend
Hours, even days, weeks, even months, going to places
And trying to find the person who can give you the
    maximum pleasure in life
As the sun hits the top of mountains but often prefers
    the hills
Where markets glint in the fading light and one's lungs
    seem filled with silver. O horrors of loneliness!
Abandon my spirit while it walks forth through the
    world and attempts to find for people
And tell them where marvelous women can be found.
    Of course, you want a very particular one.
To find her, however, you may have to look at a great
    many, and try more,
Some in the light, some in the dark. Orgies are sometimes
    organized for people,
You can try that, but I wouldn't, all life is an
Orgy, why limit oneself to a little room, full of (probably)
Mainly people who are emotionally disturbed
As you and I are not. If you could organize an orgy
Of your own, that might, I think, be something else. But
We have strayed from our subject.

Everything About Love Makes People Feel in a More Intense Way

Everything about love makes people feel in a more
    intense way,
So it seems natural enough to start right in, with "You
    are beautiful
As a) Botticelli's Venus, or b) a slice of angelfood cake,
    I want
To devour you—for my sweet tooth is the ruling tooth
    of my life!"

Later you can cry to her, when alone with her, "Oh you
    are the enslaving of me,
Dear sweet and irrefutable love!" And when you are
    dancing with her
Or anywhere in public, you may even wish to praise her
In a secret language which no one else will understand—
"Gah shlooh lye bopdoosh," for example, may mean
    "Your left leg
Is whiter even than the snow which on Mount
    Kabanayashi
Tops all Japan with its splendor!" and "Ahm gahm doom
    bahm ambahm glahsh": "I
Would like to tie you to this bannister and
Kill you with my kisses all night!" For if you believe
There is a magic in love, to get to it you will go to any
    extremes.

And one goes on looking, and talking. And neither the
    tongue
Nor the eyes wear out, and the streets are filled with
    beautiful breasts and words.

Happy the Man Who Has Two Breasts to Crush . . .

Happy the man who has two breasts to crush against
    his bosom,
A tongue to suck on, a lip to bite, and in fact an entire girl!
    He knows a success
Not known by Mount Aetna or Vesuvius or by any major
    volcano of the world!
He has someone to come into, and stay there, and tremble,
    and shake about, and hold
And dream about, and come back to, and even discuss
    party politics with if he wants to,

Or poetry, or painting. But where shall you find this bird?
  On a gondola in Venice
The tour guide said, "Look at those buildings" and I felt
  my chest crushed against your
Bosom, and the whole earth went black; when I awoke we
  were in Brindisi,
You had nailed me to a canoe, you were standing on my
  stomach, you had a rat in your hand
Which you were waving in the summer breeze, and saying
  "This is from the Almanach
Of Living, attention, please pay attention, greeniness and
  mountains, oh this is the art of love!"

STANLEY KUNITZ

The Mulch

A man with a leaf in his head
watches an indefatigable gull
dropping a piss-clam on the rocks
to break it open.
Repeat. Repeat.
He is an inlander
who loves the margins of the sea,
and everywhere he goes he carries
a bag of earth on his back.
Why is he down in the tide marsh?
Why is he gathering salt hay
in bushel baskets crammed to his chin?
"It is a blue and northern air,"
he says, as if the shiftings of the sky
had taught him husbandry.
Birthdays for him are when he wakes
and falls into the news of weather.
"Try! Try!" clicks the beetle in his wrist,
his heart is an educated swamp,
and he is mindful of his garden,
which prepares to die.

The Portrait

My mother never forgave my father
for killing himself,
especially at such an awkward time
and in a public park,
that spring
when I was waiting to be born.
She locked his name
in her deepest cabinet
and would not let him out,
though I could hear him thumping.
When I came down from the attic
with the pastel portrait in my hand
of a long-lipped stranger
with a brave moustache
and deep brown level eyes,
she ripped it into shreds
without a single word
and slapped me hard.
In my sixty-fourth year
I can feel my cheek
still burning.

An Old Cracked Tune

My name is Solomon Levi,
the desert is my home,
my mother's breast was thorny,
and father I had none.

The sands whispered, *Be separate,*
the stones taught me, *Be hard.*
I dance, for the joy of surviving,
on the edge of the road.

The Illumination

In that hotel my life
rolled in its socket
twisting my strings.
All my mistakes,
from my earliest

bedtimes,
rose against me:
the parent I denied,
the friends I failed,
the hearts I spoiled,
including at least
my own left ventricle—
a history of shame.
"Dante!" I cried
to the apparition
entering from the hall,
laureled and gaunt,
in a cone of light.
"Out of mercy you came
to be my Master
and my guide!"
To which he replied:
"I know neither the time
nor the way
nor the number on the door . . .
but this must be my room,
I was here before."
And he held up in his hand
the key,
which blinded me.

NAOMI LAZARD

Ordinance on Winning

Congratulations.
The suspense is over. You are the winner.
The doubts you have had
concerning the rules of the contest,
about the ability and fairness of the judges,
were illfounded. The rumors
pertaining to a "fix"
have been exposed as nonsense.
The contest is fair and always has been.

Now that the results are in
your prize will be sent to you
under separate cover. Be sure you have
your social security number
or other proper identification
for the postman.
                    Upon receiving it
contact us immediately in order that you
may be notified of further developments,
ensuing publicity,
other honors which will be forthcoming.
If by some chance your prize does not arrive
as scheduled, do not bother to inform us.

Our responsibility is discharged
with this announcement.
In the event that you do not receive
your prize, there is no authority
to whom you can turn
for information or redress.
We advise you to wait patiently
for your prize
which will either come or not.

In Answer to Your Query

We are sorry to inform you
the item you ordered
is no longer being produced.
It has not gone out of style
nor have people lost interest in it.
In fact, it has become
one of our most desired products.
Its popularity is still growing.
Orders for it come in
at an ever increasing rate.
However, a top-level decision
has caused this product
to be discontinued forever.

Instead of the item you ordered
we are sending you something else.
It is not the same thing,
nor is it a reasonable facsimile.

It is what we have in stock,
the very best we can offer.

If you are not happy
with this substitution
let us know as soon as possible.
                                As you can imagine
we already have quite an accumulation
of letters such as the one
you may or may not write.
To be totally fair
we respond to these complaints
as they come in.
Yours will be filed accordingly,
answered in its turn.

AUDRE LORDE

The Workers Rose on May Day or
Postscript to Karl Marx

Down Wall Street
the students marched for peace
Above, construction workers looking on remembered
how it was for them in the old days
before their closed shop white security
and daddy pays the bills
so they climbed down the girders
and taught their sons a lesson
called Marx is a victim of the generation gap
called I grew up the hard way so will you
called
the limits of a sentimental vision.

When the passion play was over
and the dust had cleared on Wall Street
500 Union workers together with police
had mopped up Foley Square

with 2000 of their striking sons
who broke and ran
before their fathers chains.

Look here Karl Marx
the apocalyptic vision of amerika!
Workers rise and win
and have not lost their chains
but swing them
side by side with the billyclubs in blue
securing Wall Street
against the striking students.

W. S. MERWIN

Assembly

Nomads gather in autumn
driving herds to the great auctions
of animals on the gold earth
by then there is blood in the trees
nights are already cold
daybreak white
some of them open stalls by the river
and hang up for sale
loose pelts of different animals
and fur garments stitched with sinews
at moments during the summer
in upland pastures among birds
some play instruments
others sing clapping their hands

Trees

I am looking at trees
they may be one of the things I will miss
most from the earth
though many of the ones that I have seen

already. I cannot remember
and though I seldom embrace the ones I see
and have never been able to speak
with one
I listen to them tenderly
their names have never touched them
they have stood round my sleep
and when it was forbidden to climb them
they have carried me in their branches

Vision

What is unseen
flows to what is unseen
passing in part
through what we partly see
we stood up from all fours
far back in the light
to look
as long as there is day
and part of the night

The Horse

In a dead tree
there is the ghost of a horse
no horse
was ever seen near the tree
but the tree was born
of a mare
it rolled with long legs
in rustling meadows
it pricked its ears
it reared and tossed its head
and suddenly stood still
beginning to remember
as its leaves fell

The Hosts

You asked what
were the names of those two
old people who lived under the big tree
and gods in disguise visited them though they were poor

they offered the best they had to eat
and opened the oldest wine in the house
the gods went on pouring out pouring out wine
and then promised that it would flow till the ends of
    their lives

when the shining guests were out of sight he turned to her
by the table and said
this bottle has been in the cave all the time
we have been together

HOWARD MOSS

The Refrigerator

The argument of the refrigerator wakes me.
It is trying to tell me it doesn't want to be cold,
It never wanted to be cold, it didn't choose
This life where everyone around it hates it.
"People only use me for their own convenience,"
It says. With a shudder, it starts off again,
Undergoing an electrical seizure,
Rambling on about its hurts and troubles:
People think it's heartless, stolid, frigid,
When, deep down, it craves for warmth and wants . . .
Well, it hesitates to say it, but
All it *really* wants is to be a stove.
Oh, how it dreams each night of the paired
Gas jets switching on their tropical blue,
The swoosh just after the match catches on,
The rectangular, passionate grid of flame
In the oven, the romance of changing things

Into other things. "The egg of the Real
Becoming the soufflé of the Ideal—
That's what I call the creative life."

"You perform an important function," I say,
"Without you, where would we be, these days . . ."
"Yes, yes, I know," it impatiently replies,
"But do you"—pause—"think I'm attractive?"
My silence, I fear, gives the show away.
"Of course," I stumble on, "for what you do,
You're remarkably well made, so few things work . . ."
Coldly, it opens, then slams its door.
"I didn't mean . . ." I say. But it will not respond.
At midnight, with a premeditated click,
It detaches itself from the circuits of the world,
Manages to shut itself off completely,
And gives up the ghost. By morning, all is lost.
"Damn it," I say to my coffee, black
(The milk's turned sour overnight),
"Unfulfillment's claimed yet another victim,"
Just as the stove speaks up to say,
"Do you think? . . . I hear . . . in the frozen north . . ."

Long Island Springs

Long Island springs not much went on,
Except the small plots gave their all
In weeds and good grass; the mowers mowed
Up to the half-moon gardens crammed
With anything that grew. Our colored maid

Lived downstairs in a room too small
To keep a bird in, or so she claimed;
She liked her drinks, sloe-gin, gin-and . . .
When she was fired, my grandma said,
"Give them a finger, they'll take your hand."

So much for the maid. My grandma lived
In a room almost as small. She gave
Bread to the birds, saved bits of string,
Paper, buttons, old shoelaces, thread . . .
Not peasant stock but peasant—the real thing.

What stuff we farmed in our backyard!
Horseradish that my grandma stained beet-red—
Hot rouge for fish—her cosmos plants
With feathery-fine carrot leaves, and my
Poor vegetables, no first class restaurant's

Idea of France. "Your radishes are good,"
My sister said, who wouldn't touch the soil.
My mother wouldn't either. "Dirt, that's all."
Those afternoons of bridge and mah-jongg games,
Those tournaments! Click-click went forty nails

That stopped their racket for the candy dish.
"Coffee, girls?" came floating up the stairs.
Our house was "French Provincial." Chinese mirrors
Warred against the provinces. The breakfast nook
Had a kind of style. But it wasn't ours.

I'd walk down to the bay and sit alone
And listen to the tide chew gum. There was
An airport on the other shore. Toy-like,
It blew toy moths into the air. At night,
We'd hear the distant thunder of New York.

Grandpa, forgive me. When you called for me
At school in a sudden rain or snow, I was
Ashamed that anyone would see your beard
Or hear you talk in broken English. You
Would bring a black umbrella, battle-scarred,

And walk me home beneath it through the lots,
Where seasonal wild roses took a spill
And blew their cups, and sumac bushes grew
Up from the sand, attached to secret springs,
As I was secretly attached to you.

Friday night. The Bible. The smell of soup,
Fresh bread in the oven, the mumbling from
The kitchen where my grandma said her prayers.
Reading the Bible, she kept one finger under
Every line she read. Alone, upstairs,

The timelessness of swamps came over me,
A perpetual passing of no time, it seemed,
Waiting for dinner, waiting to get up
From dinner, waiting, waiting all the time.
For what? For love, as longed-for as a trip

A shut-in never takes. It came to me.
But what Proust said is true: If you get
What you want in life, by the time you do,
You no longer want it. But that's another
Story, or stories, I should say, much too

Pointless to go into now. For what
Matters to me are those lifelong two
Transplanted figures in a suburb who
Loved me without saying, "I love you."
Grandpa, tonight, I think of you.

Envoi:
Grandma, your bones lie out in Queens.
The black funeral parlor limousines
Just make it up the narrow aisles.
When flowers on your headstone turn to moss,
Russian cossack horses leap across
The stone, the stone parentheses of years.

STANLEY MOSS

Clams

Ancient of Days, bless the innocent
who can do nothing but cling,
open or close their stone mouths.
Out of water they live on themselves
and what little sea water they carry with them.
Bless all things unaware, that perceive
life and death as comfort or discomfort:
bless their great dumbness.

We die misinformed
with our mouths of shell open.
At the last moment, as our lives fall off,
a gull lifts us, drops us on the rocks, bare
because the tide is out. Flesh sifts the sludge.
At sea bottom, on the rocks below the wharf,
a salt foot, too humble to have a voice,
thumps for representation, joy.

Prayer

Give me a death like Buddha's. Let me fall
over from eating mushrooms Provençal,
a peasant wine pouring down my shirt-front,
my last request not a cry but a grunt;
kicking my heels to heaven, may I succumb
tumbling into a rose bush after a love
half my age; though I'm deposed, my tomb
shall not be empty, may my belly show above
my coffin like a distant hill, my mourners come
as if to pass an hour in the country,
to see the green, that old anarchy.

An Exchange of Hats

I will my collection of hats,
straw the Yucatan, fez Algiers 1935,
Russian beaver, Irish fisherman's knit,
collapsible silk opera, a Borsalino,
to a dead man,
the Portuguese poet, my dear Fernando,
who without common loyalty,
wrote under seven different names
in seven different styles.
He was a man of many cafes,
a smoker and non-smoker.
His poets had come to live in Lisbon,
had different sexual preferences,
histories and regional accents.

The poets had a common smell
and loneliness that was Fernando's.
His own character
was to him like ink to a squid,
something to hide behind.
What did it matter, writing in Portuguese
after the first World War?
The center was Paris, the languages French and English.
In Lisbon, workers on the street corner were arguing
over what was elegance, the anarchist manifesto,
the trial of Captain Artur Carlos De Barros,
found guilty of "advocating circumcision"

and teaching Marranos no longer to enter church
saying "When I enter I adore neither wood nor stone
but only the Ancient of Days who rules all."
The Portuguese say
they have the "illusion" to do something,
meaning they very much want to do it.

He could not just sit in the same cafe
wearing his own last hat, drinking port
and smoking *Ideals* forever.

RAYMOND R. PATTERSON

Birmingham 1963

Sunday morning and her mother's hands
Weaving the two thick braids of her springing hair,
Pulling her sharply by one bell-rope when she would
Not sit still, setting her ringing,
While the radio church choir prophesied the hour
With theme and commercials, while the whole house
   tingled;
And she could not stand still in that awkward air;
Her dark face shining, her mother now moving the tiny
   buttons,
Blue against blue, the dress which took all night making,
That refused to stay fastened;
There was some pull which hurried her out to Sunday
   School
Toward the lesson and the parable's good news,
The quiet escape from the warring country of her feelings,
The confused landscape of grave issues and people.

But now we see
Now we see through the glass of her mother's wide
   screaming
Eyes into the room where the homemade bomb
Blew the room down where her daughter had gone:
Under the leaves of hymnals, the plaster and stone,

476

The blue dress, all undone—
The day undone to the bone—
Her still, dull face, her quiet hair;
Alone amid the rubble, amid the people
Who perish, being innocent.

from **Riot Rhymes U.S.A.**

1

We are the same in our despair
Who now disturb your peace with riot—
The dark oppressed of yesteryear
Who swallowed grief and bled in quiet.

7

When I passed by
They were tearing up that store.
Electric appliances all over the floor.
And I said to myself, Sure, stealing is bad
But all those things you never had.
What are you waiting for!

16

I hear they plan to investigate
All the violence, all this hate—
What made us Negroes make a fuss—
And put the blame right back on us.
If you've any doubt,
Check it out.

37

I said, Leroy
You better come back
On this stoop and sit.
But Leroy gets up. He says,
Man, this is it!
I said, Leroy,
Put down that garbage can.
But Leroy says, Baby,
I'm going to meet the man.
I said, Leroy, cool it. They got the law

And they got the guns.
The best you can get is a busted head.
But Leroy says,
Ain't no way I can cool it no more.
All my life
I been playing dead.

45

Oh Lord
We are in this land.
But they don't seem to understand.

59

My mama hadn't said one word
To my daddy for two whole years.
But after the riots, she was so happy
She was crying tears when he got released
From Disturbing the Peace, and come back home
From jail.
Nothing suits a family like a big strong male,
She said. Even if you are a jailbird,
Now you can raise your head!

72

Some people
You just have to scare—
Then they let you get somewhere.

84

To tell the truth,
Most people went home and stayed,
And some prayed.
Being frightened of violence ain't no sin.
But some of us were more afraid
To keep on living like we been.

KENNETH PITCHFORD

Homosexual Sonnets

1

Bob, nothing in me wants to tell you again
about those seven years—we in our twenties,
a poet and a pianist, both in our first passionate sexual
physically satisfied love affair, but I never fail

to remember seeing your spotlit face brooding over
a Brahms intermezzo late at night in a deserted building
as my weekend pass ran out and I had to get back
to my infantry rifle company at Fort Lewis.

In the spring you took me to the Seattle Arboretum
so that I would learn the names of trees and plants, both
exotic and ordinary, and it began to rain and everyone left

but I kissed your wet lips, our clothes drenched, discarded,
before we escaped home to our attic, leaning against the
    warm chimney
for a dozen naked hours of coming and coming.

2

I don't know what to think of the years in New York.
I can remember all the bad times in a row and say that's
    how it was,
or all the good times and see how much we shared.
Mixed all together, we still gave more love than most people
    dream of.

It was the bitter nineteen-fifties, retrenchment of
every fresh hope, and we played scales, made sonnets,
loved a lot of other people together, between us in our bed,
and didn't really believe how genocidally we were hated.

By ourselves? our friends? our enemies? our straight
compatriots who wanted to be seduced by expert artistic
hands like ours—to tell tales about afterward, hateful tales,

lying about the secret we always tried to tell everyone,
even each other: that male bodies together can learn
to lay aside their weapons and sleep in each other's arms.

When it comes to sex with other men, we both admit how easy
it is to be "natural," each in his chosen scenario, though we choke
on our own reluctance to tell each other about it, much less *show* it,
spontaneous in our oppression, awkward only in revolution:

with each other. We say that we are "in struggle" and that we don't
want to play Avis to some straight man's Hertz. And we know how
all of this makes any show of affection, much less passion, difficult,
stilted and arbitrary. But not impossible if we believe

that through struggle we will somehow learn at least to defy
the oppression we cannot defeat except through the worldwide
anti-gender revolution of which we are part. Changing ourselves

to begin with, beginning now. A commitment of years, until
we walk openly arm in arm down public streets, laughing.
That's the dream denied us in one-night stands of first names only.

6

We put Blake to sleep between us, lying in both our arms.
Some kind of miracle, too beautiful to describe.
I think of his two years stretching to twenty, when you'll
be nearly fifty, I nearly sixty—if we live that long.

Will we have been able to unteach ourselves man-ness enough
to help him from having to learn it to the same depth as we?
He'll need more than one un-male to stand with him against
all the hate he'll get, whatever ways he chooses to love.

But short of prison, et cetera, I can see all of us together sharing
poetry-music-dance, swimming, camping out, learning how to put

the straight-imperialist male of our species out of his
    misery,
gore-maddened from gorging on even his own eviscera.

We have already entered history together, Michael—I can't
think of anything like us before. No wonder it scares me.

RALPH POMEROY

Looking at the Empire State Building

It is still The Tallest Building in the World.
(Although they are already busy changing that.)
Coming as I do from the Great Plains,
it has been my Holy Mountain from the beginning.
When it disappears past clouds, I imagine
the gods holding a picnic—for once
happily masked from our stares.

At night when the top is lighted
I see it as my Holy Volcano
and the biggest penny-bank anywhere.
It is the only present I would ever
have liked to give Jean Harlow.
Planes and birds are known to crash into it.

I can't help expecting any minute
to see poor King Kong fall from the dirigible mast
or spot lovely Melisande leaning out from an upper floor
to let down her long golden hair.

English Train, Summer

Quite often, when I look out,
I see a canal and some cows
Or sheep cropping permissive green
Under air expressive with crow-eyebrows.

The silver flat water winds in neat turns
And slips suddenly beneath us, past
A bridge, aroused and shaking—its arousal lasting
Longer than the image we just saw.

The evening light increases the tone of poppies
To a blast of hues
To challenge a nearby acre of even louder yellows.
All of which is surprising; the sky being soppy.

It's odd, this loudness in softness,
But odd in a way very English, if you know what I mean:
Gentle pastel pastoral exquisitely folded,
Disturbed by a pack of red coats suddenly seen.

Or the stone knife of some ambitious spire
Tense with righteousness. Its mighty roar
Slashing upwards through the landscape's linen,
Upsetting the civilities of green tablescapes we so admire.

Oh yes, kings die here and saints did.
Don't be bemused by lawns laid out like lunch.
It's this fierceness in finery I must remember,
Travelling slowly in the direction of Oxford.

NAOMI REPLANSKY

The Mistress Addresses the Wife

Do not tremble, wife,
When you think of me.
Your castle may be sand
But I am not the sea.

Nor am I a refuge,
Nor am I a throne.
I am the dark streets
A man walks alone.

Alone, alone he walks,
And he sings at will,
And at will departs,
And my streets are still.

Though at moments I
Heard his helpless cry,
It was not you he yielded
In that yielding sigh.

Guilt ties my tongue,
Rage makes you blind.
Let your eyes just once
Fasten upon mine.

An Inheritance

*Five dollars, four dollars, three dollars, two,
One, and none, and what do we do?*

This is the worry that never got said,
But ran so often in my mother's head

And showed so plain in my father's frown
That to us kids it drifted down.

It drifted down like soot, like snow,
In the dream-tossed Bronx, in the long ago.

I shook it off with a shake of my head,
I bounced my ball, I ate warm bread,

I skated down the steepest hill.
But I must have listened, against my will:

When the wind blows wrong, I can hear it today.
Then my mother's worry stops all play

And, as if in its rightful place,
My father's frown divides my face.

In the Sea of Tears

Tentacled for food,
You range your underwater neighborhood.

To look, to like, to eat, to break your fast!
Before you move an inch an hour is past,

Your prey is past, a swarm of scales, an eye,
A round fish eye, a rude unblinking eye.

You close on nothing; slowly you untwine
Your many arms and trail them through the brine.

Now sailors at the surface hear you cry,
And from those heights they cannot fathom why.

For there are agile creatures all around
Who dart like flames through this rich hunting-ground,

And others who lie still and gaping wide
And make no move; but armies come inside.

ADRIENNE RICH

Rape

There is a cop who is both prowler and father:
he comes from your block, grew up with your brothers,
had certain ideals.
You hardly know him in his boots and silver badge,
on horseback, one hand touching his gun.

You hardly know him but you have to get to know him:
he has access to machinery that could kill you.
He and his stallion clop like warlords among the trash,
his ideals stand in the air, a frozen cloud
from between his unsmiling lips.

And so, when the time comes, you have to turn to him,
the maniac's sperm still greasing your thighs,
your mind whirling like crazy. You have to confess
to him, you are guilty of the crime
of having been forced.

And you see his blue eyes, the blue eyes of all the family
whom you used to know, grow narrow and glisten,
his hand types out the details
and he wants them all
but the hysteria in your voice pleases him best.

You hardly know him but now he thinks he knows you:
he has taken down your worst moment
on a machine and filed it in a file.
He knows, or thinks he knows, how much you imagined;
he knows, or thinks he knows, what you secretly wanted.

He has access to machinery that could get you put away;
and if, in the sickening light of the precinct,
and if, in the sickening light of the precinct,
your details sound like a portrait of your confessor,
will you swallow, will you deny them, will you lie your way
    home?

1972

From a Survivor

The pact that we made was the ordinary pact
of men & women in those days

I don't know who we thought we were
that our personalities
could resist the failures of the race

Lucky or unlucky, we didn't know
the race had failures of that order
and that we were going to share them

485

Like everybody else, we thought of ourselves as special

Your body is as vivid to me
as it ever was: even more

since my feeling for it is clearer:
I know what it could and could not do

it is no longer
the body of a god
or anything with power over my life

Next year it would have been 20 years
and you are wastefully dead
who might have made the leap
we talked, too late, of making

which I live now
not as a leap
but a succession of brief, amazing movements

each one making possible the next

1972

MURIEL RUKEYSER

St. Roach

For that I never knew you, I only learned to dread you,
for that I never touched you, they told me you are filth,
they showed me by every action to despise your kind;
for that I saw my people making war on you,
I could not tell you apart, one from another,
for that in childhood I lived in places clear of you,
for that all the people I know met you by
crushing you, stamping you to death, they poured boiling
    water on you, they flushed you down,
for that I could not tell one from another
only that you were dark, fast on your feet, and slender.
    Not like me.

For that I did not know your poems
And that I do not know any of your sayings
And that I cannot speak or read your language
And that I do not sing your songs
And that I do not teach our children
> to eat your food
> or know your poems
> or sing your songs

But that we say you are filthing our food
But that we know you not at all.

Yesterday I looked at one of you for the first time.
You were lighter than the others in color, that was neither
   good nor bad.
I was really looking for the first time.
You seemed troubled and witty.

Today I touched one of you for the first time.
You were startled, you ran, you fled away
Fast as a dancer, light, strange and lovely to the touch.
I reach, I touch, I begin to know you.

from **The Gates**

6. The Church of Galilee

As we climb to the church of Galilee
Three harsh men on the corner.
As we go to the worship-meeting of the dismissed,
three state police on the street.
As we all join at the place of the dispossessed,
three dark men asking their rote questions.
As we go ahead to stand with our new friends
that will be our friends our lifetime.
Introduced as dismissed from this faculty, this college,
this faculty, this university.
"Dismissed" is now an honorary degree.
The harsh police are everywhere,
they have hunted this fellowship away before
and they are everywhere, at the street-corner,
listening to all hymns,
standing before all doors,
hearing over all wires.
We go up to Galilee.

Let them listen to the dispossessed
and to all women and men who stand firm and sing
wanting a shared and honest lifetime.
Let them listen to Galilee.

Islands

O for God's sake
they are connected
underneath

They look at each other
across the glittering sea
some keep a low profile

Some are cliffs
The bathers think
islands are separate like them

GRACE SCHULMAN

Burn Down the Icons

What happened to Cassandra? She who cried
In me "Love is war!" has died, loving.
And Daphne, whose flesh grew leaves?
Breasts now, and twig-shaped nerves.
Fathers, forgive me. It had to be.
I never promised to be Saint Veronica
When you pressed images on me, printed in blood
On a white scarf. Or when you carved me in marble,
And gazed into the dry wells of my eyes,
Did you think I would not dissolve?

Well, burn down the icons. I have moved
Out of the Prado. Your best fresco
Cracks from the ceiling. I have gone
Beyond my body, five-feet-eleven and three-quarters
Inches of tangled philodendron. I am water.

Call out the curia. Unsanctify me.
Erase my feast day from the calendar.
Shatter the stained-glass windows of my mind.
They were idolators who cut the palm,
Two anchors and an arrow on my tomb
Found in the catacombs. I am no martyr.

Love was my habit. I know my heart moved trees.
Love called my eyes to change things of this world.
But I did not believe it. And how could I persuade you
That those visions you admired was astigmatism.
Makers of images, what you created in me
I was. But see me new! My nipples are cathedrals,
My flesh is a miracle. I flow to the ocean
Where all the rivers of the earth come together.
My body is a holy vessel. I am fire and air.

Do not desert me now, although I pray
To a genital god, and have let blaze
Strange images, my means of transportation.
I have established my chapel in water.
I would move through mountains. But fathers,
Let me return to a safe harbor; like the waves'
Slate-sheets, crash in the jetties of your arms.

The Law

My grandfather's mind was a covered ark
with doors that sprang shut when the truth was in.
"Pines bend with winds that snap oak.
They stand who bend before God."

Curtains and an ornamental lock
can light the law, as black soil shines at night;
dazzled by that law, I stood in wonder,
and trembled in the shadow of his hands.

Standing beside him in the synagogue,
I turned and saw a cage of women's faces—
fish leaping in nets—and one of them
my face, when I grew higher than his shoulder.

Stained glass grew leaves of light across the floor;
I saw a various truth with radiant shadows:
"Fathers, forgive me. I cannot follow."

Blue Max

His castrating wife is at the controls.
Blue Max, she says,
Take off.
They take off, winging it for
Haiphong, Taipei,
The China Seas.
Miles below, the dolphins
Heave and soar. It's their jet
Trails that streak the blue.
Friend or foe, friend or foe,
She shouts.
The question doesn't apply,
He'd like to explain—
If the intercom would work
Or the picture were real
Or if he hadn't just stepped out.

Riding Westward

It's holiday night
And crazy Jews are on the road,
Finished with fasting and high on prayer.
On either side of the Long Island Expressway
The lights go spinning
Like the twin ends of my tallis.
I hope I can make it to Utopia Parkway
Where my father lies at the end of his road.
And then home to Brooklyn.
Jews, departure from the law
Is equivalent to death.
Shades, we greet each other.
Darkly, on the Long Island Expressway,
Where I say my own prayers for the dead,
Crowded in Queens, remembered in Queens,
As far away as Brooklyn. Cemeteries
Break against the City like seas,
A white froth of tombstones

Or like schools of herring, still desperate
To escape the angel of death.
Entering the City, you have to say
Memorial prayers as he slides overhead
Looking something like my father approaching
The Ark as the gates close on the Day of Atonement
Here in the car and in Queens and in Brooklyn.

Where I Am Now

Every morning I look
Into the world
And there is no renewal.
Every night, my lids clamped,
I concentrate
On the renewal to come.

I am on the lookout for
A great illumining,
Prepared to recognize it
Instantly and put it to use
Even among the desks
And chairs of the office, should
It come between nine and five.

JUDITH JOHNSON SHERWIN

The Balance

darling here's my head
on a platter I promised you. if
you don't care for it that
much it doesn't matter. you can see the head
I trust, mine all right, but it's been
polished, a high shine put
onto the temples. to do that I had to take
everything wet off, sorry, or spill it out.

if you'd rather
I can give you my heart as usual it's all
wet (you can keep the platter) I have
a sieve at hand for the heart and though the head
is dead the heart can live
a while in the sieve it can turn around it can puff
in and out in and out like a frog's sides, fret, it can rub
a fine stinging rain through the fine cutting mesh
of the sieve it can fall on you
and wet you through.

you're the one has to weigh
please a merry measure
whether for one more time now
with that clear sterile skull to take
your pleasure or that soft pulsing slime.

MARK STRAND

Courtship

There is a girl you like so you tell her
your penis is big, but that you cannot get yourself
to use it. Its demands are ridiculous, you say,
even self-defeating, but to be honored somehow,
briefly, inconspicuously in the dark.

When she closes her eyes in horror,
you take it all back. You tell her you're almost
a girl yourself and can understand why she is shocked.
When she is about to walk away, you tell her
you have no penis, that you don't

know what got into you. You get on your knees.
She suddenly bends down to kiss your shoulder and you
know
you're on the right track. You tell her you want
to bear children and that is why you seem confused.
You wrinkle your brow and curse the day you were born.

She tries to calm you, but you lose control.
You reach for her panties and beg forgiveness as you do.
She squirms and you howl like a wolf. Your craving
seems monumental. You know you will have her.
Taken by storm, she is the girl you will marry.

My Life by Somebody Else

I have done what I could but you avoid me.
I left a bowl of milk on the desk to tempt you.
Nothing happened. I left my wallet there, full of money.
You must have hated me for that. You never came.

I sat at my typewriter naked, hoping you would wrestle me
to the floor. I played with myself just to arouse you.
Boredom drove me to sleep. I offered you my wife.
I sat her on the desk and spread her legs. I waited.

The days drag on. The exhausted light falls like a bandage
over my eyes. Is it because I am ugly? Was anyone
ever so sad? It is pointless to slash my wrists. My hands
would fall off. And then what hope would I have?

Why do you never come? Must I have you by being
somebody else? Must I write *My Life* by somebody else?
My Death by somebody else? Are you listening?
Somebody else has arrived. Somebody else is writing.

MAY SWENSON

Feel Me

"Feel me to do right," our father said
on his death bed. We did not quite
know—in fact, not at all—what he meant.
His last whisper was spent as through a slot in a wall.
He left us a key, but how did it
fit? "Feel me
to do right." Did it mean

that, though he died, he would be felt
through some aperture, or by some unseen instrument
our dad just then had come
to know? So, to do right always, we need but feel his
spirit? Or was it merely
his apology for dying? "Feel that I
do right in not trying, as you insist, to stay

on your side. There is the wide
gateway and the splendid tower,
and you implore me to wait here, with the worms!"
Had he defined his terms, and could we discriminate
among his motives, we might
have found out how to "do right" before *we* died—
supposing
he felt he suddenly knew

what dying was.
"You do wrong because you do not feel
as I do now" was maybe the sense. "Feel me, and emulate
my state, for I am becoming less dense—
I am feeling right, for the first
time." And then the vessel burst, and we were kneeling
around an emptiness.

We cannot feel our
father now. His power courses through us, yes, but *he*—
the chest and cheek, the foot and palm,
the mouth of oracle—is calm. And we still seek
his meaning. "*Feel* me," he said,
and emphasized that word.
Should we have heard it as a plea

for a caress—A constant caress,
since flesh to flesh was all that we could do right
if we would bless him? The dying must feel
the pressure of that
question—lying flat, turning cold
from brow to heel—the hot
cowards there above

protesting their love, and saying,
"What can we do? Are you all
right?"—While the wall opens

494

and the blue night pours through. "What
can we do? We want to do what's right."
"Lie down with me, and hold me, tight. Touch me. Be
with me. Feel with me. *Feel* me, to do right."

After the Dentist

My left upper
lip and half

my nose is gone.
I drink my coffee

on the right from
a warped cup

whose left lip dips.
My cigarette's

thick as a finger.
Somebody else's.

I put lip-
stick on a cloth-

stuffed doll's
face that's

surprised when one
side smiles.

The Secret in the Cat

I took my cat apart
to see what made him purr.
Like an electric clock
or like the snore

of a warming kettle,
something fizzed and sizzled in him.
Was he a soft car,
the engine bubbling sound?

Was there a wire beneath his fur,
or humming throttle?
I undid his throat.
Within was no stir.

I opened up his chest
as though it were a door:
no whisk or rattle there.
I lifted off his skull:

no hiss or murmur.
I halved his little belly
but found no gear,
no cause for static.

So I replaced his lid,
laced his little gut.
His heart into his vest I slid
and buttoned up his throat.

His tail rose to a rod
and beckoned to the air.
Some voltage made him vibrate
warmer than before.

Whiskers and a tail:
perhaps they caught
some radar code
emitted as a pip, a dot-and-dash

of woolen sound.
My cat a kind of tuning fork?—
amplifier?—telegraph?—
doing secret signal work?

His eyes elliptic tubes:
there's a message in his stare.
I stroke him
but cannot find the dial.

ROBERT WINNER

Miss Alderman

By the high steel hospital bed
a thousand miles from anyone I knew,
she sat while I slept;
Miss Alderman, night duty student nurse
with auburn hair, blue eyes, a perfect body.

Sixteen, just inside girl hunger,
paralyzed, sleeping on my side,
I dreamt of her in my fever,
my spine like a broken chair
on one of their broken Southern porches.

Coming out of sick half-sleep, I found her
pressing my face with her parted lips.
Desire leaped in me, all my body
helpless to respond like a sack of gravel.
I could see her breast.
A warm deep wave of her carried me off.
She kissed me, fondled me; she cared enough
to want to give me
some of that womanly fire
which haunts my manhood,
heals me, makes things right.

It haunts me now, that only chance with her,
that tenderness
lost to me in some provincial Southern city,
a nurse still maybe, or a housewife.

I knew it was no more
than kindness
by the blank calm way
she fixed her hair at the mirror
and scraped her lipstick
with her fingernail
and buttoned her dress
afterwards.

JAMES WRIGHT

Two Postures Beside a Fire

1.

Tonight I watch my father's hair,
As he sits dreaming near his stove.
Knowing my feather of despair,
He sent me an owl's plume for love,
Lest I not know, so I've come home.
Tonight Ohio, where I once
Hounded and cursed my loneliness,
Shows me my father, who broke stones,
Wrestled and mastered great machines,
And rests, shadowing his lovely face.

2.

Nobly his hands fold together in his repose.
He is proud of me, believing
I have done strong things among men and become a man
Of place among men of place in the large cities.
I will not waken him.
I have come home alone, without wife or child
To delight him. Awake, solitary and welcome,
I too sit near his stove, the lines
Of an ugly age scarring my face, and my hands
Twitch nervously about.

In Terror of Hospital Bills

I still have some money
To eat with, alone
And frightened, knowing how soon
I will waken a poor man.

It snows freely and freely hardens
On the lawns of my hope, my secret
Hounded and flayed. I wonder
What words to beg money with.

Pardon me, sir, could you?
Which way is St. Paul?
I thirst.
I am a full-blooded Sioux Indian.

Soon I am sure to become so hungry
I will have to leap barefoot through gas-fire veils of shame,
I will have to stalk timid strangers
On the whorehouse corners.

Oh moon, sow leaves on my hands,
On my seared face, oh I love you.
My throat is open, insane,
Tempting pneumonia.

But my life was never so precious
To me as now.
I will have to beg coins
After dark.

I will learn to scent the police,
And sit or go blind, stay mute, be taken for dead
For your sake, oh my secret,
My life.

Expatriates

Blessings Are

Blessings are
at hand

Empty
receives most.

I'm a Baby . . .

I'm a baby. I
shit in my pants and
wait for the mama

to come and clean me.
Clear me of the mess
I have made for her—

for you—my love—my
love. Or dont you yet
get what I'm saying?

Without You

Without you
no shadow
and the night

night. To see
heaven one
wants a star.

Cincinnati

The hatred the
bum greeted me
with—in passing—

503

each a stranger
to the other—
brings my eyes tears—

for one enough
like me to be
me made him feel

like that. Now years
later I see
I met a friend.

The Toy

I had so little
given me, as a
child. Patience, patience,
they said. It will all

be yours in the end.
I've waited, not that
there was that much choice,
but I have waited

to come finally
into the night room
and find myself with
my erector set.

It's Food ...

It's food. And
if you *are*
hungry,

you know it.
Nevermind
calling

it shit—
shocking us
into sense.

The sense is
this. Come and
get it.

504

This Is the Non-Existent Beast

This is the non-existent beast.
They didnt know it but somehow—
its movement, its manner, its throat,
even its quiet eye's gleam—loved.

True, it *wasnt*. But loving it
it became. They always left space.
And in the space, clear, allowed-for,
it lifted its head hardly had

to be. They fed it on no grain,
but only possibility.
And this gave such strength to the beast

it was crowned with a horn. One horn.
To a maiden it came, white, near—
and in her mirror was and in her.

The Old Pines

The old pines
axed. Lumber.
And some stumps.

More space at
the temple
now. But roots

alone are
meaningless—
buried mouths.

So Little Wanted

So little wanted
already too much.
Assume your breath as

what it is—your fate.
And in the name of
God—abandon hope.

ROBERT FRIEND

In the Orchard

(for Elizabeth)

We sat in the Cambridge orchard drinking tea.
Above, the apples rounded to a fall.
Preserving balance, cup upon a knee,
   we thought no thought at all,

but rumoured idly with the idle bees
deep in the heart of flowers, who triggered thus
another generation's histories.
   But what was that to us?

A cheek may flush, a heart may miss a beat.
I am not master of such languages.
I settled back into the rural seat,
   "Another biscuit, please."

Master or not, was she not signaling?
And was I not interpreting her eyes?
For suddenly I felt it like a sting:
   Why, this was Paradise!

and almost dropped my cup. Something was slithering.
Well, here was one man it could not deceive.
I laughed—as if I hadn't heard a thing.
And she laughed back—as if her name were Eve.

The Riders

The riders underneath the sea
are streaming somewhere silently.
Green in the green wave they go—
to victory or overthrow.

On motorcycles, a grim tide,
dark-caped, dark-helmeted they ride,
moving with resistless pace
towards the age-long trysting place.

I cannot waken from my dream.
I cannot halt that mindless stream,
whose will is my necessity,
overthrow or victory.

The Doll

Dollmaker, snug in your house
with your shelf piled with dolls, how can
you sleep? Yesterday in the grass
I saw, with her head full of bran
and her eyes one dead blue stare,
a doll that a child had flung
down carelessly, running off elsewhere
with a shrieking, living tongue.
But careless of that neglect,
she simpered as she lay,
still stiffly circumspect
beneath the changing day.
And if she blushed, it was not
anger, or shame for that fickle child—
merely a painted spot.
She would drive no parents wild,
whose cry was a built-in cry,
and not for pleasure, not for woe.
Not from that wax thigh
would the thick blood flow.

Dollmaker, do you not fear
that on the Judgment Day,
her limbs will begin to stir,
her Cupid lips say:
"He has much to answer for,
who to satisfy his pride,
out of wax, paint and straw,
insolently has made,
though with a craftsman's art,
this body I could not live,
perfect, without a heart
to suffer and forgive."

507

Identity

Words are written
on the Wailing Wall
I cannot read.
My Name?

I have come to read my name
where even the birds are Jewish
and the cats yowl
in the holy language,

whose mystery I master,
its stubborn consonants
and its warm vowels,
but not that mystery

I shroud in English.
Robert, I say,
pronouncing who I am
in the cold syllables

of the tongue I love.

The Test

But was the language alive?
Bialik wished he knew,
thoughtfully slapped a child.
Was the pain Hebrew?
Knowledge was not denied.
The child proved unforgiving.
"*Hamor*," (donkey) he cried,
and proved the language living.

PATRICIA GOEDICKE

The Great Depression

All of our fathers are old but lately

Lately I am beginning to see
More and more of them.

508

On streetcars, walking across bridges
In threadbare suits on a cold day

Rubbing their hands together like ghosts

Puffs of sadness flicker above the grates,
Over the subways and windows of the basements

One by one they are beginning to come
Like Eskimos, out of the smokeless North

An army of ancient pushcarts
Gathering like smudgepots to warn us

With extreme politeness and all their belongings
How they left their grandfathers behind them in the snow

Which melts, my God, in the spring
The corpses poke up like thin sticks,

In wheelchairs, on canes, crutches
Horned hands begging

Which cannot be avoided, which must
Our scrawny and tramp fears cry out

Like beggars gathering in the dust.

Young Men You Are So Beautiful Up There

Young men on the roof watching the stars,
Young men your silhouettes are like tall bears
Standing against the night sky.

Young men leaning on the railing / eagerly
Watching the fire balloons you have sent up sail away

Into the heavens like burning pumpkins,
Eagles bearing messages in golden bottles,

Young men you are so beautiful up there
What if one of your fire balloons

Should pass through the open belfry of a church
And sail on, into the desert beyond,

Instead of blazing / in a bush
What if you should incinerate a small hut
A farmhouse, maybe even the whole world

What if one of your fire balloons should land
On the heart of the wife who is sleeping below you

Dreaming of you, turning and turning
So that she rises up

Like paper, all aflame
Passionately shaking herself into ashes ...

Young men you are so beautiful up there
Surely you must understand
Nobody can stop them, the fire balloons

Once they have sailed away
They will keep on going and going

Over the heads of a few farmers watching for satellites,
Over the body of your dead mother

Who is sleeping below you,
Who is breathing the heaviness of lead,

Who is waiting and waiting for you to come down
Out of the heavens into her arms.

TED JOANS

Up Out of the African

Up out of the African
ocean came the animals
with legs as long as giraffes'
necks   and noses as long as
elephants' trunks   and eyes
as bright as birds that
sing   and ears as acute as
scorpions that sting   and feet
as hard as turtles' backs   and
mouths as wide as hippos'
wet and black   these huge
animals of the ocean came

510

Chickitten Gitten!

C'MON GODAMYA C'MON GIMME THAT PUSSY!
LET IT GO FREE LET IT COME RIGHT ON OVER
   HERE TO ME
LET IT HAVE THIS MILK I GOT AFTERALL ITS
   FREE!
C'MON GODAMYA! TURN A LOOSE THAT PUSSY,
   GIRL
LET IT BE ITS SELF DONT KEEP IT FROM ME
TAKE IT OFF THAT LEASH LET THE DAMN THING
   WALK!
C'MON DAM IT C'MON PLEASE LET ME RUB THAT
   PUSSY
ITS GOT A MIND OF ITS OWN FURTHERMO IT
   DIGS ME
C'MON LET GO THAT THERE PUSSY WOMAN!
SET THE PRETTY PUSSY FREE SO THAT IT MAY
   MEOW
AND JUMP HAPPY ALL OVER PUSSY LOVING ME!!

Watermelon

Its got   a good shape/the outside color is green/its one of
   them foods from Africa
its got stripes sometimes like a zebra   or Florida prison
   pants
Its bright red inside/the black eyes are flat and shiney/it
   wont make you fat
Its got heavy liquid weight/the sweet taste is unique/some
   people are shamed of it/
I aint afraid to eat it/indoors or out/its soul food thing/
   Watermelon is what I'm
talking about   Yeah watermelon is what I'm talking
   about   Watermelon

Knee Deep

to hold my own hand in some secret place away from
   television
to caress the insides of my own thighs hidden under no
   clothing

to rub face cheeks against my buttock's cheeks bearing no
    storebought stains
I standing naked with my nude body pressed against my
    bareness
I opening my openings to receive my tongue my forefinger
    wearing nobody's wedding ring but my marriage vows
to suck my earlobe in the shadows of overturned overplayed
    baby Grand pianos
to kiss my own armpits and elbow my way down into my
    own spread legs
to blow soft storms of hot air from my own lips down the
    spine
I lying naked uncovered with nudity wanting everything I
    can give myself
I opening and closing pushing and shoving giving and taking
breathing hard and shaking rising upward fast tumbling
    down so slow
coming into my one and only self gasping and gasping
    hanging on banging on until the cool calm
narcissistic self satisfying ego ridden climax flows gently all
    over my beautiful body
and I drown
in my own
juices
of
joy

Zoo You Too!

WHEN I VISIT EUROPE & AMERICA'S ZOOS
I SEE CAGED/FENCED/AND ALL LOCKED UP
AFRICAN & ASIA ANIMALS
I OFTEN DEPART FROM THESE PRISONS WITH
                    BLUES
I OFTEN DEPART
FROM THESE PRISONS   WITH *BLUES*!
WHY DO Third World animals
have to pay . . . such heavy/lifetime dues?

To Fez Cobra

Up against the wall
this *IS* a cobra!
He will do what you
know he's known to do

He will sink his poisonous
fangs deep into you
he will bite but will
not chew

After he strikes you'll
turn blue   what usually
happens when cobra does his bit
Usually most people—just shit!

SHIRLEY KAUFMAN

The Burning of the Birds

Flight songs the way they build their nests—
all were miraculous.

Montezuma's water birds had ten lakes
emptied cleaned and refilled every day.
Salt water for sea birds
seven thousand feet high
and private pools for birds
from marshes and streams.

He could watch from the palace balcony
a ring of ibises herons flamingos
feeding at his gold-sandaled feet.

Hundreds of keepers cared for them
collecting molted feathers to make
bracelets and banners feathered fans
robes trailing shadows of the gods.

513

Bird-gods or god-birds shapes that flew
or skimmed the lakes like tropical flowers.
Sun was the quail or was the quail the sun?
Lord of them all the war god
beak of a bird's head covered with down.

And Cortes burned them
quetzals lovely cotingas hyacinth macaws.

To see how their wings like torches
filled with flame and remember that burning
every burning when the end is ashes
and the wings tip over in the smoke

to think of their pampered wings
the well-laid fire
how their colors flaked into it
beating against that brilliance till they fried

to hear the air scream their panic
turned into outrage into words
repeated like birds or seasons
or the outrage of history repeated
which is the same as fire or burning feathers.

Plumes of the quetzal
god-filled iridescence and the human blood
shriek in the air over and over
bright birds falling scorched
in the oven of their wings
as dead as any dream of paradise.

Mothers, Daughters

Through every night we hate,
preparing the next day's
war. She bangs the door.
Her face laps up my own
despair, the sour, brown eyes,
the heavy hair she won't
tie back. She's cruel,
as if my private meanness
found a way to punish us.

514

We gnaw at each other's
skulls. Give me what's mine.
I'd haul her back, choking
myself in her, herself
in me. There is a book
called *Poisons* on her shelf.
Her room stinks with incense,
animal turds, hamsters
she strokes like silk. They
exercise on the bathroom
floor, and two drop through
the furnace vent. The whole
house smells of the accident,
the hot skins, the small
flesh rotting. Six days
we turn the gas up then
to fry the dead. I'd fry
her head if I could until
she cried love, love me!

All she won't let me do.
Her stringy figure in
the windowed room shares
its thin bones with no one.
Only her shadow on the glass
waits like an older sister.
Now she stalks, leans forward,
concentrates merely on getting
from here to there. Her feet
are bare. I hear her breathe
where I can't get in. If I
break through to her, she will
drive nails into my tongue.

Appendix: Directories

Poetry Mail Order Services

The following U.S. direct mail booksellers specialize in inexpensive contemporary poetry and fiction and provide mail order catalogues on request.

	EMPHASIS & SPECIAL FEATURES
Before Columbus*† c/o Yardbird Reader Box 2370, Station A Berkeley, CA 94702	Small presses Black, Hispanic, Native American, Asian, & European-American writing
Casa Editorial† 3128 24th Street San Francisco, CA 94110	Small press poetry & magazines Includes new, rare, & used Postage/handling free with prepayment
Christopher P. Stevens, Bookseller, Inc.*† 325 West 38th Street New York, NY 10018	New, used, & rare Includes separate catalogues for detective fiction, science fiction, experimental writing, & minority literature Postage/handling free
Cold Mountain Press† 4705 Sinclair Avenue Austin, TX 78756	Small press poetry Includes rare & used
Cosmep/South*† P.O. Box 209 Carrboro, NC 27514	Southern small presses Postage/handling free

* indicates that the seller offers introductory copies of magazines or subscriptions to magazines.
† means the seller sells books and miscellaneous publications.

Energy Blacksouth
  Distributors*†
2805 Southmore
Houston, TX 77004

Small press
Includes Black & Women's

Gotham Book Mart†
Small Press Department
41 West 47th Street
New York, NY 10036

Small presses
Includes rare & used

LPSC (Literary Publishers of
  Southern California)*†
1639 W. Washington
  Boulevard
Venice, CA 90291

Southern California small
  presses

Magazine*
1 West 30th Street
New York, NY 10001

All titles discounted

NESPD (New England Small
  Press Distribution)*†
45 Hillcrest Place
Amherst, MA 01002

New England small presses

Plains Distribution Service*†
P.O. Box 3112
Rm. 406, Block 6
620 Main
Fargo, ND 58102

Midwestern presses & authors
Discount on sample magazine
  subscriptions

Quarto Book Service†
P.O. Box 4727
Columbus, OH 43202

Poetry from trade, university
  & small presses
Postage/handling free

Sand Dollar Booksellers &
  Publishers†
1205 Solano Avenue
Albany, CA 94706

Includes rare & used

Serendipity Books
  Distribution†
1790 Shattuck Avenue
Berkeley, CA 94709

Small presses
Includes rare & remaindered
Postage/handling free

Small Press Book Club†
Box 100
Paradise, CA 95969

Small presses

Small Press Book Center*†
38415 24th Street
San Francisco, CA 94114

West Coast small presses
Postage/handling free

Spring Church Book Co.†
P.O. Box 127
Spring Church, PA 15686

Poetry from trade & university
  publishers
All titles at discount (10%-
  15% avg.)

Truck Distribution Service*†
1141 James Avenue
St. Paul, MN 55105

Small presses
Includes sev ral U.K. small
  presses
Discount on sample magazine
  copies

University Place Book Shop†
821 Broadway
New York, NY 10003

Afro-American literature
Includes rare & foreign
  language

Women's Distribution
  Cooperative*†
c/o Out & Out Books
44 Seventh Avenue
Brooklyn, NY 11217

Small press publications
  edited or written by women

Poetry Centers

Poetry Center of the
  University of Arizona
1086 North Highland Avenue
Tucson, AZ 85719
Att: Lois Shelton, Director

The Woodberry Poetry Room
Lamont Library
Harvard College
Cambridge, MA 02138
Att: Stratis Haviaras, Curator

Poetry Room—Main Library
University of Cincinnati
Cincinnati, OH 45221
Att: Jim Cummins, Curator,
  Room 407

The Poetry Center
San Francisco State University
1600 Holloway Ave.
San Francisco, CA 94132

The Poetry Center
YMHA
Lexington Ave. & 92nd St.
New York, NY 10028

Twelve of the Biggest Poetry Collections

	RANGE	SAMPLE HOLDINGS
Special Collections Boston University Libraries 771 Commonwealth Avenue Boston, MA 02215 Att: Dr. Howard Gotlieb, Director	Contemporary American poetry	Ben Bellitt Richard Frost Nikki Giovanni William Heyen Maxine Kumin Loren Niedecker Lucien Stryk Andrew J. Young
The Harris Collection John Hay Library Brown University Providence, RI 02912 Att: Rosemary Cullen, Special Collections Librarian, Harris Collection	20th century American and Canadian poetry and plays	*Aphra* *Ark River Review* *Beloit Poetry Journal* *Northern Journey* *Poesie* *Wormwood Review*
The Bancroft Poetry Archive University of California at Berkeley Berkeley, CA 94710 Att: Leslie Clarke, Rare Books Librarian	Postwar Bay Area and California poetry	Robert Duncan Thom Gunn Josephine Miles Jack Spicer City Lights Archive Auerhahn Press Archive

	RANGE	HOLDINGS
Archive for New Poetry The University Library University of California at San Diego La Jolla, CA 92037 Att: Michael Davidson, Director	Poetry in English published since 1945	Paul Blackburn Archive Clayton Eshleman Ken Friedman and the Fluxus poets Marianne Moore Lew Welch Archive
Lilly Library Indiana University Bloomington, IN 47401 Att: Acquisitions Department	American poetry from the 1930's to the present	A. R. Ammons James Broughton Stanley Kunitz David Meltzer Howard Moss Muriel Rukeyser David Shapiro Robin Skelton Mary Ellen Solt
The Library of Congress Washington, DC 20540 Att: David Kresh, Recommending Officer for Poetry in English	Poetry in English including most work sent for copyright registration	Sam Cornish Eloise Loftin Thomas Lux Tony Towle John Stevens Wade
Poetry Collection 207 Lockwood Library State University of New York at Buffalo	20th century poetry in English and in translation (probably the largest collection in the world)	Kayak Archive Sonya Dorman Siv Cedering Fox Anselm Hollo

Buffalo, NY 14214 Att: K. C. Gay, Curator, or Beverly Ruth Vander Kooy		Richmond Lattimore Stanley Plumly Louis Simpson John Tagliabue Byron Vazakas Paul Zweig
Special Collections Northwestern University Library Evanston, IL 60201 Att: Russell Maylene, Curator	Underground and young writers of the U.S., Canada, and England, from the late 1950's to the present	Carol Berge Douglas Blazek Edward Dorn Sandra Hochman Don Lee D. A. Levy Diane Wakoski
Sterling Memorial Library 1603A Yale Station New Haven, CT 06520 Att: Susan Steinberg, American Studies Bibliographer	American literature	*Grilled Flowers* *Hot Water Review* *Sun and Moon* Michael Davidson Rochelle Ratner Martin J. Rosenblum Primus St. John
Humanities Research Center University of Texas P.O. Box 7219 Austin, TX 78712 Att: F. W. Roberts, Director	20th century English and American literature	Gregory Corso Charles Henri Ford Gerard Malanga James Tate Louis Zukofsky Archive

	RANGE	HOLDINGS
Rare Books and Special Collections Olin Library Washington University St. Louis, MO 63130 Att: Holly Hall, Acting Chief	20th century American and British poetry	Donald Finkel James Merrill John N. Morris Howard Nemerov Robert Sward May Swenson Constance Urdang Mona Van Duyn
Little Magazines Collection Rare Books Department Memorial Library University of Wisconsin Madison, WI 53706 Att: Cristine Rom, Assistant to the Curator	20th century little magazines in English (probably the largest collection there is)	*Assembling* *Circus Maximus* *Experiment* *Moving Out* *Room of One's Own* *Woman Poems*

More Collections

Special Collections
University of Arizona Library
Tucson, AZ 85721
Att: Patrick Murphy,
Acquisitions

W. H. Auden
W. S. Merwin
Gary Snyder
Philip Whalen

Beloit College Library
Beloit, WI 53511
Att: Clyde Peterman,
Associate Director

Vanity presses

Special Collections
Shields Library
University of California at
Davis
Davis, CA 95616
Att: Donald Kunitz, Head of
Special Collections

Helen Adam
Daisy Aldan
Ron Bayes
James Bertolino
John Brandi
Joanne Kyger

Special Collections and Rare
Books
University Research Library
University of California at
Los Angeles
Westwood, CA 90024
Att: Brook Whiting, Assistant
Head of Special Collections

Imamu Amiri Baraka
Tom Clark
Clark Coolidge
Kenneth Rexroth
Aram Saroyan

Special Collections
U.C.S.B. Library
Santa Barbara, CA 93106
Att: Christian Brun, Head of
Special Collections

Charles Bukowski Archive
Bob Brown
David Kherdian
Cafe Solo
Painted Cave Books
Water Table Press

Special Collections
University of California at
Santa Cruz
Santa Cruz, CA 95064
Att: Rita Bottoms, Head of
Special Collections

Kenneth Patchen Archive
William Everson
George Hitchcock
Perishable Press
IO
Caterpillar

Special Collections
California State University
Library
Hayward, CA 94542
Att: Elsa Glines, Acquisitions
Librarian

Oyez Press
Mary Norbert Kate
Philip Lamantia
Michael McBride
Michael McClure

Harriet Monroe Modern
  Poetry Collection
Joseph Regenstein Library
University of Chicago
Chicago, IL 60637
Att: Charles Helzer, Head of
  Acquisitions

Archives of *Poetry* of Chicago
Allen Ginsberg
Rochelle Owens
Mark Strand
Toothpaste Press

Special Collections
University of Connecticut
  Library
Storrs, CT 06268
Att: R. H. Schimmelpfeng,
  Curator

Black Mountain Poets
Charles Olson Archive

Rare Books Division
Library West
University of Florida
Gainesville, FL 32602
Att: Laura V. Monti,
  Chairman

Duane Locke
Peter Meinke
William E. Taylor

Special Collections
University of Hawaii Library
2550 The Mall
Honolulu, HI 96822
Att: Eleanor Chang, Head of
  Special Collections

Black Sparrow Press
Hawaiian poets and presses
Phyllis Thompson

New American Poetry
  Collection
Kenneth Spencer Research
  Library
University of Kansas
Lawrence, KS 66045
Att: Alexandra Mason,
  Spencer Librarian

Jack Kerouac
Kirby Congdon
Larry Eigner
Kenneth Koch

New Mexico State University
  Library
Las Cruces, NM 88001
Att: Dr. James Dyke, Director
  of the Library

All books stocked by Gotham
  Book Mart in New York
  City

Special Collections
S.U.N.Y. at Stonybrook
Stonybrook, NY 11794
Att: Evert Volkersz, Head of
  Special Collections

Conrad Aiken
Jack Hirschman
Robert Kelly
Toby Olson
Joel Oppenheimer
Rosemary Waldrop

Morris Library
University of Southern Illinois
Carbondale, IL 62901
Att: Alan Cohn, Humanities
    Librarian

Denise Levertov
Diane di Prima
Robert Bly
Midwestern and Illinois poets
Kulcher Foundation
    Publications

Contemporary Culture
    Collection
Temple University Library
Philadelphia, PA 19122
Att: Elliott Shore

Insect Trust Gazette
Yarrow Stalks
Small presses of the late
    1960's

Watkinson Library
Trinity College Library
Hartford, CT 06106

Small press examples of fine
    printing
David R. Godine publications

Special Collections
University of Washington
    Library
Seattle, WA 98195
Att: Robert Monroe

Theodore Roethke Archive
William Stafford
David Wagoner

Large Public Libraries with Special Collections

Brooklyn Public Library
Grand Army Plaza
Brooklyn, NY 11238
Att: Monte Olenick, Chief of
    Language and Literature
    Division

Brooklyn small presses
Marianne Moore

Detroit Public Library
5201 Woodward Avenue
Detroit, MI 48202
Att: Ann Rabjohns, Head of
    Language and Literature
    Department

Michigan poets and presses
Broadside Press
Bardic Echoes Press
Ghost Dance Press
Red Hanrahan Press
El Soplon Press
Zeitgeist

Milwaukee Public Library
814 West Wisconsin Avenue
Milwaukee, WI 53203
Att: Acquisitions Department

Milwaukee poets and presses
California poets
Women poets

New York Public Library
Fifth Avenue and 42d Street
New York, NY 10018
Att: Stephen Green, Room
   108, Current Periodicals
   Section

Big Deal
Glassware
Not Guilty
Stroker
Sun
Sunbury

San Francisco Public Library
Civic Center
San Francisco, CA 94102
Att: Mrs. Nancy Nee, Head of
   Literature, Philosophy, and
   Religion

Bay Area small presses

Independent Poetry Libraries

Academy of American Poets
1078 Madison Ave.
New York, NY 10028

The Andrew W. Mellon
   International Collection of
   Contemporary Poetry
Carnegie Library
4400 Forbes Ave.
Pittsburgh, PA 15213

The Beyond Baroque Library
   of Small Press Publications
1639 W. Washington Blvd.
Venice, CA 90291

Community Writers Library
McKinley Foundation
809 S. 5th St.
Champaign, IL 61820

Coordinating Council of
   Literary Magazines (for
   literary magazines)
80 Eighth Ave.
New York, NY 10011

Poetry Society of America
16 Gramercy Park S.
New York, NY 10003

Biographical Notes

Ai (b. 1947 in Texas) Grew up in Arizona and considers herself a southwest poet. Now lives in Michigan where she teaches at Wayne State U. *Cruelty* (Houghton Mifflin, 1973).

Alta (b. 1942 in Reno, Nev.) Publisher of the feminist Shameless Hussy Press in the Bay Area. *I Am Not a Practicing Angel* (Crossing Press, 1975).

A. R. Ammons (b. 1926 in Whiteville, N.C.) Winner of National Book Award and Bollingen Prize. Teaches at Cornell U. *Selected Poems: 1951-1977* (Norton, 1977).

Jack Anderson (b. 1935 in Milwaukee, Wis.) Lives in New York City where he writes dance criticism. *Toward the Liberation of the Left Hand* (U. of Pittsburgh Press, 1977).

John Ashbery (b. 1927 in Rochester, N.Y.) His book *Self-Portrait in a Convex Mirror* (Viking, 1975) won the Pulitzer Prize, the National Book Award, and the National Book Critics Circle Award. Art critic, editor, and teacher. Lives in New York City.

Alvin Aubert (b. 1930 in Lutcher, La.) Teaches in Fredonia, N.Y. Editor of *Obsidian: Black Literature in Review*. *Feeling Through* (Greenfield Review Press, 1975).

Amiri Baraka (b. 1934 in Newark, N.J.) Well known as beat poet under name of Leroi Jones. Active as playwright (*Dutchman, The Slave*), and member of the Anti-Imperialist Cultural Union. Lives in Newark, N.J.

David Barker (b. 1948 in Chicago) Grew up in southern California. Editor of Rumba Train Press.

John Beecher (b. 1904 in Alabama) In 1950 he refused to sign a loyalty oath and was fired from San Francisco State College; reinstated in 1977. *Collected Poems: 1924-1974* (Macmillan, 1974).

Marvin Bell (b. 1937 in New York City) Teaches at the U. of Iowa, writes a column for *The American Poetry Review*. *Stars Which See, Stars Which Do Not See* (Atheneum, 1977).

527

Wendell Berry (b. 1934 in Henry County, Ky.) Lives on family farmstead in Kentucky and works for Rodale Press. Active in Sierra Club. *Clearing* (Harcourt Brace Jovanovich, 1977).

Mei-Mei Berssenbrugge (b. 1947 in Peking, China) Grew up in Mass. Lives in New Mexico. *Random Possession* (Reed, Cannon and Johnson Co., 1978).

Elizabeth Bishop (b. 1911 in Worcester, Mass.) After long years in Brazil, now lives in Boston. Pulitzer prize for *Poems* (Farrar, Straus and Giroux, Inc., 1955).

Chana Bloch (b. 1940 in New York City) Lives in Berkeley and teaches at Mills College. *A Dress of Fire*, translations from the Hebrew poetry of Daylia Ravikovitch (Sheep Meadow Press, 1978).

Robert Bly (b. 1926 in Minnesota) Lives on farm in Minn. Publishes a magazine whose title changes with the decade: *The Fifties, The Sixties, The Seventies,* etc. Founded Minnesota Poets Cooperative Press. National Book Award for *The Light Around The Body* (Harper & Row, 1968).

Philip Booth (b. 1925 in Hanover, N.H.) Lives in Maine summers and teaches at Syracuse U. winters. *Available Light* (Viking, 1976).

David Bottoms (b. 1949 in Georgia) Editor of Sweetwater Press. Lives in Ga. First chapbook: *Jamming With the Band at the VFW* (Burnt Hickory Press, 1978).

Millen Brand (b. 1906 in Jersey City). In the summer of 1977 he took part in a memorial march across Japan on the anniversary of the atom bombings of Hiroshima and Nagasaki. Lives in New York City. *Local Lives* (Clarkson Potter, 1975).

John Malcolm Brinnin (b. 1916 in Nova Scotia) Teaches at Boston U. *Skin Diving in the Virgins* (Delacorte Press, 1970).

William Bronk (b. 1918 in Hudson Falls, N.Y.) Lives in upstate New York where he is in business. *Finding Losses* (Elizabeth Press, 1976).

Gwendolyn Brooks (b. 1912 in Topeka, Ka.) First Black writer to win the Pulitzer Prize. Lives in Chicago. *Selected Poems* (Harper & Row, 1963).

James Broughton (b. 1913 in California) Filmmaker, on faculty of San Francisco Art Institute. *A Long Undressing* (Jargon Society, 1971, reissued 1978).

Michael Dennis Browne (b. 1940 in England) Teaches at U. of Minnesota. *The Sun Fetcher* (Carnegie-Mellon, 1977).

J. V. Brummels (b. 1951 in Nebraska) Teaches at Wayne State College in Nebraska.

Charles Bukowski (b. 1920 in Andernach, Germany) Has lived in Los Angeles since the age of two. *Burning in Water, Drowning in Flame* (Black Sparrow, 1974).

Olga Cabral (b. 1910 in the West Indies) Has lived in New York City from the age of ten. *Occupied Country* (New Rivers Press, 1976).

Henry Carlile (b. 1934 in San Francisco) Teaches at Portland (Ore.) State U. *The Rough-Hewn Table* (U. of Missouri Press, 1971).

Hayden Carruth (b. 1921 in Waterbury, Conn.) Lives in Vermont. On the staff of *Harper's* and *Hudson Review*. Edited the monumental anthology *The Voice That Is Great Within Us* (Bantam, 1970).

Rick Casillas (b. 1944) Has lived in the Southwest desert all his life.

Turner Cassity (b. 1929 in Jackson, Miss.) Lives in Atlanta, Ga., where he works in the Emory U. Library. *Yellow for Peril, Black for Beautiful* (Braziller, 1975).

Lucille Clifton (b. 1936 in Depew, N.Y.) Lives in Baltimore. Writes children's books. *An Ordinary Woman* (Random House, 1974).

Victor Contoski (b. 1936 in St. Paul, Minn.) Lived for several years in Poland. Now teaching at the U. of Kansas. *Broken Treaties* (New Rivers, 1973).

Cid Corman, editor and publisher of *Origen* magazine. Lived in Japan for many years, but is in the process of moving to Boston.

Gregory Corso (b. 1930 in New York City). One of the founders of the beat movement. *Elegaic Feelings American* (New Directions, 1970).

Robert Creeley (b. 1926 in Arlington, Mass.) Divides his time between teaching in Buffalo, N.Y., and his home in Bolinas, Calif., where a number of poets have settled recently. *A Day Book* (Scribner's, 1972).

Philip Dacey (b. 1939 in St. Louis) Lives in Cottonwood, Minn., where he teaches at Southwest State U. First book: *How I Escaped from the Labyrinth and Other Poems* (Carnegie-Mellon, 1977).

Ann Darr (b. 1920 in Bagley, Iowa) Wrote and performed on radio. Pilot in World War II. Now lives in Washington, D.C.

Guy Davenport (b. 1927 in South Carolina) Teaches at the U. of Kentucky. Has published translations from the Greek, critical works, poetry, and stories.

Madeline DeFrees (b. 1919 in Oregon) Until 1973 was known as Sister Mary Gilbert and belonged to the order, Sisters of the Holy Names. Teaches at the U. of Montana. *When Sky Lets Go* (Braziller, 1978).

James Dickey (b. 1923 in Atlanta, Ga.) Football hero, fighter-pilot in World War II, advertising executive, National Book Award Winner, best-selling novelist (*Deliverance*), and actor in the movie based on it. Lives in Columbia, S.C.

William Dickey (b. 1928 in Bellingham, Wash.) Teaches at San Francisco State College. *More Under Saturn* (Wesleyan U. Press, 1971).

R.H.W. Dillard (b. 1937 in Roanoke, Va.) Teaches at Hollins College in Virginia. Worked on the screenplay of *Frankenstein Meets the Space Monster* (1964). *After Borges* (Louisiana State U. Press, 1972).

Diane di Prima (b. 1934 in New York City) Lives in Northern California. Editor of *The Floating Bear*, one of the founders of N.Y. Poets Theatre, founded Poets Press, five plays produced in New York City and San Francisco. *Selected Poems: 1956-1975* (North Atlantic Books, 1975).

Alan Dugan (b. 1923 in Brooklyn, N.Y.) Winner of the National Book Award and the Pulitzer Prize. Lives mostly on Cape Cod. *Poems 4* (Yale, 1974).

Robert Duncan (b. 1919 in Oakland, CA.) Lives in San Francisco. *Bending the Bow* (New Directions, 1968).

Stephen Dunn (b. 1939 in New York City) Lives and teaches in New Jersey. *A Circus of Needs* (Carnegie-Mellon, 1978).

Richard Eberhart (b. 1904 in Austin, Minn.) Member of the National Inst. of Arts and Letters. Winner of Bollingen Prize and Pulitzer Prize. Divides his time between Florida and New Hampshire where he is poet-in-residence at Dartmouth. *Collected Poems* (Oxford U. Press, 1976).

Russell Edson lives in Connecticut. *The Reason Why the Closet-Man Is Never Sad* (New Directions, 1977).

Abbie Huston Evans (b. 1881 in Lee, N.H.) Lives in Pennsylvania. *Collected Poems* (U. of Pittsburgh Press, 1970).

William Everson (b. 1912 in California) For many years known as Brother Antoninus of the Dominican Order, but has recently returned to "civilian" life. Lives in California. *Man-Fate* (New Directions, 1974).

Irving Feldman (b. 1928 in New York City). Teaches in Buffalo, N.Y. *Selected Poems* (Viking, 1979).

Lawrence Ferlinghetti (b. 1919, New York) Founder and publisher of the City Lights Bookshop and Press. Lives in San Francisco. *Who Are We Now?* (New Directions, 1977).

Edward Field (b. 1924 in Brooklyn, N.Y.) Lives in New York City. *A Full Heart* (Sheep Meadow Press, 1977).

Donald Finkel (b. 1929 in New York City) Lives in Missouri where he teaches at Washington U. Married to poet Constance Urdang. *A Mote in Heaven's Eye* (Atheneum, 1975).

Robert Francis (b. 1901 in Pennsylvania) Lives in Amherst, Mass. *Collected Poems* (U. of Mass. Press, 1976).

Elliot Fried (b. 1944 in St. Louis, Mo.) Teaches at Calif. State U. in Long Beach. *Poem City* (Rumba Train Press, 1977).

Robert Friend (b. 1913 in Brooklyn, N.Y.) Teaches at Hebrew U. in Jerusalem. Translator of Hebrew poetry. *Selected Poems* (Seahorse Press, London, 1976).

Vi Gale (b. 1917 in Sweden) Publisher of Prescott Street Press. Lives in Portland, Ore. *Clearwater* (Swallow Press, 1974).

Tess Gallagher (b. 1943 in Port Angeles, Wash.) Has recently taught in New York and Montana. *Instructions to the Double* (Graywolf Press, 1976).

Isabella Gardner lives in New York City. Her larger poetic life has been spent in Chicago and the Midwest, though she says "my heartland is New England."

Gary Gildner (b. 1938 in Michigan) Contributing editor of *New Letters* magazine. Lives in Iowa where he teaches at Drake U. *The Runner* (U. of Pittsburgh, 1978).

Allen Ginsberg (b. 1926 in Newark, N.J.) Famous throughout the world as spokesman for counter-culture. Teaches at Naropa Institute in Colorado.

Nikki Giovanni (b. 1943 in Knoxville, Tenn.) Lives in New York City where she works at *Encore* Magazine. *The Women and the Men* (William Morrow, 1975).

Louise Glück (b. 1943 in New York City) Lives in Vermont where she teaches at Goddard College. *The House on Marshland* (Ecco Press, 1975).

Patricia Goedicke (b. 1931 in Boston, Mass.) Lives in Mexico. *The Trail That Turns on Itself* (Ithaca House, 1978).

Judy Grahn is part of a women's collective that runs Diana Press in Oakland, Calif. *A Woman Is Talking to Death* (Women's Press Collective, 1974).

Arthur Gregor (b. 1923 in Vienna) Director of Creative Writing Program at Hofstra U. Lives in New York City. *The Past Now* (Doubleday, 1975).

Susan Griffin (b. 1943 in California) Lives in Berkeley and teaches at San Francisco State U. and at the U. of California. *Like the Iris of an Eye* (Harper & Row, 1976).

Marilyn Hacker (b. 1942 in New York City) National Book Award for her first book. *Separations* (Knopf, 1976).

John Haines (b. 1924 in Norfolk, Va.) Long a homesteader in Alaska, he now lives in Montana. *In Five Years Time* (Smoke-Root Press, 1976).

Kenneth O. Hanson (b. 1922 in Shelley, Id.) Teaches at Reed College in Portland, Oregon, but spends a lot of time in Greece. *The Uncorrected World* (Wesleyan, 1973).

William J. Harris (b. 1942 in Yellow Springs, Ohio) Recently taught at U. of California, Riverside. *Hey Fella Would You Mind Holding This Piano a Moment* (Ithaca House, 1974).

Robert Hayden (b. 1913 in Detroit) Presently Consultant in Poetry to the Library of Congress. Teaches at U. of Michigan. *Angle of Ascent: New and Selected Poems* (Liveright, 1975).

Gwen Head (b. 1940 in New Orleans) Lives in Seattle. *The Ten Thousandth Night* (U. of Pittsburgh Press, 1979).

Eloise Klein Healy (b. 1943 in El Paso, Tex.) Lives in Los Angeles. Has taught at Immaculate Heart College. *Building Some Changes* (Beyond Baroque Foundation, 1975).

Tom Hennen (b. 1942 in Morris, Minn.) Still lives in the town where he was born. Does the printing for the Minnesota Writers' Publishing House in his garage. *The Heron with No Business Sense* (Minnesota Writers' Publishing House, 1974).

William Heyen (b. 1940 in Brooklyn, N.Y.) Lives upstate New York where he teaches at the State University College. *Swastika Poems* (Vanguard, 1977).

Jim Heynen (b. 1940 in Sioux Center, IA.) Lives in Port Townsend, Wash. Has translated Sioux songs. *Notes from Custer* (Bear Claw Press, 1976).

Daryl Hine (b. 1936 in British Columbia) Was editor of Poetry (Chicago) for 10 years. Teaches at U. of Chicago. *Daylight Saving* (Atheneum, 1978).

George Hitchcock (b. 1914 in Hood River, Ore.) Teaches at U. of California, Santa Cruz. Editor of *Kayak* Magazine. *Lessons in Alchemy* (West Coast Poetry Review, 1976).

Sandra Hochman (b. 1936 in New York City) Has published three novels, produced a film, *Year of the Women*. Lives in New York City. *Futures* (Viking, 1974).

Daniel Hoffman (b. 1923 in New York City) Teaches at U. of Pennsylvania. *The Center of Attention* (Random House, 1974).

Michael Hogan (b. 1943) Has moved from the South to the Southwest. Edited anthology of prison writings. Associate editor of Cold Mountain Press. *Rust* (Turkey Press, 1976).

John Hollander (b. 1929 in New York City) Teaches at Yale U. *Spectral Emanations* (Atheneum, 1978).

Richard Howard (b. 1929 in Cleveland, OH.) Won Pulitzer Prize for *Untitled Subjects* (Atheneum, 1969). Has translated over 100 books from the French. Lives in New York City.

Barbara Howes (b. 1914 in New York City) Helped organize the Southern Tenant Farmers Union. *A Private Signal* (Wesleyan U. Press, 1978).

Robert Huff (b. 1924 in Evanston, Ill.) Teaches at Western Wash. State College, Bellingham, Wash. *The Ventriloquist* (The University of Virginia Press, 1977).

Richard Hugo (b. 1923 in Seattle) Director of the Writing Program at the U. of Montana. *What Thou Loves Well Remains American* (Norton, 1975).

David Ignatow (b. 1914 in Brooklyn, N.Y.) Poet-in-Residence at York College, City University of N.Y. Bollingen Award 1977. *Tread the Dark* (Atlantic Monthly Press, 1978).

Lawson Fusao Inada (b. 1938 in Fresno, CA.) Teaches at Southern Oregon State College.

Will Inman (b. 1923 in Wilmington, N.C.) Lives in Tucson, Arizona, where he founded the Prickly Pears Poetry Society. *Voice of the Beech Oracle* (ManRoot, 1977).

Josephine Jacobsen (b. 1908 in Coburg, Ont.) Has been the poetry consultant for several terms to the Library of Congress. Lives in Baltimore and New Hampshire. *The Shade Seller* (Doubleday, 1974).

Louis Jenkins (b. 1942 in Oklahoma City) Works as printer in Minnesota. *The Well Digger's Wife* (Minnesota Writers' Publishing House, 1973).

Ted Joans (b. 1928 in Cairo, Ill.) Is thought by his publishers to live in Timbuctu. *Afrodisia* (Hill & Wang, 1970).

Erica Jong (b. 1942 in New York City) Best selling novelist. Lives in Connecticut. *Loveroot* (Holt, Rinehart & Winston, 1975).

Donald Justice (b. 1925 in Miami) Teaches at the U. of Iowa. *Departures* (Atheneum, 1973).

Shirley Kaufman (b. 1923 in Seattle, Wash.) Lives in Jerusalem. *The Floor Keeps Turning* (Pittsburgh U. Press, 1970).

David Kherdian (b. 1931 in Racine, Wis.) Founder of Giligia Press. Lives in Oregon. *Any Day of Your Life* (The Overlook Press, 1975).

Linda King was born in Utah. Editor of *Purr* magazine, runs "art, poetry and pool bar in Phoenix, Arizona." *Sweet and Dirty* (Vagabond, 1974).

Galway Kinnell (b. 1927 in Providence, R.I.) Lives in New York City. *The Book of Nightmares* (Houghton Mifflin, 1971).

Carolyn Kizer (b. 1925 in Spokane, Wash.) Studied with Theodore Roethke. Founded *Poetry Northwest*. Lives in Berkeley, CA. *Midnight Was My Cry* (Doubleday, 1971).

William Kloefkorn (b. 1932 in Kansas) Teaches at Nebraska Wesleyan U. *Not Such a Bad Place to Be* (Windflower Press, 1978).

Etheridge Knight (b. 1931 in Corinth, Miss.) "Self-educated at various prisons, jails." *Belly Song* (Broadside Press, 1973).

Kenneth Koch (b. 1925 in Cincinnati) Teaches at Columbia U. Famous teacher of poetry to the young and the old. Playwright. *The Art of Love* (Random House/Vintage, 1975).

Ronald Koertge (b. 1940 in Olney, Ill.) Teaches at Pasadena City College. *The Hired Nose* (MAG Press, 1974).

Ted Kooser (b. 1939 in Ames, IA.) Lives in Lincoln, Neb., where he works for an insurance company. Publishes Windflower Press. *Old Marriage and New* (Cold Mountain Press, 1978).

Karl Kopp (b. 1934 in Havre de Grace, Md.) Lives in New Mexico. Has edited an anthology of Southwest poets. *Yell County Machine Shop* (Three Herons Press, 1976).

Maxine Kumin (b. 1925 in Philadelphia) Pulitzer Prize in 1973. Lives in New Hampshire. *The Retrieval System* (Viking, 1978).

Stanley Kunitz (b. 1905 in Worcester, Mass.) Pulitzer Prize, 1959. Teaches in the Graduate writing program at Columbia U. *Poems New and Old: 1928-1977* (Atlantic-Little, Brown, 1971).

Greg Kuzma (b. 1944 in Rome, N.Y.) Teaches at the U. of Nebraska. Publisher of Best Cellar Press. *Village Journal* (Best Cellar, 1978).

Paul Lawson (b. 1916 in Virginia) Lives in Washington, D.C. Publisher of The Charioteer Press.

Naomi Lazard lives in New York City. *The Moonlit Upper-deckarina* (Sheep Meadow Press, 1977).

Don L. Lee (b. 1942) *Don't Cry, Scream* (Broadside Press, 1969).

Meridel LeSueur (b. 1900 in Murray, Iowa) Lives in Minnesota. Considered "the local Earth Mother." *Rites of Ancient Ripening* (Vanilla Press, 1975).

Denise Levertov (b. 1923 in England) Lives in Massachusetts. *The Freeing of the Dust* (New Directions, 1975).

Philip Levine (b. 1928 in Detroit) Lives in Fresno, CA. *The Names of the Lost* (Atheneum, 1976).

Gerald Locklin (b. 1941 in Rochester, N.Y.) Teaches at California State U. at Long Beach. *The Criminal Mentality* (Red Hill Press, 1976).

Ron Loewinsohn (b. 1937 in the Philippines) Teaches at the U. of California, Berkeley. *Goat Dances* (Black Sparrow, 1976).

Audre Lorde (b. 1934 in New York City) Teaches at The City University of New York. *Coal* (Norton, 1977).

Cynthia MacDonald (b. 1929 in New York City) Teaches at the U. of Houston. *Transplants* (George Braziller, 1976).

Morton Marcus (b. 1936 in New York City) Lives in California where he teaches. *Where the Oceans Cover Us* (Capra Press, 1975).

Richard Mathews (b. 1944 in Washington, D.C.) Founding editor of *Florida Quarterly*. Publisher, Konglomerati Press. Teaches at Eckerd College in Florida.

Michael McClure (b. 1932 in Marysville, KS.) A playwright (*The Beard*). Lives in San Francisco. *September Blackberries* (New Directions, 1974).

Howard McCord (b. 1932 in El Paso) Teaches at Bowling Green State U. in Ohio. *Hard Tack and Chilled Whisky* (Crossing Press, 1978).

Thomas McGrath (b. 1916 in North Dakota) Founded *Crazy Horse* Magazine. Lives in Minnesota. *The Movie at the End of the World* (Swallow Press, 1972).

Sandra McPherson (b. 1943 in San Jose, CA.) Married to poet, Henry Carlile. Lives in Oregon. *Radiation* (Ecco Press, 1973).

Peter Meinke (b. 1932 in Brooklyn, N.Y.) Lives in Florida where he teaches at Eckerd College. *The Night Train and the Golden Bird* (U. of Pittsburgh Press, 1977).

David Meltzer (b. 1937 in Rochester, N.Y.) Lives in Berkeley where he is editor and publisher of *Tree* Magazine and Tree Books. *Six* (Black Sparrow Press, 1976) and *The Secret Garden*: Anthology of the Classical Kabbalah (1976).

James Merrill (b. 1926 in New York City) Won National Book Award. Lives in Connecticut and Greece. *Country of a Thousand Years of Peace* (Atheneum, 1970).

W. S. Merwin (b. 1927 in New York City) Pulitzer Prize in 1971. Divides time between New York City and various parts of the world. *The Cactus Flower* (Atheneum, 1977).

Josephine Miles (b. 1911 in Chicago) Teaches at U. of California, Berkeley. *To All Appearances* (U. of Illinois, 1974).

Jim Wayne Miller (b. 1936 in Leicester, N.C.) Teaches German at Western Kentucky U. *Dialogue with a Dead Man* (U. of Georgia Press, 1974).

Vassar Miller (b. 1924 in Houston, Tex.) Lives in Houston. *Approaching Nada* (Wings Press, 1977).

Robert Morgan (b. 1944 in Hendersonville, N.C.) Teaches at Cornell U. *Land Diving* (Louisiana State U. Press, 1976).

John N. Morris (b. 1931 in Oxford, England) Teaches at Washington U. in Missouri. *The Life Beside This One* (Atheneum, 1975).

Howard Moss (b. 1922 in New York City) On staff of *New Yorker* Magazine. Won National Book Award in poetry. *A Swim Off the Rocks* (Atheneum, 1976).

Stanley Moss (b. 1925 in New York) Art dealer, publisher of Sheep Meadow Press. Lives in New York City. *Skull of Adam* (Horizon, 1978).

Lisel Mueller (b. 1924 in Hamburg, Germany) Lives in Illinois and teaches at Goddard College in Vermont. *The Private Life* (Louisiana State U. Press, 1976).

Leonard Nathan (b. 1924 in Los Angeles) Teaches at U. of California, Berkeley. *Returning Your Call* (Princeton, 1975).

Howard Nemerov (b. 1920 in New York City) A pilot in World War II, now teaches at Washington U. in St. Louis. *The Collected Poems* (U. of Chicago Press, 1977) won the National Book Award.

Bink Noll (b. 1927 in Orange, N.J.) Teaches at Beloit College in Wisconsin. *The Feast* (Harcourt, Brace, 1967).

Kathleen Norris (b. 1947 in Washington, D.C.) Manages family farm in South Dakota. *Falling Off* (Big Table/Follett, 1971).

Harold Norse (b. 1916 in New York City) Editor of *Bastard Angel* Magazine. Lives in Bay Area. *Carnivorous Saint: Gay Poems* 1941-1976 (Gay Sunshine Press, 1977).

nila northSun (b. 1951 in Schurz, Nev.) Shoshoni-Chippewa. Co-edits *Scree* Magazine with Kirk Robertson. *Diet Pepsi & Nacho Cheese* (Duck Down Press, 1977).

Ed Ochester (b. 1939 in Brooklyn, N.Y.) Under name of Spring Church Book Co. sells poetry books by mail order. Teaches at U. of Pittsburgh. *The End of the Ice Age* (Slow Loris Press, 1977).

George Oppen (b. 1908 in New Rochelle, N.Y.) Member of Objectivist group in the 30s. Won Pulitzer Prize in 1969. *Collected Poems* (New Directions, 1976).

Steve Orlen (b. 1942 in Holyoke, Mass.) Teaches at the U. of Arizona. *Permission to Speak* (Wesleyan U. Press, 1978).

Simon J. Ortiz (b. 1941 in Albuquerque, N.Mex.) Works with Bay Area Indian community. *Going for the Rain* (Harper & Row, 1976).

Robert Pack (b. 1929 in New York City) Director of Bread Loaf Writers' Conference. Lives in Vermont. *Keeping Watch* (Rutgers U. Press, 1976).

Raymond R. Patterson (b. 1929 in New York City) Teaches at City University of New York. *26 Ways of Looking at a Black Man* (Award Books, 1969).

Gerda Penfold was born in Germany and grew up in Saskatchewan. Works as secretary on the west coast. *Done with Mirrors* (Vagabond Press, 1975).

Robert Peters (b. 1924 in Wisconsin) Teaches at U. of California at Irvine. *Selected Poems* (Crossing Press, 1978).

Robert Peterson (b. 1924 in Denver) Lives in New Mexico, though he considers himself a Bay Area poet. *Under Sealed Orders* (Cloud Marauder Press, 1976).

Marge Piercy (b. 1936 in Detroit) Lives on Cape Cod. *Living in the Open* (Knopf, 1976).

Kenneth Pitchford (b. 1931 in Moorhead, Minn.) Married to poet Robin Morgan. Lives in New York City. *The Contraband Poems* (Templar Press, 1976).

Frank Polite (b. 1936 in Youngstown, OH.) Lives in Youngstown.

Ralph Pomeroy (b. 1926 in Evanston, Ill.) Art critic/curator, freelance writer. Lives in New York City. *In the Financial District* (Macmillan, 1968).

Leroy V. Quintana (b. 1944 in Albuquerque, N.Mex.) Teaches at El Paso Community College. *Hijo Del Pueblo* (Puerto Del Sol Press, 1976).

Carl Rakosi (b. 1903 in Berlin, Germany) Until retirement, worked as social worker and psychotherapist. Lives in Minneapolis. *Ex Cranium, Night* (Black Sparrow, 1975).

Eugene B. Redmond (b. 1937 in St. Louis) Teaches at California State U. in Sacramento. *In a Time of Rain & Desire* (Black River Writers, 1973).

Naomi Replansky (b. Bronx, N.Y.) Lives in New York City where she works as computer programmer. *Ring Song* (Scribner's, 1952).

Kenneth Rexroth (b. 1905 in South Bend, Ind.) Artist, composer, and father of the San Francisco Renaissance. Lives in Santa Barbara. *New Poems* (New Directions, 1974).

Adrienne Rich (b. 1929 in Baltimore, Md.) Lives in New York City. Won National Book Award for *Diving into the Wreck*. *The Dream of a Common Language* (Norton, 1978).

A. A. Rios (b. Nogales, Ariz.) Student at U. of Arizona.

Kirk Robertson (b. 1946 in Los Angeles) This year lives in California. Publisher of Duck Down Press and co-editor of *Scree* Magazine. *Under the Weight of the Sky* (Cherry Valley Editions, 1977).

Carolyn M. Rodgers (b. Chicago) Lives in Chicago. *How I Got Ovah* (Doubleday, 1975).

Larry Rubin (b. 1930 in Bayonne, N.J.) Teaches at Georgia Tech in Atlanta. *All My Mirrors Lie* (Godine, 1975).

Muriel Rukeyser (b. 1913 in New York City) Lives in New York City. Member, Institute of Arts and Letters. *The Gates* (McGraw-Hill, 1976).

Vern Rutsala (b. 1934 in McCall, Id.) Teaches at Lewis and Clark College in Portland, Or. *Paragraphs* (Wesleyan, 1978).

Sonia Sanchez (b. 1935 in Birmingham, Ala.) Lives in Philadelphia. *A Blues Book for Blue Magical Women* (Broadside Press, 1974).

Reg Saner (b. 1931 in Jacksonville, Ill.) Expert mountaineer and photographer, teaches at U. of Colorado. *Climbing into the Roots* (Harper & Row, 1976).

May Sarton (b. 1912 in Belgium) Well-known novelist. Lives on Maine coast. *Selected Poems* (Norton, 1978).

Tom Schmidt (b. 1939 in San Francisco) Lives on American River near Sacramento. Plays woodwinds in own band, Bluebop. *One More for Gunilla Liljequist* (Deerprint Press, 1978).

Grace Schulman (b. New York City) Lives in New York City where she teaches at City University, is poetry editor of *The Nation*, and director of the YMHA Poetry Center. *Burn Down the Icons* (Princeton, 1977).

Herbert Scott (b. 1931 in Norman, Okla.) Spent many years in grocery business. Now teaches at Western Michigan U. *Groceries* (U. of Pittsburgh Press, 1976).

Harvey Shapiro (b. 1924 in Chicago) Editor at the *N.Y. Times*. *Lauds and Nightsounds* (Sun, 1978).

Karl Shapiro (b. 1913 in Baltimore) Teaches at U. of California, Davis. Won Pulitzer Prize. *Collected Poems* (Random House, 1978).

Richard Shelton (b. 1933 in Boise, Id.) Lives in Tucson. Teaches at the U. of Arizona and at the Arizona State Prison. *The Road to Veracruz* (U. of Pittsburgh Press, 1978).

Judith Johnson Sherwin (b. 1936 in New York City) President of the Poetry Society of America. *Transparencies* (Countryman Press, 1978).

Naomi Shihab (b. 1952 in St. Louis) Lives in San Antonio, Texas, where she works in poets-in-the-schools program. *Eye-to-Eye* (Texas Portfolio Press, 1978).

Charles Simic (b. 1938 in Yugoslavia) Teaches at U. of New Hampshire. *Charon's Cosmology* (George Braziller, 1977).

Louis Simpson (b. 1923 in Jamaica, W.I.) Teaches at State U. of N.Y. in Stony Brook. Pulitzer Prize winner. *Searching for the Ox* (William Morrow, 1976).

Knute Skinner (b. 1929 in St. Louis) Teaches in Bellingham, Wash. Lives half the year in Ireland. Co-editor of *The Bellingham Review. A Close Sky Over Killaspuglonane* (Dolmen Press, 1968).

W. D. Snodgrass (b. 1926 in Wilkinsburg, Pa.) Won Pulitzer Prize. Teaches at Syracuse U. *The Fuhrer Bunker* (BOA Editions, 1977).

Gary Snyder (b. 1930 in San Francisco) Pulitzer Prize for *Turtle Island* (New Directions, 1975). Lives on "Sierra pine forest melon patch."

Gary Soto (b. 1952 in Fresno, CA.) Ex-farm worker, teaches at U. of California, Berkeley. *The Elements of San Joaquin* (U. of Pittsburgh Press, 1977).

Barry Spacks (b. 1931 in Philadelphia) Teaches at M.I.T. *Imagining a Unicorn* (Godine, 1978).

William Stafford (b. 1914 in Hutchinson, KS.) Teaches at Lewis and Clark College in Oregon. "Biker, hiker, photographer." *Someday, Maybe* (Harper & Row, 1973).

Ann Stanford (b. 1918 in La Habra, CA.) Teaches at Calif. State U. in Northridge. *In Mediterranean Air* (Viking, 1977).

Charles Stetler (b. in Pittsburgh) Teaches at California State U., Long Beach. *Roger, Karl, Rick, and Shane Are Friends of Mine* (MAG Press, 1973).

Leon Stokesbury (b. 1945 in Oklahoma City) Graduate student at U. of Arkansas. *Often in Different Landscapes* (U. of Texas Press, 1976).

Ruth Stone (b. 1915 in Roanoke, VA.) Lives in Vermont. *Cheap* (Harcourt Brace Jovanovich, 1975).

Adrien Stoutenburg (b. 1916 in Dafur, Minn.) Writes children's books. Lives in California. *Greenwich Mean Time* (U. of Utah Press, 1978).

Mark Strand (b. 1934 in Summerside, P.E.I., Canada) Lives in New York City. *The Late Hour* (Atheneum, 1978).

Lucien Stryk (b. 1924 in Chicago) Teaches at Northern Illinois U. Translator of Zen poetry. *Selected Poems* (Swallow, 1973).

Dabney Stuart (b. 1937 in Richmond, VA.) Teaches at Washington and Lee U. in Virginia. *Round and Round* (Louisiana State U., 1977).

May Swenson (b. 1919 in Logan, UT.) Lives on Long Island shore. *Things Taking Place: New & Selected Poems* (Atlantic/Little, Brown, 1978).

John Tagliabue (b. 1923 in Cantu (Como), Italy) Teaches at Bates College, Maine. *The Buddha Uproar* (Kayak, 1970).

James Tate (b. 1943 in Kansas City, MO.) Teaches at the U. of Mass. *Viper Jazz* (Wesleyan, 1976).

John Thomas lives in Los Angeles. *Epopoeia and the Decay of Satire* (Red Hill Press, 1976).

Eve Triem (b. 1902 in New York City) Lives in Seattle where she teaches poetry workshops. *The Process* (Querencia, 1976).

Constance Urdang (b. 1922 in New York City) Married to poet Donald Finkel. Lives in St. Louis. *The Picnic in the Cemetery* (George Braziller, 1975).

Mona Van Duyn (b. 1921 in Waterloo, IO.) Won National Book Award. Lives in St. Louis. *Merciful Disguises* (Atheneum, 1973).

Mark Vinz (b. 1942 in Rugby, N.D.) Teaches at Moorhead State U. in Minnesota. Editor of *Dacotah Territory* and the Territorial Press. *Songs for a Hometown Boy* (Solo Press, 1977).

David Wagoner (b. 1926 in Massillon, OH.) Teaches at the U. of Washington. Editor, *Poetry Northwest*. Novelist. *Collected Poems* (Indiana U. Press, 1976).

Diane Wakoski (b. 1937 in Whittier, CA.) Writer-in-residence at Michigan State U. *The Man Who Shook Hands* (Doubleday, 1978).

Robert Penn Warren (b. 1905 in Kentucky) Professor Emeritus of English at Yale. Pulitzer Prize winner for both fiction and poetry. *Selected Poems: 1923-1976* (Random House, 197?).

Cary Waterman (b. 1942 in Bridgeport, Conn.) Lives in Minnesota "on an acreage." *First Thaw* (Minnesota Writer's Pub. House, 1975).

Charles Waterman (b. 1933 in McCook, Neb.) Married to Cary Waterman. *Talking Animals* (Juniper Press, 1977).

Robert Watson (b. 1925 in Passaic, N.J.) Lives in North Carolina. *Selected Poems* (Atheneum, 1975).

Theodore Weiss (b. 1916 in Reading, Pa.) Teaches at Princeton. Editor of *Quarterly Review of Literature. Fireweeds* (Macmillan, 1976).

Don Welch (b. 1932 in Hastings, Neb.) Teaches at Kearney State College in Neb. *Dead Horse Table* (Windflower Press, 1975).

James Welch (b. 1940 in Browning, Mon.) Lives in Montana. Novelist. *Riding the Earthboy 40* (World, 1971).

Joanie Whitebird (b. 1951 in Houston, Tex.) Co-edited *Travois*, an anthology of Texas poetry. Editor of Wings Press. Lives in Houston. *Birthmark* (Second Coming Press, 1977).

James Whitehead (b. 1936 in St. Louis) Teaches at the University of Arkansas. Novelist. *Domains* (Louisiana State U. Press, 1966).

Reed Whittemore (b. 1919 in New Haven, Conn.) Teaches at the U. of Maryland. *The Mother's Breast and the Father's House* (Houghton Mifflin, 1974).

Richard Wilbur (b. 1921 in New York City) Extraordinary translator of Moliere. Pulitzer Prize and National Book Award winner. *The Mind-Reader* (Harcourt Brace Jovanovich, 1976).

Peter Wild (b. 1940 in Easthampton, Miss.) Teaches at U. of Arizona. *Chihuahua* (Doubleday, 1976).

Jonathan Williams (b. 1929 in Asheville, N.C.) Publisher and editor of Jargon Press. Divides time between England and America. *The Loco Logodaedalist in Situ* (Cape Goliard Press/Grossman, 1972).

Miller Williams (b. 1930 in Hoxie, Ark.) Teaches at U. of Arkansas and the Arkansas State Penitentiary. *Why God Permits Evil* (Dutton, 1978).

Keith Wilson (b. 1927 in Clovis, N.Mex.) Teaches at N.Mex. State U. *Midwatch* (Sumac Press, 1972).

Robert Winner (b. 1930 in New York City) A businessman, lives in New York City.

John Woods (b. 1926 in Martinsville, Ind.) Teaches at Western Michigan U. *Striking the Earth* (Indiana, 1976).

Charles Wright (b. 1935 in Hardin County, Tenn.) Teaches at U. of California, Irvine. *China Trace* (Wesleyan, 1977).

James Wright (b. 1927 in Martin's Ferry, Oh.) Pulitzer Prize winner. Member of National Institute of Arts and Letters. Teaches at Hunter College in New York. *To a Blossoming Pear Tree* (Farrar, Straus, and Giroux, 1977).

Al Young (b. 1939 in Ocean Springs, Miss.) Novelist. Teaches at Stanford U. Editor of *Yardbird* Magazine. *Geography of the Near Past* (Holt, Rinehart and Winston, 1976).

Marya Zaturenska (b. 1902 in Kiev, Russia) Won Pulitzer Prize in 1938. Married to poet Horace Gregory. Lives in Rockland County, N.Y. *The Hiden Waterfall* (Vanguard, 1974).

Paul Zimmer (b. 1934 in Canton, Oh.) Has been Associate Director of U. of Pittsburgh Press and currently moving south. *The Zimmer Poems* (Dryand Press, 1976).

COPYRIGHTS AND ACKNOWLEDGMENTS
(continued from page iv)

543

544

547

the Forest, *published by Juniper Press, Wisconsin; copyright © 1977 by Lisel Mueller; by permission of the author. Other poems from* The Private Life; *copyright © 1976 by Lisel Mueller; by permission of Louisiana State University Press.*

NATHAN, LEONARD: *All poems from* The Likeness; *copyright © 1975 by Leonard Nathan. By permission of the author.*

NEMEROV, HOWARD: "Ginkgoes in Fall," *from* The Western Approaches. *By permission of the author.*

NOLL, BINK: "Shutting the Curtains" *(originally in* Equal Time, *1972) and* "Wedlock" *are reprinted by permission of the author.*

NORRIS, KATHLEEN: "The Middle of the World," *copyright © 1976; and* "Focus" *are reprinted by permission of the author.*

NORSE, HAROLD: *All poems from* Hotel Nirvana; *copyright © 1974 by Harold Norse. By permission of City Lights Books.*

NORTHSUN, NILA: *All poems from* Diet Pepsi & Nacho Cheese, *published by Duck Down Press, Box 996, Carpinteria CA 93103; copyright © 1977 by nila northSun. By permission of the author.*

OCHESTER, ED: "Snow White," *from* Nausea; *by permission of Russ Haas Press. Other poems from* Dancing On the Edge of Knives; *copyright © 1973 by Ed Ochester; by permission of the University of Missouri Press.*

OPPEN, GEORGE: *All poems from* Collected Poems; *copyright © 1962, 1965, 1972 by George Oppen. By permission of New Directions Publishing Corporation.*

ORLEN, STEVE: "Bar Mitzvah" *(originally in a chapbook,* Separate Creatures, *published by Ironwood Press, Tucson, Arizona), copyright © 1976 by Steve Orlen; and* "In praise of Beverly" *are reprinted by permission of the author.*

ORTIZ, SIMON: *All poems from* Going for the Rain; *copyright © 1976 by Simon J. Ortiz. By permission of Harper & Row, Publishers, Inc.*

PACK, ROBERT: "The Mugger," *from* Keeping Watch; *copyright © 1976 by Rutgers University, the State University of New Jersey. By permission of the publisher.*

PATTERSON, RAYMOND R.: *All poems from* 26 Ways of Looking at a Black Man; *copyright © 1969 by Raymond Patterson. By permission of the author.*

PENFOLD, GERDA: "The Lust for Murder" *(originally in* Bear) *and* "A Pesadilla" *(originally in* Beloit Poetry Journal), *from* Done With Mirrors, *published by Vagabond Press; copyright © 1975 by Gerda Penfold. By permission of the author.*

PETERS, ROBERT: "Allen Ginsberg Blesses a Bride and Groom . . . ," *from* The Poet As Ice-Skater, *published by ManRoot Books; copyright © 1975 by Robert Peters; by permission of the author and publisher.* "Claremont," *from* A Gift to Be Simple, A Garland for Ann Lee; *copyright © 1973, 1974, 1975 by Robert Peters; by permission of Liveright Publishing Corporation.* "The Beach," *from* Songs for a Son; *copyright © 1967 by Robert L. Peters; by permission of W. W. Norton & Company, Inc.*

PETERSON, ROBERT: *All poems from* Under Sealed Orders; *copyright © 1976 by Robert Peterson. By permission of the author.*

PIERCY, MARGE: "To the Pay Toilet" *and* "A Proposal for Recycling Wastes," *copyright © 1975, 1976 by Marge Piercy, from* Living in the Open. *By permission of Alfred A. Knopf, Inc.*

PITCHFORD, KENNETH: "Homosexual Sonnets," *copyright © 1973 by Kenneth Pitchford, are reprinted by permission of the author.*

POLITE, FRANK: *All poems are reprinted by permission of the author.*

POMEROY, RALPH: "Looking at the Empire State Building," *copyright © 1968 by Ralph Pomeroy, and* "English Train, Summer" *are reprinted by permission of the author.*

QUINTANA, LEROY V.: "Legacy II," *from* The Face of Poetry, *edited by L. H. Clark and Mary MacArthur; copyright © 1976 by Gallimanfry Press, Arlington, Virginia; and* "Last Night There Was a Cricket in Our Closet" *are reprinted by permission of the author.*

RAKOSI, CARL: "Poetry," "Tune," "Being Natural," *and excerpt from* "The Indomitable," *from* Ex Cranium, Night; *copyright © 1975 by Carl Rakosi; by permission of Black Sparrow Press. Other poems from* Ere-Voice; *by permission of the author.*

REDMOND, EUGENE B.: *All poems from* In a Time of Rain & Desire: New Love Poems; *copyright © 1973 by Eugene B. Redmond and Black River Writers Press. By permission of the publisher.*

REPLANSKY, NAOMI: "The Mistress Addresses the Wife," *from* Poetry *(February, 1954): copyright 1954 by The Modern Poetry Association; by permission of the editor of* Poetry. "In the Sea of Tears," *published as*

Index of Poets

Index of Titles

555

START A COLLECTION

With Bantam's fiction anthologies, you can begin almost anywhere. Choose from science fiction, classic literature, modern short stories, mythology, and more—all by both new and established writers in America and around the world.